The values of God, family, and country are a [...] Harris and what he represents. A true inspir[...]

BRIGADIER GENERAL JOHN M. RHODES,
U.S. Army National Guard

The incomprehensibly long ordeal of the Harris family is agonizing. Their love, faith, loyalty, and courage epitomize all that is good about America.

LT. COL. ORSON SWINDLE, USMC (ret.), POW,
Hanoi, 11/11/1966 to 3/4/1973

Tap Code is an incredible story about two American heroes. Col. "Smitty" Harris and his wife, Louise, epitomize the definition of *commitment*—to God, to country, and to family. This tale of extreme perseverance will restore your faith in the human spirit.

BRIGADIER GENERAL JOHN NICHOLS, USAF

Tap Code is a hard road of reminiscence for those of us who were there, but an excellent history for those who have never known the terrors of war behind the lines of the enemy. The prison camps of North Vietnam were hell on earth, and those who know little about the POWs held captive will do well to read this book.

SAM JOHNSON, former U.S. representative
from Texas, Colonel USAF (ret.),
and ex-"Alcatraz" POW

"Smitty" Harris is one of the truest examples of our Air Force core values—integrity, service before self, excellence. As a pilot, I can attest to how Smitty's Tap Code is an integral piece of our training today as we cultivate bold, innovative leaders who will continue the Long Blue Line and be ready, lethal pilots in the world's greatest Air Force.

COLONEL SAMANTHA WEEKS, Commander,
14th Flying Training Wing, Columbus
Air Force Base, Mississippi

Col. "Smitty" Harris proudly served our great nation during the Vietnam War, and it is an honor to call him a trusted friend. He is known for his unwavering faith and loyalty to America.

TRENT KELLY, U.S. representative from Mississippi

Tap Code tells the true story of Col. Carlyle "Smitty" Harris, who was shot down in North Vietnam on April 4, 1965. From the first sentence you find yourself thrust from his fighter jet and into the hands of people who want to kill the young pilot. Smitty has the reader living his stay in the Hanoi Hilton, surviving brutal interrogations, and celebrating his homecoming. This is a remarkable story of the unbreakable American spirit forged by combat, capture, and faith.

PHIL BRYANT, governor of Mississippi

If you're interested in what it was like to be a POW of the North Vietnamese, or to be the wife of one, grab a copy of *Tap Code* immediately. No one has told this story better.

GENERAL CHUCK BOYD, USAF (ret.)

TAP CODE

THE EPIC SURVIVAL TALE
OF A VIETNAM POW
AND THE SECRET CODE THAT
CHANGED EVERYTHING

A TRUE STORY

COL. CARLYLE "SMITTY" HARRIS (RET.)
AND SARA W. BERRY

ZONDERVAN BOOKS

Tap Code
Copyright © 2019 by Carlyle S. Harris and Sara W. Berry

Published in Grand Rapids, Michigan, by Zondervan. Zondervan is a registered trademark of The Zondervan Corporation, L.L.C., a wholly owned subsidiary of HarperCollins Christian Publishing, Inc.

Requests for information should be addressed to customercare@harpercollins.com.

Zondervan titles may be purchased in bulk for educational, business, fundraising, or promotional use. For information, please email SpecialMarkets@Zondervan.com.

ISBN 978-0-310-37011-6 (softcover)
ISBN 978-0-310-35913-5 (audio)
ISBN 978-0-310-35912-8 (ebook)

Art direction: Curt Diepenhorst
Cover design: Tim Green / Faceout Studio
Cover photography: Getty Images
Interior design: Kait Lamphere

To all prisoners of war
who endured untold hardship,
this is for you.
To all the families of these POWs
who endured untold heartache,
this is for you.
To all captives everywhere,
whether captives in body or in soul,
this is for you.

May the words you find here
fill you with enduring hope, strength, and peace.
May you, with unveiled faces,
see the glory of the One
who came to set the captives free.

"This is what the Lord, the God of Israel, says: 'Write in a book all the words I have spoken to you. The days are coming,' declares the Lord, 'when I will bring my people Israel and Judah back from captivity and restore them to the land I gave their ancestors to possess,' says the Lord."

JEREMIAH 30:2-3

FOREWORD

You are about to venture into a story so amazing that it's difficult to imagine. As one who has known Smitty and Louise Harris for almost fifty years, I can tell you that it's true and they are the real deal. These two are bright, wise, adventurous, and highly successful at everything they do. At the same time, they are highly regarded by others for their kindness and strong faith. They are also down-to-earth, fun-loving, and delightful to be around. They are unique—a married couple where both are superstars and both are elegantly humble.

On April 4, 1965, Smitty was the sixth American POW captured in the air war over North Vietnam. By the time I arrived two-and-a-half years later, he had already survived some of the worst treatment of the entire POW experience. Though a quiet captain and not the senior leader in the camp, Smitty had a monumental impact on the POW experience.

When writing and speaking about life as a POW, I refer to Smitty as the code bearer. As a young man spurred by his insatiable curiosity, Smitty learned a communication technique that we later called "the Tap Code." What seemed like happenstance at the time now seems like a divine intervention to equip Smitty, one of the early arrivals in the camps, with a tool we all would desperately need in the days ahead.

In that medieval bastille known as the Hanoi Hilton, our captors' goal was to divide and conquer the POWs. The prison's sixteen-inch masonry walls were designed to isolate prisoners. Smitty took great risk and through resourcefulness and creativity spread the code that enabled our covert communication. Using the code, we could softly tap messages of encouragement to lonely neighbors and pass along resistance policies from our leaders. These vital communications lifted our spirits and gave us a united front throughout the camps. Admiral Stockdale (senior Navy POW) has commented that communications were the blood and sinew that kept us alive. Smitty was the code bearer who enabled us to connect and communicate—the two most vital needs of every POW.

Smitty and I were in the same camp for more than five years and cellmates for almost two years. Since he was the most experienced POW in our group, we looked to him for wisdom and sought his counsel on tactics for our resistance and survival.

Back in "the land of the free," as we called it, Louise was proving to be a true warrior as well. As one of the first MIA wives of the war, she suffered the learning curve. The Air Force had virtually no policies in place to deal with her situation. Louise's initiative solved problems for her and their three young children and paved a smoother path for spouses of future POWs.

Eventually the war ended, and we came home. For Smitty and Louise, it had been just two months shy of eight years. Most of us had a wonderful reunion and moved on. It seemed that the Harris family just stayed in the reunion mode—relishing their time together again. They are one of the closest families I've ever known. Smitty and Louise continue to be as amazing as ever. Though they are among the most senior of the Traditionalist Generation, they are always a charming couple, blending smoothly with the four generations that cycle through their home and social lives.

As you read this inspiring story, you will see that the strong adjectives I used above to describe Smitty and Louise fall short. Their life story may seem beyond imagination, but I know them well and have seen it firsthand—it's real. Moreover, the way they have bounced back from suffering and sacrifice can be an inspiration to today's weak culture. Their lessons of character, courage, and commitment could rescue and restore our nation. I'm inspired by their example, and I believe you will be as well. They are my role models, and I hope you will let them be yours too.

Col. Lee Ellis (ret.), former POW

CARLYLE SMITH "SMITTY" HARRIS

APRIL 4, 1965
11:00 A.M.

In one split second, I passed from the known to the unknown—from a comfortable, safe, and ordered life into a hostile environment filled with danger and trauma.

When I ejected from my crippled airplane, I had no thoughts of what lay ahead. I was too busy trying to survive the crash. It was a spontaneous act of desperation, conditioned by years of emergency training, that would give me some chance for survival.

I had trained for this. I knew exactly what to do and what would happen. My seat would fly off with great velocity and force, just after the glass canopy of the plane flew hundreds of feet up in the air. My mind and my emotions were on autopilot as I went through the motions.

In my frantic efforts to keep my F-105 flying, I had waited until the last moment to radio my squadron mates that I was ejecting. As a result, my left hand was still on the mike button when I pulled the trigger that would catapult me from my burning and lifeless craft. As my parachute snapped open, I felt a sharp, searing pain in my left shoulder. I had not placed my arm in the armrest that would prevent it from flailing in the wind blast when my body was hurled into space. For a moment I thought I was blinded, but I reached up to my face and found that my oxygen mask had slipped up over my eyes. Pulling it down, I saw my F-105 as it struck the ground and burst into a huge ball of fire.

Looking up, my parachute was beautiful. There was absolute silence and serenity as I floated noiselessly earthward. What a contrast from the screaming, frantic scene moments before.

Suddenly, my mind raced to my predicament. I must have been briefly mesmerized or possibly in shock. A Vietnamese village was directly below me, and I could see people running around. It finally sank in—I was in enemy country and would probably be there a long time.

There were no trees or other cover in the area—just open rice paddies and the village. My chances for evasion were nil. I reached up and grabbed my parachute risers with my right hand and was successful in slipping my chute sideways so I would float away from the village. I landed less than 100 yards from the thatched-roof huts and immediately tried to open my survival kit to get my emergency radio so I could alert my friends that I was safely on the ground. My left arm was limp and useless, which made it very difficult to open the emergency kit. Before I could get to the radio, loud, angry voices were yelling at me.

Villagers had already surrounded me and were closing in. I saw a few rifles, but most had sticks and hoes. Many of the men seemed almost as frightened of me as I was of them. As I looked around, the men in my line of sight would duck down behind a small levee or clump of grass as if I could harm them with my stare. However, the circle of men tightened, and a few brave ones finally rushed me and knocked me to the ground. I was armed with a snub-nosed .38 revolver strapped to my chest, but it had not even occurred to me to try to fight my way out of these impossible odds, so the gun was still in its holster.

The villagers quickly began to strip me of all my gear. However, the process was as frustrating for them as for me because they had trouble with all the snaps and zippers on my flight gear. While several men held my upper torso on the ground, two men tried to pull my flight suit over my heavy high-top boots, but that didn't work, so they began to remove the boots. A heavy zipper ran down each boot for quick donning, but the Vietnamese ignored the zippers and laboriously unlaced each boot down to the toe before pulling it off. Finally, I was clothed only in my shorts and was yanked to my feet and pushed toward the village. I heard several angry voices, and one irate young man pushed me off the narrow levee into ankle-deep water. He raised his gun to shoot me on the spot, but an older man grabbed the barrel of his rifle, and I was pulled back onto the levee.

As we proceeded toward the village, a violent argument broke out among the men. Several, armed with rifles, seemed to gain control of the mob. On the edge of the village was a partial brick wall, and three men pushed me with my back against it. One was the man who had pushed me off the levee. He put his forefinger to my forehead and jabbered instructions to his cohorts. The crowd, now including some women and children, moved back to leave about a fifteen-foot clear area in front of me.

Three men positioned themselves with rifles directly in front of me, and their leader backed away to join them. I knew I was about to be killed, but somehow my mind refused to accept the seriousness of the situation. I kept thinking, *Stand tall and straight; I must stand tall and straight.* Despite being stripped and bruised and broken, my body stood tall and straight, with a soldier's back, and my thoughts turned to the source of my strength—prayer: *Our Father which art in heaven, hallowed be thy name.*

I was unable to finish my prayer due to the distraction of angry voices, livid faces, and the electric excitement of the mob scene. It was almost as if I were watching a movie from afar. I wanted only to keep my composure and at least die bravely, as all movie heroes are supposed to do. As the pitch of excitement of the mob increased, there were more angry voices, and some men milled into the circle, arguing violently with my executioners. Other men came over to me and started leading me away from the wall. I shivered violently. Was what had just occurred a bad dream or was it real? It was only later that the full impact of what had almost happened sank into my muddled brain. I still shudder when I recall those moments that are engraved indelibly in my mind.

LOUISE LAMBERT HARRIS

2

APRIL 5, 1965
5:00 A.M.

I lay alone in our double bed, sleeping soundly. It had taken me a while to get used to sleeping alone, but after many nights, weeks, and months of separation throughout our five years of marriage, I had overcome the anxious agitation that had once plagued me. I no longer jumped at every creak or awakened at every bark from our beloved German Shepherd, Schotze. No, I had grown accustomed to the life of an Air Force wife. I knew what I had signed up for. And I was sure that this indeed was the life I had chosen—the life I wanted. God had blessed me indeed.

I had not always possessed this assurance—this deep-rooted certainty that I had chosen well my path of life. Though my love for Carlyle Smith Harris had grown into deep wells of love in a relatively short amount of time, I had insisted on a full six months of engagement. It took me years to tell Smitty why I had insisted on this time frame. With his scheduled assignments, a quicker engagement would have been more convenient. But I needed to be absolutely certain. And as the months melted one into another, our hearts melted into one as well, and my resolve—my determination that this would be the best life, the best path, for me as well as for Smitty—came to live in my heart.

My time of testing quickly came, even before we had the opportunity to say, "I do." If Smitty ever doubted that I would be an understanding wife, his fears were dispelled when one month before our wedding, he announced it would have to be delayed for an additional month. By now I was as anxious as Smitty was to be married, and I regretted the six-month engagement. Just as I began counting down the days to our blessed event, Smitty was asked if he would take a six-week trip to make demonstration flights all over the Pacific area in the T-37 jet trainer. He was to fly in Hawaii, Tokyo, Korea, the Philippines, Hong Kong, Singapore, and Australia. Between demonstration flights, he and his crew would dismantle the wing of the T-37, and they would be transported in a C-130 transport aircraft.

I knew the trip would be a once-in-a-lifetime opportunity for Smitty. I also knew this would be a test of my resolve to be a supportive and faithful Air Force wife, so I joyfully acquiesced in delaying our wedding. I say joyfully because even at a young age I had learned the difference between happiness and joy. Happiness is dependent on our circumstances, whereas joy is another thing entirely. Joy involves looking at the whole situation and seeing the benefits for others as well as for ourselves. Joy is not dependent on our circumstances and is not removed through our situations. Joy is a gift, and joy is a choice. I quickly learned to choose this eternal gift of joy, and this mind-set would prove to be tested far beyond what I could have fathomed.

The delay of our wedding, of course, did not make me happy. It did, however, make me joyful that Smitty had been granted the opportunity, so I chose to joyfully support him. As it turned out, the whole trip was canceled, and our wedding occurred as scheduled.

But I had passed the test. My resolve—my surety in this life I had chosen—was set in stone, and all of life's chiseling would never change this commitment.

——— ◆◆◆ ———

In the wee hours of the early morning of April 5, 1965, I slept soundly—that is, until the dream. Oh, it was so clear, so vivid. I heard the beloved voice of my Smitty calling my name. *Louise, Louise!* I sat straight up in bed. *Smitty?* I replied, half to myself, half to the voice I had heard. *Why, it can't be Smitty. He's in Korat, Thailand. He'll be there for at least four more days*, I thought. Still, the voice had been so clear.

I quickly rose and put on my bathrobe and slippers. I tied the bathrobe as tightly as I could around my almost-eight-months-pregnant body and walked quickly down the hallway. The sound of flapping slippers seemed too loud against the hardwood floor, and I slowed a bit to keep from waking the girls. I didn't have to wake Schotze, who already stood as if at attention when I entered the kitchen. I took the leash off the hook by the back door and went out into the dark, cool night. I walked all around the house, feeling silly, knowing it couldn't have been Smitty. Even so, I had to check. The voice—his voice—had been so real. Not surprisingly, our walk around the house did not produce a reunion with my Smitty. I replaced the leash by the door and watched as Schotze lay contentedly back down on his bed on the floor.

I, however, did not lie down as contentedly. As I tried to shake off the dream and fall back to sleep, my mind kept traveling backward through my years with Smitty. I smiled as I remembered.

● ● ●

Carlyle Smith Harris had thoroughly enjoyed being a bachelor officer in the Air Force. He had particularly enjoyed the training flights he took all over the United States with students when he was an instructor pilot and in flights of fighters when in an operational unit. Las Vegas, Miami, San Francisco, New York, and other exciting places were easily within reach of his cross-country flights.

Marriage was simply out of the question for Smitty. He thought it would put a damper on his restless spirit. He persistently avoided any long-term commitments, while actively enjoying meeting and dating girls at every opportunity.

But as almost inevitably happens, he soon became very interested in a girl who showed little interest in him. I had dated a friend of Smitty's who was about to enter pilot training. He introduced me to Smitty. Soon, instead of trying to avoid any amorous entanglement with the opposite sex, Smitty was actively seeking ways to win my heart and my love.

The early years of our marriage had been idyllic. Robin and Carolyn, our two precious daughters, were three and four years old when Smitty received orders in 1964 to transfer from McConnell Air Force Base in Kansas to Kadena Air Base in Okinawa, where he would fly the F-105 fighter-bomber. We had been happy here for more than a year now.

When Smitty received the assignment, we were all excited and hoped for an opportunity to visit Japan, Hong Kong, and the Philippines while we were there on our two-to-three-year tour. Smitty had been a flight commander in the F-105 at McConnell and thoroughly enjoyed this high-performance aircraft, which he had been selected to fly in international skies. But not everyone was as excited as the two of us were. While we visited my family prior to departure, my mother had expressed fear that Smitty would become involved in the war in Vietnam. Smitty had assured her—and me—that the F-105 was much too large and fast to be successfully used in the close air support role that would be required in the war in South Vietnam. At that time, the air war had barely begun over North Vietnam, where the interdiction of supply routes and bombing of military targets could utilize the F-105's capabilities. We proceeded blissfully to our new assignment.

The girls and I arrived in late January 1965 after Smitty had been there long enough to buy a home on the island and get settled in his new job. Soon after we arrived, it became apparent that the air war might expand rapidly to North Vietnam. Everett Alvarez Jr., a Navy pilot, had been shot down and captured on August 5, 1964, during a reprisal bombing mission following the Tonkin Gulf incident. Thus, he became the first American POW held in North Vietnam.

In February, Bob Shumaker, another Navy pilot, was shot down and captured over Dong Hoi. In March, one of Smitty's first missions from Korat was a bombing mission in northern Laos near the Vietnam border. The target, an ammo dump, had been completely destroyed, but one Air Force F-105 pilot had been shot down and later rescued. Also in March, a squadron strength unit made up of men and aircraft from the three F-105 squadrons at Kadena was sent on temporary duty to Korat Air Base in Thailand. The obvious use for this detachment would be an expanded air war over North Vietnam.

Smitty never held back information from me. We were equal partners with different parts in the story of our life together. Even as I lay in the dark, my agitation was not fear. I knew he was a fighter pilot when I married him. This is what he chose to do. He loved it, believed in it, and was committed to it. And I was committed to him. With that thought, the familiar resolve returned, and peaceful sleep returned with it. It was the last peaceful sleep I would enjoy for quite some time.

SMITTY

3

In the village I was led into a dirt-floored building, and several people pushed in with me. An older man started giving instructions, and all left but two men with rifles and him. He was holding my .38 revolver.

Just to be safe, my hands, which had been tied behind my back, were now tied to a post that supported the roof. After about an hour, I saw a uniformed man pull up to the hut on a bicycle. After a short conversation among my captors, my hands were untied, and someone brought in my flight suit and boots. After donning them, I was taken out and motioned to start walking. The older man led the way, and the two men with rifles followed. Ten or twelve other villagers joined our group.

When we came to the edge of the village, we passed over a narrow levee with a deep trench dug beside it. The older man stopped and talked to the men behind me. I guess I was still shaken up by my previous experience with a firing squad, for I was sure that at any moment a bullet would crash into my head and I would be pushed into the trench. Instead, he turned around, and we started walking again. My injured shoulder was giving me much pain, so I pulled the zipper of my flight suit down to my waist and rested my arm in it like a sling. Also, my knee had gotten stiff and sore while I was sitting in the hut. It turned out to be a bad sprain, but I hadn't even known it was hurt until then.

We walked for about an hour on small paths and levees between the rice paddies until we reached another larger village. The people were out in force to see me. I was surprised to see almost no hostility in their faces—only curiosity. I also noticed the bare subsistence level of their existence. I saw only two or three bicycles and no cars. Most of the thatched-roof huts had bare floors, and no appliances or luxury items were visible through the open doorways. An outside well provided water. There was, however, a loudspeaker in each village blaring out some Vietnamese radio program. I supposed that the people were too poor to own radios of their own.

We passed through the village and continued to walk for another half hour or so. It was now early afternoon, and I was extremely hot and thirsty. We stopped in a small group of trees, and I was tied to one, with the two men with rifles still guarding me. The rest of the group found some comfortable spots in the shade and took a nap. Soon, some Vietnamese women brought food and drink. The men awakened and took the food but offered me none. I made some motions that I was thirsty, and finally one of the guards untied my hands and gave me a bowl of hot, salty soup that did little to quench my thirst.

Soon we were walking again. This time my knee was almost completely stiff. After about a mile, we came to a river with a pontoon bridge and crossed to the other side. The hot sun and humidity were oppressive. I was perspiring freely and suffering from acute thirst. I would gladly have drunk the river water if given the opportunity. We walked up a bank near the river, and in the distance I could see another small village, with some trees and foliage near it. I had been looking for even the slightest possibility for escape, but to this point there had been no cover in which I could hide. Our group walked through the village, and again the people were alerted and stared curiously at me.

Just past the village was what I believed to be a police station. Several uniformed men in unpressed khakis were standing around. I was led behind a large building to a small brick hut that was obviously a place of detention.

There were bars in the high windows and a heavy padlock on the thick wooden door. I was pushed inside, and the door slammed behind me. I sat on the only piece of furniture, a wooden platform that was used for a bed. Within a short time, I began to hear many voices outside and a loudspeaker blaring something in Vietnamese.

The voices got louder and angrier and began to chant. I was unable to see out of the high windows but knew a large number of people were out there. Suddenly, the cell door opened, and two policemen led me out into the crowd. They had placed two ropes as an aisle for me to walk in and to separate me from what was now an angry mob. When I appeared in the cell door, there was a loud yell, and a sea of hostile faces met my gaze. I was led a short distance to a cleared circle about thirty feet across, in the middle of which were my helmet, dinghy, parachute, survival seat pack, and other personal objects. These things had not accompanied me on the walk, and I wondered how they had gotten here.

There were at least a half dozen men with cameras and one large 35mm movie camera. A ring of fifteen or twenty uniformed men kept the mob of people out of the circle. One of my guards pushed on my head, indicating for me to bow. I feigned ignorance of what he wanted, and the crowd yelled madly. I was led around the circle two times and then through the corridor to my cell. When the door slammed behind me, I heaved a sigh of relief. This small, dingy cell was a welcome respite from the mob outside. Several years later, Louise was shown a picture of me taken that day by one of the photographers. It was found on the body of a North Vietnamese soldier killed in South Vietnam. She guessed that my arm was injured, because I was carrying it in the zippered front of my flight suit.

Back in my cell, I thought about the hostile, screaming Vietnamese just a few feet away. Were these the same people who a short time before had passively watched me walk through their village? Their lack of sophistication and childlike response to an emotional appeal over the loudspeaker were revealing. Apparently, their government had no problem controlling the hearts and minds of these people.

My cell door opened, and two civilians accompanied by two armed guards entered with a portable tape recorder. One of the civilians asked me in poor English to give the name of the Navy ship from which I was flying. I remained mute. He then asked the type of aircraft I was flying. Again, I remained mute. He was obviously angered by my lack of response and spoke at length with the other Vietnamese men.

Controlling his voice, he asked my name, rank, and service number. I provided this information, and he seemed pleased. Then he said, "Speak into the microphone and tell us about your bombing mission."

I shook my head—*No*. His face turned livid, and I saw him look at my left hand that was resting on my lap. He spoke to the guards in Vietnamese and then turned to me and said, "Give me the ring from your finger."

"No," I said once again. He simply nodded to the guards, and they knocked me backward on the bed. There was a short struggle with all four men participating, and they removed my wedding band.

Louise. Her name pierced my mind as one of the men held up my ring in triumph. With a sinking feeling deep in my gut, I knew I had been ripped away from her and my children, just as the ring had been ripped from my finger.

SMITTY 4

I sat up on the bed, sickened to see my wedding ring in the hands of my enemies. *Why didn't I put up more of a fight?* I wondered and then immediately knew the answer. I couldn't. My left arm was almost useless, and the scuffle had caused excruciating pain in my shoulder. My physical weakness at that moment only strengthened my mental resolve.

I was now ordered to make a statement in the microphone. I took it and spoke into the microphone: "Will someone please get a doctor to look at my shoulder?" The English speaker was again angered, and he turned and jabbered something in Vietnamese.

Abruptly, the four men left my cell, taking their tape recorder with them. I got up and began to hobble around the small cell, trying to loosen up my knee.

As I walked in circles, I began to think of escape. *I have to get out of here*, I thought with determination. I remembered from my survival training that the best time to attempt escape was immediately after capture or while en route to a permanent place of detention. I had seen the grove of trees and some underbrush that came within yards of the police station. Wanting another chance to reconnoiter the area, I began shouting for a guard. When the door opened, I indicated I needed to relieve myself. He called another guard, and the two of them escorted me to an outdoor privy with a shoulder-high bamboo screen around it. I was able to see part of the wooded area, which looked well cleared out near the ground and would provide little cover. I was unable to determine the extent of the trees and underbrush, but perhaps they would lead me to the river, and at night I could make my way down river to a better area of concealment.

Back in my cell, I examined possibilities for escape. The ceiling appeared to be bamboo with some type of plaster over it, and the roof was red clay tiles. It would be difficult to break through the ceiling, but if I could work a bed board loose, I might be able to use it to make a hole large enough to get through. My arm was going to hamper my efforts, but I began trying to loosen one of the bed boards one-handed. While I was working on removing a nail that was slightly loose, the cell door opened again, and I was motioned to come out. The crowd that had dispersed for an hour or so was back in full force, and again I was led through a corridor of shouting, fist-waving Vietnamese. This time, however, the corridor led to a vehicle, and I was pushed inside. Guards tied my hands and put a heavy blindfold over my eyes. As the vehicle pulled away, the crowd roared. The loudspeaker had again given the cues to the people, and they had responded as directed. The propaganda and control by the government were alarmingly effective.

We bumped along for several miles before coming to a paved but rough road. The darkness of the blindfold matched the darkness of my situation. My thoughts digressed from my current situation to the previous twenty-four hours.

I had returned to Korat ten days earlier after a wonderful week with my family, who were still in our little home in Okinawa. Upon my return, I had immediately noticed a quickened pace. We were flying more missions. Maintenance and armament personnel were working around the clock; pilots were briefed in the middle of the night for early-morning strikes; and a feeling of excitement was in the air.

We were all anxious to hit some really important targets. So far, we had flown many sorties in armed reconnaissance along some roads and rail lines and had hit a few small bridges, trucks, and small troop movements. We all knew this effort to stop rail and road traffic was largely futile, as most of the traffic moved at night. At this time we had no effective night capability. We were also restricted from striking far enough north to destroy major centers, loading and docking areas, and supply dumps. The enemy could move men and material with impunity to the narrow band of North Vietnam in which we were permitted to operate and then proceed at night through this area.

Each pilot at Korat was given a few days off during his combat tour to gain some rest and relaxation from the war. After several missions that were largely unproductive, some friends and I planned on R & R in Bangkok. I eagerly anticipated spending a few days in this beautiful, interesting city. However, my squadron was tasked to knock down the Hàm Rong bridge at Thanh Hóa, North Vietnam.

This was the most important target that had been assigned so far in the war. Not only was it an important rail and highway bridge used to speed war material south, but it was also psychologically important to the North Vietnamese. It was the first major bridge designed and built by the North Vietnamese since the French had left their country. It was a massive structure supporting concrete roadbeds as well as rail tracks. We were briefed that the bridge was heavily defended by 37mm and possibly 85mm antiaircraft guns and many smaller automatic weapons. I canceled my trip to Bangkok and successfully pleaded to be assigned to this mission.

Early in the morning of April 3, 1965, we were briefed for the attack on the Hàm Rong bridge. Lt. Col. Risner was to lead the mission with four flights of four aircraft armed with "Bull Pup" air-to-ground missiles. These very accurate missiles would probably drop the bridge, but in case they did not, four flights of four F-105s were to follow, each aircraft armed with eight 750-pound bombs. Though less accurate, the large bombs surely would knock down the bridge with a direct hit.

I was somewhat disappointed to be assigned as flight leader of the last flight of four F-105s. I was sure there would be no bridge left for my flight to bomb. As we neared the target, I knew from the radio chatter that the Bull Pups had not been able to knock down the bridge. There were many reports of direct hits with no apparent effect on the bridge.

As the lead flights of F-105s carrying 750-pound bombs pulled off the target, we heard Maj. Matt Matthews, who was spotting hits, report that most of the bombs were falling too far to the east. Unexpectedly strong winds carried the bombs away from the target. Armed with this information, my flight recomputed our aim points and started our bomb runs against a bridge that wasn't supposed to be standing.

My flight made several direct hits on the bridge. Lt. Ivy McCoy put the center of his group of eight bombs directly on the center span of the bridge. A huge geyser of water and smoke rose, but when it cleared, the bridge was still standing. Apparently, the inexperienced Vietnamese engineers who designed the bridge had decided it would be wiser to overstrengthen the bridge than take a chance on a mistaken calculation in the opposite direction. At any rate, the massive steel girders were essentially undamaged, but the concrete roadbeds were broken and unusable. The rail tracks, offering little resistance to bomb overpressures, appeared to be undamaged.

On the following day, April 4, another strike on the Hàm Rong bridge was planned. This time, the entire force of forty-eight aircraft would carry 750-pound bombs, as it was apparent that the Bull Pups were almost completely ineffective on this target.

It was believed that repeated hits by the bombs would drop the bridge. Because my flight had made the only direct bomb hits on the bridge the previous day, I was selected to make the first bomb run on the target with my wingman, Lt. Bob Bigrigg, staying high to observe the wind effect on my bombs before starting his bomb run.

Lt. Col. Risner was again leading the mission, but he and his wingman, Capt. Wayne Sharp, would remain at altitude over the target, armed with air-to-air missiles in case any enemy MiG aircraft came to meet us. As we approached the target area, a heavy haze and low, broken clouds made it very difficult to pick out the bridge.

Lt. Bigrigg saw it first and called out its position to me. As I started down my bomb run from about 13,000 feet, I began to see the small flicks of light on the ground that were muzzle flashes of antiaircraft guns. Although there had been heavy gunfire the previous day, none of our strike aircraft had been shot down, and I had even less reason to fear being hit today. Lt. Col. Risner's F-105 had battle damage, but he was able to nurse his crippled aircraft for a safe landing at the United States Air Force base located at Da Nang in South Vietnam.

The lead ship was rarely hit because the inexperienced North

Vietnamese (at this point in time) almost never led the target sufficiently, and the second or subsequent aircraft were more vulnerable to being inadvertently shot down. Aside from that, I was too busy tracking my target to be concerned with enemy fire. At 3,600 feet, I released all eight bombs with a perfect sight picture.

The aircraft jumped when all that weight was released, and I started my pullout from a 45-degree dive. I pulled hard to clear the ground by as much altitude as possible. As I leveled out, traveling at nearly six hundred miles per hour, I started a turn so I could observe my bombs' impact. At that moment, I felt a heavy jolt, which shook the entire aircraft. It yawed violently to the left, and smoke began to fill the cockpit. I knew the aircraft was hit, and hit badly. A conditioned response caused me to hit the disconnect switch to the automatic yaw damper system that sometimes causes these problems. I immediately regained control of the aircraft, even though the yaw had been so severe that in my peripheral vision I saw my left external fuel tank ripped from the aircraft. But now I had more severe problems: my engine had lost complete power; the aircraft was decelerating rapidly; and the cockpit warning lights were flashing *FIRE*. The panel on the left was lit up like a Christmas tree, shouting loud warnings—too many for me to have time to comprehend.

Surprisingly calm, I radioed my squadron mates who were flying on the same mission, following my lead. Using our call sign of the raid, I informed them that my aircraft was hit and burning.

Apparently, my aircraft had received a direct hit in the engine area. I tried to restart the engine on the emergency backup system and started a turn toward the sea, hoping I could get to a more favorable rescue area. The engine did not respond, and the aircraft continued to decelerate. I was now fairly close to the ground. At about a thousand feet and near stall speed, I radioed once again that I was ejecting from my crippled aircraft.

——— • • • ———

Could that have been only twenty-four hours ago? Time was moving at a different pace as I began my race of endurance. Minutes seemed like hours, hours like months. *And what lies ahead? How much time will pass before I see Louise and my little girls? Will I ever lay eyes on them again? Will I ever meet my little one yet to be born?* I immediately squelched the brief, dark thought. I could not go there. Not now. Not yet.

After what seemed hours, though it was probably less than one hour, I could tell by the sounds of other traffic, outdoor radio speakers, and frequent stops that we were entering a city, most likely Thanh Hóa. We made a hard turn and lurched to a stop. I was pulled out of the vehicle, and my blindfold removed. It was dusk now, but I could see we had stopped in a prison courtyard.

Iron bars were on all the windows, and heavy padlocked doors were evidence of the cells behind. I was led down a dark corridor and pushed into one of the cells. The stench almost took my breath. At the end of one of the two concrete bunks was a French-type toilet– two footpads in the concrete with a hole between them over which one could squat. There was a bucket of water and a dipper used for flushing out the hole, but the stench remained. Since getting into the vehicle, my stomach had been rumbling, and I had a terrific urge to use a toilet. As bad as the place smelled, I took off my flying suit and tried to squat down, but to no avail. My knee was so stiff and painful that I could only lean awkwardly against the wall and hope for the best. Nature would not be delayed. On the very first day of my capture, I had the first of many cases of diarrhea. No paper was available, and I was forced to clean myself with my shorts, which I dropped in the corner. I lay down on one of the bunks, feeling miserable.

A bare lightbulb hung down from the ceiling and shone in my eyes, and a couple of lizards played on the ceiling. My body and mind were numb–I just waited for what might happen next.

My cell door burst open, and amidst giggling, a half dozen uniformed Vietnamese crowded into my cell. One of them was a fairly young woman. With sign language and a few words of broken English, they tried to communicate with me. The woman, they said, had manned the gun that shot me down, but from the levity of the group I was not sure if it was their idea of a joke. I think they were just a group of young guards who wanted to see an American; no hostility was apparent. They pointed to me and asked, "Wife, babies?" I nodded yes. They laughed and asked, "You want to make baby with her?" pointing to the young woman. I wasn't sure they knew what they were saying, but from some explicit gestures, I knew that at least in jest I had been propositioned.

An older uniformed man—I guessed an officer—and a civilian then entered my cell, and the atmosphere changed as if a switch had been thrown. Everything was strictly business.

The civilian had a pad of paper and prepared to write down my answers to his questions. In very good English he asked, "What type of aircraft were you flying, from where did you take off, and what was your target?" I responded, "I cannot answer those questions." He looked up slowly, waited a few minutes while looking me in the eyes, and then said, "Things are going to go very badly for you, Captain Harris." He stood up, and the whole group left my cell and locked the door.

Soon someone rattled a key in the padlock. I caught my breath and could almost feel my pulse quicken. I wanted only to be left alone. Another intrusion in my cell would almost surely be unpleasant. The known quantity of this stark, stinking cell with the bare lightbulb giving emphasis to its utter emptiness was preferable to the unknown consequences on the other side of that door.

My sanctuary was being invaded. A guard stood holding a bowl of rice and a cup of hot water. He said, "Eat fast; we move." I was sure he had memorized this line.

When the door closed, I almost gulped the water, but it was too hot to swallow quickly. I was so thirsty that I had considered drinking the remaining water in that rusty bucket by the toilet, but the odor and look of it made me retch at the thought. I was able to finish the cup of hot water but longed for a tall, cool drink of almost anything. The rice was completely uninteresting. The door opened. Another gulp. Four guards motioned for me to follow them. The narrow corridor, lighted only from small barred transoms over the row of cell doors, led again to the courtyard. Were there other miserable souls in each of those cells? The courtyard was dark—I had not even thought about it being night or day. The normal confines of time had been replaced by the confinement of this nightmare.

At the vehicle—perhaps the same one I had come in—I was blindfolded once again, and my hands were securely tied in front. We bumped out onto a street and rode through town for fifteen or twenty minutes. My thoughts were occupied with interpreting what was happening and what might happen. My training kicked in, and I found myself more focused on gaining information around me than on myself and my predicament. After making several turns, I felt we had gone around in a circle and fully expected to see the prison courtyard again.

Instead, I began to hear loudspeakers and a multitude of voices. Perhaps this was some big rally to bolster the people's war fervor. Could it be for my benefit? No, surely not. I had already been publicly presented to the people at the police station. The vehicle stopped, and I was pulled out. My heart sank. A deafening roar from the crowd drowned out the shrill voice over the loudspeaker. My blindfold was removed, and I saw what must have been several thousand people packed into an open square. A raised platform at one end held spotlights and loudspeakers. A man was yelling into a microphone. Surrounding me were at least a dozen uniformed guards.

I was led nearby to a motorcycle with a sidecar. A guard riding in the sidecar took one end of the rope that tied my hands and tied it to a bar on the motorcycle, giving about two feet of play. We began to move, the guards walking in front of and beside the motorcycle. The going was very slow, for they had to almost push their way through the milling people. Some crowded near and shook their fists and tried to spit at me. The loudspeaker had at least done some on-the-spot language training, for I heard over and over again, "son of bitch," with a distinct Asian accent. *They should have been more careful to include the article "a," but what more could be expected from such a rush program?* I thought defiantly.

As we pushed on, I could see the people filling the wide boulevard in front of us. Some bolder young men attempted to push past the walking guards to take a poke at me. One was able to get close enough to make a wild kick at my back. The blow landed directly in my kidney area, and I felt a deep searing pain that knocked me into the sidecar and took my breath away. Just as I was recovering from this blow, a rubber shoe someone had thrown struck me in the neck. I could feel the emotional pitch of the people rising.

There was more shouting, and people crowded in so close and tight that the motorcycle was unable to move. They threw hats, shoes, and other objects and shook their fists. My guards were trying to keep the people away from me, but the crowd wanted blood. Finally, the guards physically pushed and knocked people out of the way, and we began to move again. I remembered how much I had enjoyed parades as a boy, but it sure wasn't much fun being a parade.

Though I was hit many times with glancing fists and thrown objects, the only serious blow I received was that kick in the kidneys, which was still causing intense, throbbing pain. After hobbling with my stiff knee and bruised kidneys a distance of about eight or ten city blocks, we approached a vehicle parked in the street. The entire parade had lasted no more than an hour, but it seemed like a lifetime and easily could have been. My other life, the one with a pleasant pace and fulfilling future, seemed like a distant dream from which I had awakened, only to live in the midst of a nightmare.

LOUISE 5

**APRIL 5, 1965
6:30 A.M.**

In the fog of sleep, I heard ringing. Without opening my eyes, I reached over to the bedside table and popped the round, metal alarm clock. Still, the ringing continued. As I became more awake, I realized the ringing was not the alarm clock but the telephone in the hallway. I sat up and glanced quickly at the clock—6:30 a.m.

Who is calling me so early? I wondered as I grabbed my robe and walked quickly to the hallway. I didn't want the girls to wake up quite yet, so I practically ran down the hallway as fast as my pregnant body would allow.

"Hello?" I answered, out of breath.

"Oh, Darling! I am so sorry about Smitty!"

"Mother? What? What do you mean?"

"You don't know? Oh, Honey. They called me to tell me. I thought you knew."

"Wait. Who called?"

"Smitty's mom and dad. The casualty office told them he has been shot down! That's all I know."

"I'll call you back, Mother," I said as I abruptly hung up the phone, just as my mother was saying, "Don't hang up!"

I felt very mechanical at that point. I had to find out what my mother was talking about. I quickly dialed the number of my friend Kathy Risner, the wife of the squadron commander, Lt. Col. Robbie Risner.

"Kathy, what happened to Smitty?"

"Louise, someone will be there in a few minutes."

"What happened?"

"They are coming in just a minute, Louise. They will tell you everything." Though her words were spoken with great compassion, her answers didn't satisfy.

I rushed back to the bedroom and grabbed the first dress my hand reached. My eyes filled with tears as I saw it was my red-checked maternity dress with the white Peter Pan collar. I had worn this the last time I saw my Smitty.

On that last day, Smitty and I had talked about many things but mostly plans for the future and our new child, who was to be born in two months. We both hoped it would be a boy, and I wanted him to be named Carlyle S. Harris Jr. and to be called Lyle. Smitty objected and suggested Robert C. Harris, after his grandfather.

The week before Smitty returned to Korat and combat, he went to the base legal office to update his will and to give me a general power of attorney with an indefinite expiration date. He told me he had no worry about being shot down—he was ever the optimist—but he still thought it prudent as a head of household to keep his affairs in order. I took it all in stride. When he returned from the legal office, we had a long conversation about our home, car, and major appliances. Ostensibly to see how much money we had tied up in them, Smitty made a list of their new and current values. I guess I knew exactly what he was doing, but we both maintained the pretense that it was just an exercise in curiosity. From the day I had arrived in Okinawa, Smitty let me handle the checkbook, pay all the bills, and keep track of finances—the first time in our married life he had not handled these details.

The week was over almost before it began—or so it seemed. On the night Smitty was to leave to return to Korat, we delayed our dinner until after the girls were in bed. It was a long, leisurely dinner with good food, wine, and our best silver and china—for just the two of us.

This was not an unusual occurrence when Smitty was leaving home for more than one day. I guess I'm somewhat of a romantic.

I enjoy the little extra touches that make an event memorable. And it was. Especially now.

Smitty was to return to Korat for just two weeks, and we spent the evening making plans for all the things we would do when he returned. At 1:30 in the morning, we were still talking. I had already packed Smitty's bags and hidden little notes in his clothes, reminding him to be good and telling him how much I loved him. It was a beautiful night, interrupted when a horn honked outside. It was time for Smitty to leave. He went in and kissed our sleeping daughters, and then we said our good-byes as the horn honked once again. Just like that, our wonderful week was over, and he departed for Naha Air Base for the flight to Korat. He had been there flying missions for just six days when I got Mother's call.

———————— •◦• ————————

I forced myself back to the task at hand, dressing quickly and preparing myself to hear what very well could change the course of my life. By now, the girls were up, and I knew I must prepare them for whatever might lie ahead on this dark day. I sat them down on my bed and held their hands as I told them that some people were coming to give us news of Daddy.

"Is he okay?" Robin, our oldest daughter, asked.

"Yes, Daddy is okay. Something is wrong with his plane though." This seemed to satisfy their curiosity, and thankfully, I heard Shieko entering through the carport. Shieko was my godsend. She was my full-time maid, and if truth be told, she was my best friend in Okinawa. I told her the most basic details, and she understood the situation immediately. She was the first to give me a word of encouragement.

"You no worry, Okasan. Papasan be okay," she said confidently.

While she took over the care of the girls, I allowed myself the brief luxury of releasing the tears I had painfully held. I went into our bathroom and sat on the edge of the tub.

"Oh, God," I prayed, though prayerful words seemed to escape me. Despite my wordless prayer, I knew God had heard. With new resolve, I wiped my tears and prepared to greet the infamous blue cars that all the Air Force wives silently dreaded.

As I walked down the hallway toward the living room, I glanced around the house we called home. It was a brick ranch-style house that sat on a beautiful lot high on a cliff overlooking the Pacific Ocean. Though the ceilings were low and the house small, I felt like I lived in a castle. I had so enjoyed decorating and putting special touches on our newly purchased house. It was home.

But now, everything felt strange, as if I was walking in uncharted territory. I glanced out the window and saw two blue cars pull up and park in front of our house. My heart beat rapidly as three men got out of the cars. I recognized one as the casualty officer and soon found out the other two were the doctor and the chaplain. They walked through the carport and entered the kitchen. I quickly invited them to sit in the living room, and we all sat on the rattan sectional.

"Mrs. Harris, we are sorry to inform you that your husband's plane was shot down over enemy territory. We don't yet know if he survived the crash."

"He's alive," I said forcefully.

"We don't know that for sure, and perhaps you should prepare yourself . . ."

"He. Is. Alive," I said with a fierce confidence. "I know he is. I can feel it."

We continued to talk of the limited details of Smitty's current situation, as well as my own situation.

"We will make plans to immediately fly you back home. How long will you need to pack? We can have you on the next plane out."

"No, I'm not going."

"Well, ma'am, our procedures include getting you back to the United States and to your family."

"My family is here. I am almost eight months pregnant and have been through eight OB-GYN doctors so far. I'm not moving—not yet anyway. I have to decide what I'm going to do. I own this house, and when the time is right, I will sell this house and do what is best for me and the children."

Secretly I thought, *Maybe they will find him, and he will be home quickly.* Which, of course, was only a dream. I did not yet want to know reality.

APRIL 5, 1965
8:00 A.M.

I lay motionless on the bed. I fluctuated between grief and anger. Though the team in the blue cars was compassionate, they had treated me like a helpless woman. Especially the doctor. Yes, I was almost eight months pregnant, but that was not an ailment or an illness. As I began to speak, the doctor who was sitting beside me thrust a pill into my mouth, and I automatically swallowed in surprise.

"What did you just do?" I asked incredulously.

"I just gave you a sedative," he replied, as if popping a pill into someone's unsuspecting mouth was the most natural thing in the world.

"I didn't need a sedative," I said, forcing my voice to stay in a calm octave.

"Well, I thought . . ."

"I did not ask for a sedative. As you can see, I am very much in control of my emotions," I insisted.

"Most people in your situation are very upset," he said defensively.

"I *am* upset. I am upset with you. I am almost eight months pregnant. I don't need to be taking unnecessary medication." With that, I ended the conversation, thanked the men for their support, and told them I would be in touch with them about what I decided the next best steps for me and my girls would be.

I watched from the window as the blue cars drove away. I was relieved to see them go. I had to think, and now I was afraid my thoughts would be muddled—not only with grief but also with medication. I tried to close my eyes to rest for just a bit, but I couldn't. The pill did not faze me, so great were the thoughts rolling in my mind. *Think, Louise*, I instructed myself silently. Immediately, a new strategy came to my mind. *Pray, Louise.* This gentle reminder seemed like a whisper to my spirit, and with it came a renewed resolve.

I got up from the bed and walked quietly to the bathroom—a huge room with white tile on floors and walls. At that moment, it almost seemed heavenly. And that is where I directed my attention. Heavenward.

I began to pray, as I had earlier, with a simple cry of "Oh, Lord." Silent tears streamed down my face, and suddenly more words came to my heart. Though not Catholic, I had gone to St. Genevieve of the Pines boarding school in North Carolina for ten years. The words learned from the nuns each day in chapel flowed from my lips: "Dear blessed Virgin Mary, never was it known that anyone who fled to thy protection, sought thy intercession, was left unaided. Inspired by this confidence, I come to thee, virgin of virgins, Mother of God." Then the conversation between me and my Lord continued as friend to friend.

"Blessed Jesus, may you enfold Smitty in your loving arms. Guide him and guard him, protect him, and bring him safely home. Bless my children and this baby. Help us make it through this day and the days to come. I place my total trust in you, Jesus. I rest all my confidence in you and in our heavenly Father." The words flowed freely now, as my tears also flowed freely down my cheeks. An unexplainable peace and strength filled me as I ended my prayer in the same way the Lord Jesus ended his in the garden: "yet not my will, but yours be done."

I stood up and wiped my tears. There was much to do, and I had to make myself ready. As I left the bathroom, my resolve was set. I knew deep in my heart that my husband was alive, though I shuddered to think of what he might be enduring.

If Smitty can do what he is doing right now, I can do this. I have to be strong for our girls, I thought as I walked through the house, ready to face the future.

35

SMITTY

APRIL 6, 1965

After leaving Thanh Hóa and the parade, we traveled a short distance out of the city and waited in a line of vehicles that inched forward slowly. I was blindfolded but could hear other engines start and stop, and by tilting my head back I could glimpse a line of taillights in front of us. Time seemed to have stopped. With the side curtains up, the vehicle was steaming hot, but I took some consolation in the knowledge that the two guards sandwiched on each side of me on the narrow backseat must be suffering too. They, however, were surely not suffering from thirst as I was and certainly weren't bothered by aches and pains.

Finally, I understood the delay. We embarked on some kind of ferry that would carry us across the river. I thought of my failed mission at the Hàm Rong bridge. *Surely, there is no bridge still standing,* I thought as we bumped across the river. I would learn several years later that the Hàm Rong bridge was not finally dropped into the water until August 11, 1967, with 3,000-pound laser-guided "smart bombs."

We traveled all night over paved but bumpy roads. The guards had brought food with them, and they gave me a piece of heavy French-style bread and poured a few ounces of water in a tin cup for me. Even with the water, my mouth was too dry to swallow the bread, although truth be told, I still was not hungry. The pain in my body and the uncertainty of my situation had stolen my appetite, just as the Vietnamese had stolen my freedom.

The vehicle stopped two or three times for fuel and to give the guards a chance to stretch their legs. I, however, was not permitted to move, nor was I sure I would be able to move. Throughout the long, arduous trip, the jeep remained stifling hot, and my thirst was unquenched.

Midafternoon of the following day, we entered a town large enough to have a trolley or streetcar. The sound was unmistakable, even though my eyes could not see through the blindfold. On the long journey, I passed the time by guessing where we were headed. I assumed our destination was Hoa Lo Prison, which had come to be known as the infamous "Hanoi Hilton" among the U.S. prisoners of war. The city of Hanoi, located in the northern region of Vietnam, has been the capital for almost a thousand years. The prison's actual name, Hoa Lo, is commonly translated as "stove" or "fiery furnace," or even "hell's hole." I would soon find out the accuracy of that translation as I entered my own personal hellhole.

I guessed correctly that we were in Hanoi and at least took heart that we would probably stop here and this tortuous trip would finally end. *And water! Surely, they must have water*, I thought as we slowed to a stop. I didn't know how terribly acute thirst could be.

My blindfold was finally removed. We had stopped in a courtyard with shrubs and trees that made me wonder if we were indeed at a prison. I tried to disembark but was unable to move my knee from its bent position in the crowded backseat. Guards pulled me roughly from the vehicle and half carried me through a corridor into a smaller courtyard and then into a narrow, dark hall with four cell doors facing it. Now I could clearly see that this indeed was a prison.

The cell was similar to the one in Thanh Hóa, except there was no toilet—just a rusty bucket. At the rear of the cell was a barred window above eye level, through which I could see a high wall. Embedded in the concrete on top of the wall were thousands of pieces of broken glass—old wine bottles—and above that three strands of wire strung between electrical insulators. I knew immediately that this was French construction because I had seen identical walls, minus the wires, surrounding French villas in the city of Casablanca when I had been stationed in French Morocco.

My first concern was my knee. Painfully, I was able to straighten it out, and I walked stiff-legged between the two concrete beds that were staggered, one at each end of the cell, which was about fifteen by seven and a half feet. There was no other furniture, only a short broom made of a bunch of twigs tied together and an old worn-out shoe. The previous occupant had obviously not used the broom—the place was filthy.

I sat on one of the beds, keeping my injured leg straight so that when it stiffened up, at least I could walk. I found that when I was sitting, my shoulder continued to give me much pain, so I lay on my right side with my arm resting on my left side. Just as I was getting more comfortable, I heard the keys rattle in my door. Again, I felt myself tense up and felt great apprehension. Those damn keys! For the next almost eight years, I would almost always feel some apprehension when I heard my cell door being opened.

An old guard motioned for me to follow him. We went to a windowless room, draped at one end by a dirty blue cloth. The same type of cloth covered a table in the center of the room, and a bare lightbulb hung down over the table. I was directed to sit on a short stool in front of the table. Two Vietnamese officers in uniform and a young man in civilian attire entered. I rose and saluted the older man. We had been taught to recognize senior officers when in captivity. He did not return the salute but motioned me to sit.

The young man, an interpreter, began with a well-rehearsed spiel that I was not a POW but a criminal who had perpetrated heinous crimes against the Democratic Republic of Vietnam. My mind wandered as he droned on about the righteousness of the Vietnamese cause and how my Yankee imperialistic government persisted in the warmongering, obdurate falsehood that the United States was legitimately involved in the Vietnam War. *He looks like an owl but acts like a parrot*, I thought, as I listened to his memorized lines. From then on, I called him "the Owl." Suddenly he stopped.

The older man spoke at length in Vietnamese. The Owl said, "Tell us about your mission. From what base did you fly? What type of aircraft did you fly? What is your squadron?"

Ignoring his questions, I replied, "Please have a doctor look at my shoulder and give me some water."

38

Comments were exchanged between the Vietnamese, and the Owl said, "Now you return to your cell."

Back in my cell, I felt my first real depression. I was tired, thirsty, and injured. The realization finally sank in that I was not going home to my family—today, tomorrow, or perhaps ever.

The Owl had said I would be punished for my so-called crimes. What did he mean?

I noticed for the first time the French and Vietnamese names carved in the stocks at the end of my bunk. Had they been punished? How? Where were they now?

This was undoubtedly the "Hanoi Hilton." *What an awful place! Room service, food, and accommodations are terrible*, I thought, trying to keep a semblance of my former sense of humor.

Keys rattled in my door. The old guard stood there with articles in his hands. He put them on the floor and slammed the door closed. *Stoneface*, I thought. I had never seen such an unemotional countenance. *He must be completely inured to the human suffering he has seen in this god-awful place.* But Stoneface had brought me water! It was in an old, stained, galvanized metal pitcher, and my tin cup was even more disreputable, with most of its original porcelain coating chipped off and rusting. Nevertheless, this was water, and my parched mouth eagerly emptied the cup again and again. He also had brought a too-small set of pajamas, a bowl, and a mosquito net.

Later, he brought some rice with a few small pieces of an unknown meat and gravy. I was really surprised. For some reason, I had not expected them to bring food that day. My survival training had stressed that the enemy would try to keep us alive, for we were more valuable to them alive than dead.

At least, I surmised, *they want to keep me around for now.*

SMITTY 8

For the next several days, I was interrogated two or three times a day—sometimes in the middle of the night. When I would not answer their questions, they became angry and told me that their superiors demanded answers and were losing patience with me. But mostly the Vietnamese officer would speak at length and Owl would translate.

I was given the entire history of Vietnam, stressing how they had repeatedly defeated foreign "aggression." The long war and final defeat of the French at Dien Bien Phu were covered in detail.

After about three days, I noticed that some minor burns on my neck from my parachute were becoming infected. Stoneface led me from my cell for my first bath in the DRV. The bathroom, for lack of a better name, faced the small courtyard adjacent to my cell. The dark room contained a recessed tiled area and a rusty showerhead. I turned the handle, but no water came out of the shower. Stoneface pointed to a spigot near the floor and with sign language told me to fill my bowl and pour water over my body. Only a trickle came out of the spigot, but I tried my best to clean myself, particularly my neck. It felt wonderful! My flight suit and boots had been taken away and replaced with a second set of too-small pajamas. About every two days I was permitted to bathe with strong lye soap, and I found pleasure in washing myself and one set of pajamas in the ten minutes allotted for this purpose. However, my infected neck continued to get worse.

The patience of my interrogators wore thin. The older man often got up and took a swing at me when my lack of response infuriated him. He did not use his fist as an American would but hit me with the heel of his palm. What a punch for a little man! One blow to my head often knocked me sprawling from my stool. I tried to control my emotions and be absolutely impassive. The armed guards standing in the doorway were a reminder that physical resistance would be a losing endeavor.

In one session, my interrogator seemed very pleased with himself. He said that my knee clipboard had been recovered. I knew he was lying. It had been on my knee when I ejected, but I believed it very improbable that my maps and charts could ever be found. However, he told me I had taken off from Korat, Thailand, in an F-105 and described my route of flight.

Although it was true, he must have been guessing. I would not confirm this information. In succeeding sessions, it became clear to me that indeed he did have my papers. My heart sank. Not only did my charts reveal my base and flight plan, but a careful analysis would reveal speeds and the capabilities of my aircraft. Times between checkpoints and fuel consumption were carefully annotated on my paper—all information I did not want our enemies to have.

I was taken to the blue room for another interrogation. The interrogator gave me a friendly greeting and said he had good news for me.

"You will be permitted to go home," he said proudly.

My heart leaped. "When?"

"Very soon. Perhaps one or two weeks."

I sat dumb and incredulous. I was completely unprepared for this but finally managed, "Why? Is the war over?"

"No, the war continues. Our president, Ho Chi Minh, is a very reasonable and caring man who loves the American people but hates the warmongering reactionaries who control your government and military forces. To show his love for peace and as proof of his reasonable concern for peace-loving Americans, he has agreed to release one American prisoner."

I thought it significant that this was the first time I had not been referred to as a criminal, even though I still was not given the correct title of "prisoner of war." However, I was still dubious.

"Why me?" I asked. "What must I do now?"

I knew there were other American POWs (Alvarez, Shumaker, and Lockhart), and my captors had bragged of capturing other American "criminals."

"You must show your appreciation to the government of the Democratic Republic of Vietnam by writing a letter to Ho Chi Minh thanking him for his leniency and telling him you are sorry for your acts against the DRV."

So that's what they want—some kind of confession that they can use for political purposes, I thought, as my tiny window of hope shut decidedly in my mind. *How dumb could I be to even get my hopes up? These people have no regard for humane treatment or leniency. They only want to exploit their captives for political purposes.*

"No," I answered as firmly as I could.

My answer visibly shook my interrogator. His face reddened with anger, but he retained his outward composure and asked me to be reasonable and to think about my family and loved ones. "It is only a small thing for you to do, and since Ho Chi Minh himself has showed his concern for you, it is only proper that you should show your appreciation."

Grasping at a fleeting straw, I said, "I can thank Ho Chi Minh for releasing me, but I cannot state that I am sorry for my acts. I was following a legitimate order of my government that was justified by your government waging war against South Vietnam, against the Geneva Agreements of 1954."

Again, with difficulty, he retained his composure. "Now you return to your cell and think about what I have told you."

For the next three days, my interrogators pressed me to be reasonable, but finding that I would not agree to provide them a propaganda statement, they dropped the subject. My struggle was only beginning.

SMITTY 9

As I sat in my concrete bunk in that stinking, squalid cell, the events of my life that had led to my presence there passed in an array before my mind. *What would I change? What mistakes did I make? How was I singled out for this despicable end?* Yet I felt certain that the pattern of my life had led almost inevitably to a career in the Air Force. I had not thought consciously and deeply about patriotism and duty, but my religious beliefs, family, school, and cultural background had imbued in me a deep love of my country. A large part of my satisfaction with an Air Force career was derived from the sure knowledge that I was contributing to a vital instrument of our national power.

But here I sat—miserable, dejected, and sweating in the tropical spring heat of Hanoi. My cell was dirty, dark, and depressing. Drawings and names carved in the walls told a poignant story of their own—a crude drawing of a bird and one of a sunrise, a lewd sketch of a couple fulfilling a basic human drive, a crucifix and chalice, a dagger dripping blood. All reflected the moods, fears, aspirations, and thoughts of previous inhabitants.

Some of the carvings in the cell had almost been obliterated by repeated coats of whitewash many years in the past; for now, the walls were dark gray and splotched with water marks and mold, giving the cell a look of antiquity. It was almost as if someone had purposely tried to create a dungeon that would contribute to breaking the minds and spirits of hapless inmates.

The passing of time and political regimes was attested to by the names C. Duprey, Nguyen Van Tho, Richleau, and Minh Quoc Chi

43

carved into the same heavy wooden stocks on the end of one of the concrete bed platforms. The stocks themselves, which could lock the ankles in two undersized apertures, were worn smooth by years of use in inflicted misery. I wondered how many victims in the past had shared my abode and the almost incomparable odds that would operate to make me join the experiences of such people as Duprey and Nguyen Van Tho. Just a few years earlier, I had barely even heard of Vietnam or Hanoi and knew only that they were located in some part of Southeast Asia on the other side of the earth.

Why me? I thought dejectedly.

Then quickly I began to reason with myself. *Should I be depressed and regret the chain of events that led me here? Does that help anything?*

The answer was clear. This miserable cell, the pain from a broken shoulder and sprained knee, the fear of the unknown that lay ahead, the arrogant captors bent on breaking my will, and the incessant worry about my family were the source of my mental and emotional anguish. These and other factors had contributed to my depressed state, which I was having a hard time getting around.

But then I saw it. Glancing at the wall of my cell, the crucifix reminded me that I was not alone, and the sunrise sparked a ray of hope in my tortured mind.

There will be a tomorrow. That simple thought brought with it a glimmer of hope, just as a glimmer of light shone through the barred window.

Taking stock of my situation, I realized that I had gladly accepted the challenge to give my life for the things I believed in. I was not dead but alive. My conduct in the ensuing months (perhaps years) was important to my country, my family, and myself.

With God's help, I will prevail. Now is not the time to quit but the time to fight. I must recognize my own mental, emotional, and physical weaknesses. I may have other times of low morale and resolve, but I am still an Air Force officer and must be able to bounce back from whatever comes. With these thoughts, my hope continued to rise, for whoever hopes in God will never be disappointed, as the Scriptures had told me. With renewed resolve, I felt proud to be part of the fight, part of the U.S. Air Force. I would not quit.

Of course, this mental battle continued to be a constant foe. In solitary confinement, there is much time to remember, and memory is a fickle bedfellow. It often brought smiles and even a slight comfort, but in the next minute, it would bring agitation or sadness. Even so, remembering was my constant companion.

● ● ●

The first U.S. Air Force bombing mission on North Vietnam had occurred on March 2, 1965, against the Xom Bang supply dump just north of the demilitarized zone separating North and South Vietnam. I had been on temporary duty at Korat Air Base in Thailand for about one week and was extremely pleased to be on this mission. Preceding our F-105 strike aircraft, a group of F-100s flying out of Da Nang AFB in South Vietnam had flown a flak-suppressing mission over the target. Our intelligence had told us that the target was strongly defended by 37mm antiaircraft guns and a large number of smaller automatic weapons dispersed in doughnut-shaped revetments. Their predictions proved to be true.

Just before arriving over the target, we heard over our radios that one F-100 was down and that the pilot had parachuted, landing very near the target area. We were forced to delay our F-105 strike until his position was determined so we wouldn't drop our ordnance near him. Lt. Col. Robinson Risner was in the lead F-105 over the target. His wingman, Capt. Boris Baird, was hit and had to eject from his burning aircraft.

Within the next twenty minutes, two more F-105s were shot down. Maj. George Panas nursed his crippled airplane to Laos before having to eject, and Lt. Ken Spagnola flew all the way into Thailand before ejecting. All three of my squadron mates—Baird, Panas, and Spagnola—were subsequently rescued, but my initiation into combat proved the vulnerability of our aircraft to intensive ground fire surrounding military targets in North Vietnam. This was not going to be a picnic.

In mid-March, I returned to Okinawa to rejoin my family for one wonderful week. Our household goods had arrived from the States during my three-week absence, and Louise had the new home we had bought looking great. We were happy; the girls had met some playmates and were having fun; and we were all excited over the prospect of our tour in Okinawa.

I had always told Louise about the close camaraderie that existed in overseas squadrons and the lasting friendships and great times that could be had. From the moment she and the children arrived, the squadron wives fulfilled every expectation. They brought over dinner the first night she arrived, took her shopping for some of the beautiful and useful locally produced household items that would make our house a lovely home, and displayed spontaneous friendship and help-fulness. I was certain that these friends were taking care of my family.

A few nights after I returned from Korat, we hosted a small dinner party with three other couples from my squadron. The atmosphere was joyful and lively. Looking back at that night, it resembled a memorable evening when four couples who had been lifelong friends had gotten together after a long separation. There was no talk of war, even though all four of the men had recently returned from combat and would be involved again in a few days.

We went to bed tired but exhilarated after our first party in our new home. The next morning at breakfast, Louise was glancing at the *Stars and Stripes* newspaper when she read an article about Lt. Hayden Lockhart, the F-100 pilot who had been shot down over Xom Bang. He had evaded capture for one week in the rainforests of North Vietnam but had finally been captured. A Hanoi news release was quoted as saying that even after capture, Lt. Lockhart had "persisted in the warmongering, obdurate falsehood that the United States was legitimately involved in the Vietnam war and that he had mouthed the same lies of his Yankee imperialistic government."

Louise remarked, "I don't even know Hayden Lockhart, but I like him."

The following day, Louise prepared a picnic lunch for our family, and we headed out in the car, not knowing exactly where we would go. We drove along the western coast of the island and finally found a rocky area with a steep path leading down to the sea. There we found a sandy cove protected on three sides by huge rocks and laid out our picnic.

46

The girls, now three and a half and four and a half years old, giggled and laughed as they ran in and out of the shallow surf, trying to beat the waves to shore.

I wandered off for a few minutes to look around the rocks for old weapons or other evidence of the invasion that had taken place over this same beach when the U.S. Marines landed in 1944. I found only some unidentifiable chunks of rusted metal, but stumbled onto a cave that had been carved into rocks by centuries of tidal action.

I called the girls, who thought this cave was the neatest place they had ever been. There were two entrances, and they had great fun running in and out, playing hide-and-seek with me, and listening to the echo of their voices in the cave. After a while, we returned to Mommy, and two tired little girls fell asleep on the blanket as the gentle breeze, warm weather, and swishing of the sea lulled them into dreamland. At dusk the girls awoke, and we returned home.

The day before I left, I had made great preparations. If anything should happen to me, I wanted Louise to be as well prepared as possible to take care of our affairs when she would have to move and sell most of these items. *Had I known? Deep down had I known something was going to happen?* I didn't know the answer to that, but I believed Someone had known, and I had been prompted to prepare Louise for a possible future without me. How I hoped it would not be forever!

What an enjoyable week I had spent with my family, but sadly, it ended in the middle of the night with the honk of a horn. At Naha, the C-130 that was to fly me to Korat was out of commission but would be fixed momentarily. We did not depart until 3:00 in the afternoon after spending a hot, tired, frustrating night and day waiting for the aircraft to be fixed.

● ● ●

I looked up at the tiny window of my cell. Though I could not see a true picture of the outside world, the shadows in my cell indicated that it was dusk once again—a dusk that brought a swifter and darker darkness than I ever experienced in my memories.

APRIL 11, 1965

I could hear the girls playing outside with Shieko as I washed the dishes. Warm, soothing water ran over my hands and brought a respite of relaxation. The little-girl squeals and easy laughter that drifted into the house through the open window were a balm to my soul. Smitty was still considered MIA—Missing in Action—which was devastating until I thought of the other acronym that would have caused unsurpassed grief, KIA—Killed in Action. If Smitty had been captured, I knew from my casualty officer that he was most likely being held at the Hanoi Hilton. The very name sent shivers up my spine. If I let my mind wander to what he might be enduring, it would be my undoing. My motto had become "if he can do that, I can do this."

Praying became like breathing to me. If tears came, I quietly went to the safety of my white bathroom. Shieko was the only person who had any idea how difficult that time was. She would quietly take the girls outside or distract them with a game until I could regain my composure. I had to stay strong for my children. Each night, the three of us knelt by the couch before I tucked them into bed.

"Please keep Daddy safe and bring him home soon" was their standard prayer. I hoped their childlike faith would rub off on me. I had slowly come to realize that we might not see my beloved Smitty for a long, long time. But I had to control my thoughts, lest an overwhelming wave of sadness crash over me like a tsunami, washing away my strength and resolve. *No. I will take every thought captive, as the Scriptures say. I will cast down imaginations and destroy speculations,* I would often quote to myself. I had memorized that verse in

2 Corinthians 10, and it had become my go-to when despair tried to invade my thoughts.

Today was particularly challenging. I had been dreading this day for several days. It was Smitty's birthday. How I longed to prepare his birthday breakfast–eggs, bacon, toast, and fruit. Breakfast was always his favorite meal. And I would have bought him a gift, which he would have protested due to his frugality. How I longed to hold him. Since I could do none of those things, I could at least remember him. I could celebrate him. I could rejoice that he was alive. And that would have to be enough today.

"Girls!" I called out the back door. They both looked up and smiled expectantly.

"It's time!" I said as cheerfully as I could. They came running as fast as their little legs could carry them, with Shieko close behind.

We gathered around the dining room table as we paused to admire the homemade cake. It was chocolate with chocolate icing, Smitty's favorite.

"Who can tell me why we're having cake?" I asked my girls. Both raised their hands high in the air.

"Okay, Carolyn. What do you think?"

"Because it's Daddy's birthday!" she said proudly.

"That's right! It's Daddy's birthday. And that is something to celebrate."

And then I led them in a heartfelt rendition of "Happy Birthday to You." Tears filled my eyes as we sang. But I would not let them spill over. Not now in front of my girls. Later, maybe. In the safety of my white, heavenly bathroom.

As we enjoyed the delicious cake, I wondered what Smitty was eating. *Were they feeding him?* According to the terms of the Geneva Convention, they must. But I had seen photos of other prisoners of war in other wars, the memory of which sickened me. Was he sick? Was he injured? Had he lost weight? If his stay in the Hanoi Hilton was extended, would he come out looking like those photos I had seen– emaciated, weak, and sick men who looked more like sticks than robust soldiers? Oh, I couldn't bear to picture Smitty like that!

I had learned through my mother's example what it meant to be an overcomer. When I was five years old, she was diagnosed with ovarian cancer and given months to live. Of course, I didn't understand at the time. When my father received the news of her diagnosis, he simply said he could not handle any more. He left me, my mother, and my sister Janice, who was seven years older than I was, to fend for ourselves. My Grandmother and Grandfather Rindeleau came and took us to their home. When the doctor in Asheville, North Carolina, said Mother had possibly a year to live, Grandmother and Grandfather took her to Johns Hopkins Hospital in Baltimore, Maryland. Grandfather literally carried her in and said, "Fix her." It took a long time, and many return trips over the years, but miraculously they cured Mother's illness.

During this time, Grandmother and Grandfather Rindeleau swept in to care for me, my sister, and my deathly ill mother. We lived in North Carolina with them after that. Because I was little more than a baby when all that was happening, it was years before I knew this story or was greatly affected by it. I was loved and surrounded by people who cared for me and nurtured me.

When I was six, I entered St. Genevieve of the Pines in Asheville—a private Catholic boarding school for girls. Only a small percentage of the students were Catholic—the rest were Protestant and Jewish. The nuns were wonderful, loving, kind, and firm, but always reassuringly present. At St. Genevieve I received a thorough education, well rounded in Latin, French, history, math, literature, English, religion, science, and, of course, moral guidance. The nuns' sure, steady hands and soft voices guided us. We had chapel each morning, followed by breakfast, classes, phys ed, and music education. Friday nights were movie nights, and we had plays and could go off campus for concerts or special events.

I went home on many weekends and always for holidays, summers, or special times. At home, Grandmother was in charge, but Mother was loving and close to me. Janice and I had a typical big sister–little sister relationship—we loved each other and needed each other, but she was a teenager and I was a pain most of the time. We became very close after we were grown up. Mostly, we became friends. This would serve us well in the coming years.

— • • • —

As all the realities of Smitty's situation began to close in, the irony of it all dawned on me as well. Our children, at least for some time, would be without their father, just as I had been without a father. My experience growing up without my father took place during the years of World War II. Daddies were at war. My friends' fathers were away from home many times too, which made it easier to handle my own situation. Looking back, I realized that I really had a good childhood and was well loved and cared for. Not until much later did all of the story become clear. And that would be my prayer for my own children. How grateful I was for my legacy of strength passed down to me from my mother and my grandparents. They were overcomers, and I would be too.

I rose from the table to gather the dishes. Sweet Shieko stopped me and took over. She knew how tired I was. My rotund belly continued to grow. It moved in ripples whenever the baby kicked or moved, which was basically all the time.

"It won't be long now. A few more weeks and our son will be born," I said to Shieko. *Our son—why do I keep thinking that?* I wondered to myself. But I just felt that it would be a boy. Just like I felt that Smitty would survive this ordeal. And so would I.

Carlyle Smith Harris Jr. And we will call him Lyle, I thought, resolving to name our son after Smitty, regardless of what he had said. *See you soon, little one*, I thought as I patted my belly.

APRIL 16, 1965

After about ten or twelve days, my neck was a mess. Pus oozed constantly from a large scabby area. There was much swelling, and I was running a fever. I asked repeatedly for medical attention for my shoulder and neck. Although my knee was painful and stiff, I was not worried about it. The only comfortable position for my shoulder was lying on my right side. Within a few days, my right hip, knee bones, and ankle bones were almost as painful where sores had developed from lying on the concrete bed. I switched to my back, and my tailbone became sore. I thought that the Portland Cement Company would make a fortune building the Vietnamese version of mattresses.

My interrogators told me repeatedly that I would get medical attention only after I answered all their questions. After about two weeks, I was called to interrogation, and a different officer had joined my inquisitors. I noticed him looking at my neck when I sat on my stool. He actually winced, and I saw his face pale. An hour or two after the interrogation ended, Stoneface opened my cell door, and there stood the interrogator and a Vietnamese man and woman dressed in white robes.

In fairly good English, the interrogator said, "In accord with the lenient and humane policies of the DRV, the doctor will treat your injuries." He rambled on that he and the doctor hated me and my criminal government, but they always acted in strict accord with humane principles. The doctor and nurse then cleaned the scabby area on my neck with alcohol. From their rough treatment, I truly believed they hated me, but I was determined to show no evidence of emotion or pain. They sprinkled a white powder (perhaps sulfa) on the wound and bandaged it. When they finished, they started to leave.

I said to the interrogator, whom we later called "Dog," "Please have the doctor look at my shoulder."

Dog spoke in Vietnamese, and the doctor came over and lifted my arm and let it drop. My shoulder was not displaced, though broken.

Comments in Vietnamese were exchanged, and Dog said, "Your shoulder will heal in time." With that, they departed.

Though still in pain, I was elated. I had called their bluff on "no medical treatment until you talk" and won.

In my cell, I thought often about my family. I was truly worried. *How could Louise cope with the challenges of two children, another one on the way, selling our home, moving back to the States, and the uncertainty of my situation? Where and when would she move? Did she know I was alive?* I took some consolation in the knowledge that our friends, squadron mates, and the Air Force would do everything possible to help her.

At other times, I thought of our past life together. I recalled Louise telling me that after I left for Okinawa, she spent some time with her sister and brother-in-law. He asked her to deliver an old car to the dealer from whom he had bought a new car and to drive the new one home. As she parked the old car in the lot of the dealer, the main brake cylinder ruptured, losing all its brake fluid. When a salesman tried to move the car, he put it in reverse, and the car started accelerating backward down a steep incline, across a busy street, and into a tree on the opposite side. I pictured the panic of the salesman as he applied the useless brakes and his thoughts about someone trading in such a car. I broke out in laughter.

In my peripheral vision I saw someone watching me through the small barred opening in my cell door. He must have thought I was crazy, lying there on my bunk laughing. When I turned to look at him, he closed the door over the eight-inch-square peephole. I got up, walked over to the door, and peeked through a crack to see if he was still there when he opened the peephole again. Our faces were about six inches apart, and it completely startled him. He jumped back, hitting the wall on the other side of the corridor, and then left shaking his head. If there was any doubt in his mind about the sanity of Americans, it must have been removed.

My interrogations continued. Between threats and harangues, they gave me many hours of political indoctrination and their version of history. I was shown articles by Americans that supported their position. They told me that other American criminal pilots were cooperating fully with them. They named Morgan, Shumaker, Alvarez, Lockhart, and Vohden. They said that Alvarez, the first American POW, was living very comfortably and was writing and receiving several letters each week. I asked to write too. My request was ignored, but perhaps soon they would let me write also. By the Geneva Accords of 1947, to which North Vietnam was a signatory, POWs must be permitted to write letters and receive packages from the International Red Cross. Again and again I was told that their superiors were very displeased with my arrogant, die-hard opinions and lack of cooperation. Soon their patience would be exhausted, they said, and I would be punished for my crimes—by death.

During one interrogation, my interrogator was very angry and knocked me off my stool three or four times.

"My superiors have lost all patience with you," he said furiously. "You must answer my questions," he insisted as he knocked me off the stool once again.

A guard then entered the room with a piece of paper that he gave to the interrogator. He read the paper and seemed pleased. Translating the contents, he informed me it was from the Vietnamese High Command.

"My order is for you to be punished in two days if you do not cooperate with us," he threatened.

The next morning at another session, the interrogator was still in a foul mood, and again he knocked me off the stool. He threatened me, called me stupid, and asked if I wanted to die. I was sure the whole thing was an act. The interrogation lasted about three hours. In the afternoon, I was very surprised that his mood had entirely changed. Now he was very friendly, almost fatherly.

"For your own safety you must change your attitude," he said.

He spent about two hours telling me about his life, his children, and his role in the battle of Dien Bien Phu. Finally, he said, "I like you, Captain Harris. I would hate to see you die. I will see if I can talk to the High Command and persuade them to rescind the order for your punishment tomorrow."

My head was spinning. What was the truth and what was a lie? At about nine that night, I had another interrogation that lasted about two hours. No mention was made of the previous session, and the interrogator was very angry with me. I was reminded that at eight in the morning, my punishment would take place if I did not cooperate.

As I returned to my cell, I began to worry—I had called their bluff once, but 8:00 a.m. was just a few hours away. Should I continue to refuse to give them information that I knew they already had? *Yes,* I told myself, *I am more valuable to them alive. This is still a bluff.* I was resolved that I wouldn't answer their questions.

At 2:00 or 3:00 a.m., I was still awake when keys rattled in my door. *Is it eight already?* I wondered. *Are they taking me somewhere else for my punishment?* My pulse quickened.

Stoneface motioned for me to follow him. We entered the blue room. The friendly interrogator was there, but this time he was not friendly. He explained that he had asked the High Command to be lenient, but they refused because of my bad attitude. "In a few hours you will be taken to another place for your punishment," he said ominously. "If you will just tell me the type of aircraft and the base from which you flew, I may be able to get the order changed, even at this late hour. We know you flew an F-105 out of Korat, but the High Command will recognize a change in your attitude if you will just answer these questions."

I sat silently for a while, head down. I then looked up at him and affirmed that their information was correct.

Stoneface led me back to my cell. I felt crushed. I knew I had provided no useful information, but I felt duped and tricked.

How stupid of me! I berated myself. Just an hour earlier, I had resolved to call their bluff—if it was a bluff. I tried to rationalize that I was exhausted and not alert, but still I felt a terrible guilt. I had not lived up to my own standards, my code of honor. I had lost my resolve to never answer any of their questions except name, rank, service number, and date of birth.

What now? I wondered. I remembered another moment of depression and my resolve then to recognize my own weakness.

Snap out of this, Smitty, I told myself, knowing I must tame these feelings of self-pity and guilt and do my utmost to deserve the trust my country and family had placed in me.

Please help me, God, I prayed, and felt a tiny flicker of peace. I finally fell asleep, trusting that tomorrow would be better.

MAY 1965

"Why me?" I must confess this was a sentiment that often plagued me in the early days of my incarceration. Trying to find the answer to this unanswerable question, I often thought back over my childhood. I was a typical boy from a middle-income family in a small rural town. Though I hadn't thought of it back then, I realized as I sat in that dank and humid cell that my childhood had been a very happy one. I had grown up in Preston, a small farming community on the eastern shore of Maryland. My two best friends were Bobby Plutschak and Donald Brodes.

I wonder what those two are doing right now, I often thought.

Bobby lived on a farm outside of town. Around the age of twelve, I began working for Bobby's dad on the farm. I rode my bike out there with my .22-caliber rifle resting on the handlebars, just in case we had an opportunity to go squirrel hunting.

Donald was younger than I was and lived across the street from me. He helped support their family because his father was disabled. I easily fell into the role of being there to make certain Donald had fun—and for that to take place, I would walk across the street and help him finish his work. We both were interested in building model airplanes, and our favorite was the U-Control variety, powered by a motor. We would make the plane go up, up, up and then turn swiftly and fly down, down, down.

Much like I did with my F-105, yet here I am, stuck in this hellhole, I thought miserably. How I longed to be up in the clouds, defending my countrymen once again.

In the summers I worked on Bobby's farm, went camping, and enjoyed the outdoors. On reflection, I probably had my share of an adventurous disposition. I was often one of the first to go skinny-dipping in an icy cold stream in the spring, and in winter I skated on the mill pond when there was barely enough ice to hold a boy. These best friends and I were always first to test the ice and often broke through into the shallow water. Dad was a strict disciplinarian, and he took a dim view of some of my antics.

Dad, I thought sadly. *Will I ever see Dad again?* He had been diagnosed with cancer just before I was shot down. *Will he live long enough for me to see him once again? Stop. Don't go there. I can't let those types of thoughts rule my mind.* The battle of the mind was never-ending.

For as long as I can remember, I had an active interest in aviation. Throughout her life, Mother kept the scrapbook I put together of hundreds of pictures of airplanes I collected and cataloged when I was twelve to fifteen years old. During this time, I began building model airplanes and spent a large part of the money I made as a farmhand and delivering papers to buy new engines and models. I enjoyed patching up old rubber-powered models for one last flight and sent them off with a large firecracker and extra-long fuse to provide a dramatic end to their usefulness.

I dreamed of being a pilot but doubted I would ever have the chance, much less the funds, to pursue this interest. From the time I was twelve or thirteen, I frequently pedaled my bike eight miles to a grassy strip that served as a local airfield. I volunteered to sweep the hangar and wash the airplanes, and I spent many hours simply hanging around pilots and airplanes, daydreaming of becoming a pilot myself. This persistence paid off, and I was eventually invited to take a ride in a Piper Cub airplane. I was thrilled.

The pilot air races of the 1930s were of particular interest to me, and I could see myself joining the ranks of Jimmy Doolittle, Roscoe Turner, and others who had reached the pinnacle of air racing—the Cleveland National Air Race. My early ambition to fly was finally fulfilled when I was able to qualify for the Aviation Cadet Training Program in the United States Air Force. I disdained multi-engine aircraft and wanted to fly only small fighter aircraft. My early years in pilot training and later flying the F-86F day fighter aircraft were too good to be true. It was almost inconceivable that I would be paid to do the very thing for which I had longed.

Adapting to military life wasn't too difficult, for I had been used to discipline. However, I strained the regulations to the limit and occasionally broke them when I had an urge to fly too low (buzz) or to perform acrobatics not specified in the aircraft technical order.

As I grew more experienced and mature, I came to realize the importance of the Air Force mission and took a more professional approach to the ever more complex and demanding job of being an Air Force pilot.

"Why me?" I guess the better question was "Why not me?" It could have been any of my colleagues and friends sitting here. Looking back, I believed my life had prepared me for this terrible journey in a million different ways—from hard work on the farm to the discipline of my parents, from my admiration of Donald through the difficulties of his youth to the strong will I was born with. *I can do this*, I thought, as my resolve returned yet again. "I will do this." I laid back on the cold, concrete platform that served as my bed.

Yes, my days of childhood had been happy. Was that to be true of my little ones? Would my girls be able to overcome this situation? Would they grow up happy, as I did? And what of my son? Why I felt the baby Louise was carrying was a boy, I will never know. But I did. I just knew. Was he born yet? Would I ever see him? Would I ever watch him run and play? That was the great desire of my heart—to watch my children as they experienced a happy childhood. I sighed deeply and shook the thoughts from my head. *Well, it is up to Louise now. And Louise can be trusted.* I lay down on the concrete bunk and fell into a fitful sleep, dreaming of my children running and playing in the backyard of our home in Okinawa as I looked over the steep cliff to the waters of the Pacific Ocean below, where naval ships were anchored.

LOUISE 13

I sat on the rattan sectional with swollen feet propped on a pillow, thinking back over the past thirty-eight days. I still kept track of each day. Would there ever be a time that I didn't? Would the weeks turn into months? Years? I thought back to the first day of our new "normal." Soon after the blue cars left, my friends began to arrive. Word traveled fast among the Air Force family. The first to arrive was Patti McCoy, quickly followed by Shirley Meyerholt—two of my closest friends. Kathy Risner had called to tell them what had happened.

Patti arrived first. She simply hugged me, but her presence alone was a comfort. Shirley arrived soon after her. She also hugged me and challenged me with words that both helped me and haunted me at times: "Louise, you will never be tested beyond your power to endure." I spent a lot of time praying about those words. They were hard to hear and even harder to believe, but on this side of our eight-year trial, I can confidently say they were true. When I would get to the end of my perceived endurance, something would always happen to get me over the next hurdle.

These two dear friends and many others were a healing balm at a terrible time of my life. There was an understanding among us Air Force wives. We couldn't know what tomorrow would bring—especially during this time of war. We never knew when we would play the role of comforter and when we would be on the receiving end. Either way, we all knew we would stand with each other through the triumphs and the tragedies. We were prepared for either position—well, as prepared as anyone could possibly have been.

Lt. Col. Robbie Risner had gathered the wives for a meeting before our men left for Korat. He briefed us as best he could, although he was unable to tell us of their exact mission. We couldn't know that they were flying over North Vietnam, but we instinctively did know it. We knew it was war—this was the real deal. When they went on rotation, we always knew that things could happen. We knew the possibilities. At our meeting, each wife was given full power of attorney. One wife obviously didn't need power of attorney. She seemed to already wear the pants in the family.

"How much money shall I give my husband to go on rotation?" she asked, like he was going on a field trip.

"I think he can tell you how much money he will need," Risner replied and quickly moved on to the next question.

Later, with a twinkle in his eye, Smitty asked, "Well, how much money are you going let me have, Louise?" I laughed when he asked that. And it made me laugh now, though the laughter was bittersweet. I missed that aspect of our life together so very much. Smitty could always make me laugh.

The stream of friends arriving with casseroles soon became a bit of a blur. I can't really remember what I said to them—except what I said to everyone.

"Smitty is alive. I know he is."

I am sure some of them secretly shook their heads in pity, but they were all gracious, kind, and encouraging. I knew they wanted to believe as much as I did.

———— •◦• ————

I shifted my position on the rattan sofa. My lower back had been aching all day. Now the pain came in spurts, rotating from my lower belly to my lower back. I had felt this type of discomfort before. Twice before. Yes, I was in labor. I removed my swollen feet from the pillow and planted them firmly on the floor. With a great deal of effort, I lifted my body from the sofa and waddled to the phone.

With just a few words, my plan was set in motion. Shirley was on her way to pick up the girls. I walked calmly to our bedroom to retrieve the bag that had been packed for two weeks now. Thirty minutes later, my contractions had progressed into a more regular pattern. I drove our Oldsmobile to my first stop—the Officers Club. The hospital required payment up front, and I had to get a check cashed in order to pay. After I had the cash in hand, I drove quickly and yet calmly to the hospital.

Smitty would be furious with me, driving myself to the hospital, I thought between contractions. But I had resolved to do what I needed to do, and right now, I needed to get myself to the hospital. I pulled into the hospital parking lot and parked as close to the entrance as I could. I walked gingerly to the entrance and breathed a sigh of relief that I had made it. My relief was quickly snuffed when I met the nurse at the front desk.

"May I help you?" she asked, not bothering to look up from her paperwork.

"Yes, I'm in labor. I need to be checked in for my delivery," I said calmly.

She looked up and then looked at me from top to bottom, eyes finally resting on my belly.

"You aren't in labor. Come back in a couple of days and the doctor can check you."

"I most certainly am in labor," I stated with authority and a bit of indignation.

"Honey, you aren't in labor. Trust me, I see women in labor every day."

"I am in labor. This is not my first child. It is my third. And I think I am a better judge of what is going on in my body than you are," I declared, my voice rising slightly.

She continued with this argument until my doctor walked up and glared at the nurse.

"For God's sake, let's take her back and check her," he said impatiently.

Carlyle Smith Harris Jr. was born forty-five minutes later.

My doctor jubilantly announced, "You have a beautiful son!"

"Don't be silly; I only have girls," I said incredulously.

"Well, the plumbing is wrong for being a girl," he replied with a laugh.

I laughed too. And then I cried. My tears were joyful. I was so thankful for the great gift of our son. And my tears were also sorrowful. Smitty was not there to greet his firstborn son, his namesake. But once again I remembered Shirley's words: "Louise, you will never be tested beyond your power to endure." I sure hoped she was right.

MAY 1965

"High up in the sky the little stars climb, always reminding me that we're apart."

Stardust! I listened carefully. Someone was whistling that old standard. I was no longer alone. Another American was incarcerated nearby–within hearing distance. I climbed up on my bed and yelled out in the alley behind my cell.

"Hey, American, who are you?" The whistling stopped. The alley was quiet. Again, "Who are you?"

"Hayden Lockhart" came the response from a nearby cell.

My cell door started banging. A guard was hitting it and through the open peephole motioning me to get down. In a few minutes, an interpreter entered my cell and said it was against regulations for me to climb up on my bed or to make any noise. "If you try to communicate with other criminals, you will be punished."

So there are other Americans here, I thought, elated. The Owl had told me that other Americans were held somewhere else. I had noticed that almost all activity at the prison stopped for about two hours after noon. I reasoned it would be the best time to try to talk to Hayden. I felt I already knew him from being present at his shoot-down over Xom Bang and the write-up about his capture in *Stars and Stripes*.

As soon as the prison quieted down the next day, I called out in the alley, "Hi, Hayden."

He answered, "Hi. Who are you?"

We talked quietly for about ten minutes. Hayden was just down the hall from me in cell number four. I was in number one. He told me he had been permitted to write a letter home. Again there was banging at my cell door. I got down quickly.

What great news! I immediately started composing a letter to Louise in my mind. I had a million things to tell her, but most important was that I was still alive. I worked diligently to find the right words that would bolster her spirit and give her hope for the future. I thought about all the problems she must be having and got a lump in my throat.

If only I could help, I thought helplessly. I was only partially reassured when I thought how very capable and stable she was and the help she could obtain if needed.

For the next few days Hayden and I had short conversations. He believed there was a Navy pilot in another cell facing our small courtyard.

"Perhaps we could get in contact with him by passing a note in the bath area," I said.

I heard keys at my cell door. They must have heard us talking again. A guard I had not seen before made motions for me to pick up my bowl, net, pajamas, and grass mat that I now had and to follow him. I knew I was moving from this cell, but where? I guessed that I was being separated so I wouldn't be able to talk to Hayden. *Or perhaps I'm being moved to another camp*, I thought.

We walked through the corridor I had entered twenty days ago into the large courtyard with trees and shrubs. Entering another corridor, we stopped at a wide door that opened onto a dark hall. A strong smell of urine combined with human sweat produced a heavy, damp, musky odor that spoke of misery and suffering behind the eight cell doors facing the hall. The odor recalled a vision of some underground dungeon, and the foot-and-a-half brick-and-mortar walls furthered the illusion. I entered cell number four at the end of the hall. My heart sank as the cell door was closed, bolted, and locked behind me.

This cell was almost half the size of the one I had just left. In the seven-by-seven-foot area, concrete bunks on each side left a two-foot aisle, at the end of which was the only other furniture, a rusty one-gallon can. I sat on a bunk, utterly dejected.

How can I keep my sanity locked in this tiny dark cell for who knows how long? Will I ever get used to the musky odor?

I noticed a familiar-looking peephole with a door on the outside in my cell door. Above the door was a barred transom. I climbed up on the stocks at the end of each bed, straddling the aisle, and was able to look out onto the hall.

I whispered loudly, "Any Americans here?"

In a moment, an answer came back: "Yes, it's me in cell number one." So Lockhart had been moved too.

"How goes it, Hayden?"

A long pause. "Who is Hayden? I'm Scotty Morgan. Who are you?"

"I'm Smitty Harris."

"Oh. Phil Butler, a Navy lieutenant, was here last night and this morning."

The door at the end of the hall banged open. Guards opened our peepholes. "Keep silent."

A guard menacingly pointed at the leg stocks as a reminder of what would happen if we continued to talk.

Scotty and I were the only two occupants of the cellblock. Cell number eight, directly opposite Scotty, was the latrine, which explained part of the odor. Each morning, we emptied our buckets, dumping them out a four-inch drain hole at the back of the cell. A showerhead had been installed over that end of the cell that at least gave a trickle of water when we were allowed to bathe.

Guards entered the cellblock at all hours of the day and night. Rather than walking back to the drain hole, they stood in the doorway of cell number eight and urinated on the floor. Being permitted to bathe in the cell was a mixed blessing.

The door at the end of the hall was usually left open, but Scotty was able to reach outside his transom and with a spoon pull the door open enough so he could give it a good push to slam it closed. When it was closed, we could talk quietly with little chance of being caught.

Scotty said the only other American he knew of was Lt. Cdr. Ray Vohden, who was in a cell nearby. He had been able to communicate with Ray by talking out of the high, barred window that faced the courtyard. Even though he could climb up on his bed and look out, it was impossible to completely clear the area, and he had been caught talking several times. So far the Vietnamese had only threatened punishment.

Ray had been shot down on the third of April and had a compound fracture of his leg. The Vietnamese had set his leg, but it had become infected, and Ray had been in excruciating pain. This, combined with high fever from the infection, had caused him to become delirious. The Vietnamese had finally begun to give him penicillin, but he was still very weak.

My cell was closer to Ray's, so I tried to contact him, without result. Through the window I could see the doctor and nurse often enter what Scotty told me was his cell, so I assumed he was still alive.

Scotty and I talked often. One day, I called down to him and as an opener said, "Scotty, this is the crummiest hotel in the world, and the room service is terrible."

Scotty replied, "You've got that right. This is the original Heartbreak Hotel."

From then on, this block of eight cells in the "Hanoi Hilton" was called "Heartbreak Hotel." A large percentage of American POWs would spend some time here and usually shortened the name to "HBH."

● ● ●

I heard someone whistling softly, "Daddy's Little Girl," the 1950s hit song recently rereleased by Frank Fontaine: "You're Daddy's Little Girl ... my Pot of Gold, you're Daddy's Little Girl to have and hold."[*]

Tears welled in my eyes, and I was unable to swallow because of the lump in my throat. I thought about Robin and Carolyn and how much I loved and missed them.

It suddenly dawned on me that the whistling was not coming from HBH but from outside. I climbed up on my bed and without caution said, "Is that you, Ray?"

---

* Bobby Burke and Horace Gerlach, "Daddy's Little Girl" (1949), Vocal Popular Sheet Music Collection, Score 547, https://digitalcommons.library.umaine.edu/mmb-vp-copyright/547.

Ray answered immediately. We talked briefly. Ray said he was very weak but was doing better. He was from Memphis and had two children. Loud voices and men entering HBH interrupted our talk.

An interpreter and guard entered my cell, and I was thoroughly chastised for communicating with Ray. They threatened severe punishment if I talked with him again. In my opinion, it had been worth it.

My shoulder was still painful and useless, but it was much improved. As long as I didn't move it, it gave me little discomfort. I had begun an exercise program of sit-ups and some isometric exercises, moving my left arm gingerly and pressing and pulling my hands up to the point of pain in my shoulder. My right knee was still stiff, but I spent hours walking back and forth in the narrow aisle.

Despite the threats, I continued to talk daily with Ray. By watching the area carefully during siesta, we usually could talk quietly without being caught. After about a week, I thought to ask Ray if he was doing any exercises, as they might be helpful to regain his strength.

He answered, "No, today is the first day I've been able to sit up to be fed." I hadn't realized how very sick he was. His voice was strong and confident. He said the Vietnamese were going to take him to a hospital to operate on his leg when he was a little stronger.

On the tenth of May at dusk, an Army ambulance drove into the courtyard. As they carried Vohden out on a stretcher, both Scotty and I stood at our windows and yelled out, "Good luck, Ray." The guards scowled and yelled back at us in Vietnamese, but no further action ensued. I learned that he had a compound fracture of his fibula; the bones were broken in two. But his leg had become infected, and his moans and groans of pain had increased significantly. Both ends of the broken bone became infected. At the local hospital, they sawed off both ends of the infected bones. He was back in the cell that evening, and the horror of his suffering echoed through the walls. He was delirious with pain, and it was a month or more before he was coherent again.

Ray's suffering disturbed me to the deepest depths. They gave him a few shots of morphine, but when the effects wore off, he was almost out of his mind in agonizing pain. His moans echoed through the cellblock, and Scotty and I cringed in helplessness, knowing we could do nothing for him. The pain slowly subsided to the point that we could communicate again. He had been put to sleep with ether, but the hospital conditions were terrible—a dirty room with an oilcloth-covered operating table and open windows for mosquitoes to swarm in and out. Though Ray survived the grisly ordeal, he was still using crutches at the time of our release, nearly eight years later.

Scotty Morgan and I were now old friends. We had been together in HBH for what seemed an eternity but was actually less than three weeks. We talked daily and found out a great deal about each other. Scotty's principal hobby had been hunting and guns, while mine was golf. Scotty was Protestant and I was Catholic, but both of us had a deep faith that was strengthened through prayer since our capture. We found out that both of our wives were pregnant and talked of plans for our families when we were released.

Scotty closed the door at the end of the hall and called down to me. "Smitty, I know we're of different faiths and that your new child will have Catholic godparents. Nevertheless, if it's okay with you, I'd like to be an honorary godfather."

I was deeply moved. It took a few moments before I could speak. "Scotty, I would be extremely honored for you to be godfather to my child, but only under the condition that I can be honorary godfather to your and Ruth's new baby." The pact was made. Scotty promised to give my son (hopefully) his first shotgun, and I promised to give his child his first set of golf clubs. That was a happy thought, which I savored for a long time.

MAY 1965

Any time a turnkey guard arrived at our cell door other than at the standard times, we experienced a feeling of dread. One day, I received the command to change from my standard prison shorts to the long pajama-like garb, which indicated I would be taken to the blue room for more interrogation. Thankfully, the interrogation that day included repeated questions and attempts at indoctrination—which I saw right through—and not torture. I repeatedly asked to write a letter home. When my interrogators had left the blue room, Owl, with his bugged-out eyes and emotionless countenance, told me I might be able to write soon.

He seemed receptive, so I told him my wife was expecting a baby, and a letter from me would be most helpful and encouraging. He said he would talk to the authorities. I didn't hold out much hope that the attitude of the authorities toward me would change enough to permit this. On the following day, I was taken to interrogation once again.

In every camp, there were two arms of camp authority—a political arm and a military arm. All interrogators worked for the political officer in the camp. One of these we had nicknamed Dog. He was the English-speaking political officer I had spoken with about my shoulder.

Dog showed me the wallet of Major Lawrence Guarino and asked me if I knew him. I said, "No, I have never known a Major Guarino."

As a matter of fact, I did know Larry, and the picture on his ID card was very good. He was in a sister squadron at Kadena and had been with me at Korat.

I asked, "Where did you get this wallet?"

"He was shot down and perished in his burning aircraft. This is his last effects."

I knew Dog was lying. If Larry had burned with his aircraft, the wallet would not have been in perfect condition.

On June 22, Owl entered my cell while the turnkey waited outside. This was the first time he had come to my cell, and I hoped it was to tell me that I would be permitted to write home. Instead, he said, "I have come to tell you that on May 14, your wife gave birth to a son. Both are doing well."

I asked, "How do you know?"

He responded, "Guarino told me."

What great news! I was grateful to Larry for passing the information to me and was convinced my prayers had been answered.

Soon after, new guests arrived at Heartbreak Hotel. Within a few days, Air Force Lts. Bob Peel, Paul Kari, and Ron Storz were moved in. Navy Lts. Bill Tschudy and Hayden Lockhart filled up the remaining available cells. The halls buzzed with conversation. Although we were all in solitary confinement, we became very close. How true is the old cliché—misery loves company. Our morale soared with the increased contact with our new friends.

All of us had found by now that our interrogators were very ignorant and unsophisticated about flying and tactics. We all spent hours in interrogation, most of which was political indoctrination. However, we found it advantageous to answer their questions and give them deliberate misinformation about our aircraft, armament, and tactics. Generally, they did not know what questions to ask and had no concept of how we did our jobs.

For many questions we would reply, "I don't know." The interrogators would insist that we *did* know, and by letting them prod and suggest possible answers, we could find out what they thought the answer should be. In feigned resignation, we would agree with their answers, which they dutifully wrote down—and which couldn't have been further from the truth.

One technique I used in the interrogation room was very helpful. Lt. Col. Robbie Risner, my squadron commander when I was shot down, was one of the strongest, most capable air leaders I had ever known. Because I had such great respect for this man, in the interrogation room I always pretended to myself that Robbie was on a stool beside me and was observing everything I said or did. Even when I was tired from lack of sleep and both mentally and physically exhausted, his presence beside me helped me keep my mind on the task at hand.

Hayden Lockhart told me of one interrogation he had with Dog. We were continually referred to as criminals, and to make their point, our interrogators accused us of all kinds of atrocities, showing us pictures of mutilated babies, bombed churches, and so on to make us feel personally responsible. In the interrogation room, Dog accused Hayden of killing his aging mother.

Knowing it was all a lie, Hayden asked him, "How did I kill your mother?"

"My mother is very old, and in the village where she lived, I dug a trench about fifteen meters from her hut so she could protect herself when you Yankee dogs bombed and strafed innocent civilians. One day, you [shaking his finger in Hayden's face] bombed and strafed her village, and she was unable to get into the trench before she was killed."

Hayden responded, "I didn't kill your mother; you did."

Dog slapped the table with both hands, jumped up, and said, "What do you mean I killed my mother?"

Hayden answered, "If you had dug the trench closer to the hut, the old lady would have made it."

Dog was so angry that he stomped out of the room, unable to speak.

Through our windows facing the courtyard, we could see food being taken to a cell diagonally across from us. We assumed it was an American POW, perhaps Alvarez, but the distance made conversation with him impossible. How could we communicate with him? We enlisted the unwitting help of one of the somewhat-less-than-bright guards in the system.

Rudolph—so named because of his red, bulbous nose—often acted as our turnkey, opening our cell doors when we bathed, picked up our food, or dumped our buckets. He loved to talk to us. He spoke in Vietnamese, and, of course, we used English. But he never realized that our animated conversations with him were actually directed to the other cell occupants, telling them about our latest interrogation or other information—completely free from suspicion or censure.

Scotty Morgan, over several sessions, taught him to count to four—in a Southern accent. We could hear Rudolph walking outside practicing, "One, two, three, fo." Then, when he delivered food to the man across the courtyard, we heard him proudly say, "One, two, three, fo" as he opened the door.

If it was Alvarez, we wanted him to know there were other Americans here with him, so we taught Rudolph to say, "Hi, wetback." We used this good-natured ribbing, for we knew Alvarez would recognize this as coming only from his fellow pilots. Rudolph practiced his new linguistic abilities in the yard for two or three days as he walked around, and then one day we heard him say loud and clear as he opened the other cell door, "Hi, wetback." A year later, I was finally able to communicate with Alvarez and learned that indeed he had received the message.

At the end of our hallway, there was a covered peephole, which I assumed opened into another cell, although there was no door on this side. I felt compelled to look through to see if there were Americans on the other side, but I was always accompanied by a guard in the hall.

Rudolph opened my cell door holding a bucket and short broom. He indicated he wanted me to wash down the cell diagonally across the hall that was temporarily empty. I acted as if I didn't know how to do it and made motions for Rudolph to show me how. He took the bucket and broom and began sweeping. I stepped out into the hall, walked quickly to the end, and opened the peephole. On the other side was a large cell, approximately twenty by twenty feet, and inside were a large group (perhaps thirty) of dirty, bedraggled-looking Vietnamese prisoners. I closed the peephole and started back to Rudolph when he popped out of the cell, scowling and angry. He was completely ignorant of what I had done and within five minutes had forgotten the incident as I finished sweeping out the cell.

All of these efforts to gather information and to communicate were about to change. And it had all begun when a chance encounter with an instructor collided with my insatiable curiosity.

73

SMITTY 16

Looking back, I can see it clearly. It was a plan of provision orchestrated by the Supreme Maestro, wrapped in the costume of a chance encounter—insignificant at the time—which, years later, made a difference in my life and in the lives of more than 350 other POWs at the Hanoi Hilton.

It was June 1963. I was in Escape and Evasion school in Nevada. The program involved classwork, followed by hands-on instruction through the rigorous experience of being put out in the mountains all alone, with no provisions whatsoever. If we had learned well, we would return unscathed.

One of the sergeants, Claude Watkins, was my instructor. In class one day, Watkins casually mentioned that a POW in Germany used a Tap Code that, when applied to the water pipe, sent messages throughout the prison to the other POWs. I lingered after class, as my curiosity had produced a question that seemed unimportant at the time.

"How did the POWs handle the dashes?" I asked.

"Oh, I should have clarified. This was not Morse code. Got a minute? I can show you."

Sergeant Watkins went to the chalkboard and began writing down the Tap Code. It was a five-by-five matrix of the alphabet, excluding the letter K, which was indicated by a slow C.

The whole conversation appeared to be happenstance; the information was received due to my ever-inquisitive nature. But the unfolding of time would reveal a much greater purpose for that casual conversation.

———● ● ●———

Back in the Hanoi Hilton, I had an unexpected visitor on a hot and humid summer day. Stoneface, whom I had not seen since I had moved to HBH, opened my cell door, indicating for me to roll up my mat for a move. It was now June 24. I was apprehensive about leaving my friends and familiar surroundings—the very cell that had so depressed me two months earlier. We walked back past the blue room into the small courtyard but turned right, away from my first cell. Stoneface opened a cell door, and I entered.

I couldn't believe my eyes. Three grinning Americans greeted me—Phil Butler, Bob Peel, and Bob Shumaker. It was midafternoon, but we were all so excited at being together that we talked, joked, and swapped stories until dawn. All four of us had been in solitary confinement until that day. So far, we had only been able to use voice contact for communicating with other Americans. We were going to have to devise other tactics, as the Vietnamese were making greater efforts to prevent talk, and there was no way to reach HBH by voice.

And then I remembered. The memory came clearly and vividly, and I easily relayed what I had learned from my instructor that day years before. I explained to the others about a Tap Code that used a five-by-five matrix of the alphabet:

	1	2	3	4	5
1	A	B	C	D	E
2	F	G	H	I	J
3	L	M	N	O	P
4	Q	R	S	T	U
5	V	W	X	Y	Z

With two sets of taps, we could identify the column and row that designated any letter of the alphabet. For our purposes, this was superior to the Morse code because of the difficulty of sending a dash.

Although we had no need for the Tap Code at that point, I taught it to my three cellmates for possible future use. From my interrogators,

I was able to conclude that the DRV was under some pressure to live up to the Geneva agreements regarding POWs by permitting International Red Cross inspection of our camp, letter exchange, and packages. Several times they mentioned that the Red Cross wanted to meddle in their internal affairs but that we were criminals, not POWs. To relieve some of this pressure, I believe, two days after Peel, Shumaker, Butler, and I moved together, Stoneface brought us paper and ink to write letters home.

We were elated, though dubious that the letters would ever be sent. There was so much I wanted to say, but words were simply not adequate to express my love, care, and concern for Louise, Robin, Carolyn, and my new son. I had no idea where they might be, so I addressed the letter to Tallahassee, Florida, where Louise's mother lived.

Time passed much more quickly with the four of us together. We scratched a checkerboard into the seat of a stool in our cell and used bits of paper as pieces. We now bathed daily in the same bathroom I had first used. Everyone was following an exercise program. My knee was almost completely well, and my shoulder had healed, though there was still a rough spot in the socket that caused it to bump and catch when I raised my arm high. Food, as always, was brought to us two times a day.

Shumaker was still suffering from a back injury he had received upon ejection from his F-8 fighter. After repeated requests for medical attention, a week or two after he was shot down, he was taken to a hospital and was put on an operating table while a doctor and two nurses posed with him for a cameraman.

When the cameraman finished, an English speaker said it was time to return to the prison. Shumaker said, "How about my back?"

The interpreter said, "The doctor says your back will be better in time."

Shumaker returned to camp, his back never having been examined—the propaganda of war on full display.

By looking out a crack in our door, we saw two other Americans being taken to the bath. I had to see one of the men twice before I was convinced he was Larry Guarino. He had lost so much weight that I almost did not recognize him.

Partly because he was more senior (a major) but mostly because he had infuriated the senior interrogator, he was on half rations and had one ankle in the stocks. I looked down at myself and realized that I too had lost twenty or more pounds since my capture. *Larry must really be hungry*, I thought. We established contact with him, and in a few days with Commander Jeremiah Denton as well, by leaving notes in the bath area. Both were being held in the cellblock where I had first been held. Phil Butler suggested that this area of the prison be called New Guy Village or NGV.

As the senior POW, Commander Denton started issuing instructions and gave guidance through our note system. He asked that we draw up escape plans, assigning probabilities for exiting the camp and for escape from the country. We brainstormed for several days, but the probability of success seemed very small. We thought our best chance might be to turn ourselves over to the Swiss embassy for asylum if we could successfully exit the camp. We needed more information before anything could be put into effect. We had developed a simple code so that our captors would not be able to obtain useful information should our notes be intercepted. Our efforts were not wasted. A Vietnamese prisoner found one of our notes in the bath area and turned it over to the guards. Dog was furious with us and put us all back in solitary confinement.

POWs were shuffled between cells. Shumaker and I ended up in cells six and seven of HBH. Conditions had changed. Covers had been nailed over the transoms; the windows were boarded up to a narrow slot at the top; and guards roamed the hall frequently. Voice communication was difficult, so Shu and I tried the Tap Code. We were very slow at first, but our speed picked up quickly. We passed the system to the other men in HBH. We placed an ear to the wall and tapped lightly, making it difficult for a guard to hear what we were doing.

Our solitary confinement lasted only a week until we four were put back together again. I think the pressure of numbers caused this move, for new American POWs were arriving and were invariably placed in solitary confinement. Our captors simply needed the space and were not yet prepared to open up a new camp or even a new area of the Hanoi Hilton.

Our return to HBH had been very beneficial. We had passed the Tap Code to six other POWs and had set up a system of communication between HBH and NGV. Our food was brought into the prison in stacked metal containers held together by a metal strap and handle. We had stolen a pencil from an interrogation room and wrote short messages on the bottom of the strap under the handle.

When our meal containers were taken out of our cells, some of them would be mixed up at the next meal and arrive at the other part of the Hanoi Hilton, thus transporting the messages we wrote. It took about two weeks before the Vietnamese discovered our deception and put a stop to it. By this time, the names of everyone in camp, including some new arrivals, had been passed between the two areas.

Although Stoneface was our regular turnkey, Rudolph came from the HBH area one afternoon to see us. He opened our cell and entered, leaving the key in the lock. He seemed pleased to see us and talked animatedly in Vietnamese. He loved to make a shooting sound and use his hands to act out an aircraft being shot down and a pilot coming down in a parachute.

He would laugh and point to one of us. While he was so engaged, Bob Peel walked out of the open cell door into the courtyard. Seeing the key in the lock, Bob closed the door and locked it from the outside. Rudolph was beside himself. He banged on the cell door and spoke loudly in Vietnamese. Bob, fearing a not-so-simple guard would cause real trouble, reopened the cell door and entered. Rudolph scolded him, shaking his finger in Bob's face. Within a few minutes, however, we had Rudolph acting out his shoot-down story again. He had completely forgotten the incident.

Our food had been getting worse and worse. We were getting almost no meat or fresh vegetables and fruit. Our captors stopped bringing our food from outside the camp and gave us food from their own kitchen. It usually consisted of a small loaf of bread, some thin, watery soup, and an awful side dish—usually a boiled vegetable, many of which we could not identify. Sometimes it was pumpkin and sometimes sliced boiled cucumbers. How I longed for Louise's home-cooked meals. As I lay on my cot, I would sometimes eat a meal with my family—course by course, bite by bite—in my imagination.

One day, while lying on my concrete bunk, I held my small tin cup in my hand and felt the smooth metal and the rough twine wrapped around the handle. I had added the twine from a cord I had found on the ground. Though rough, it protected my hands from the uncomfortable heat of the hot water they provided from time to time. I thought of Louise and her effortless way of creating beauty in a family meal. Louise could dress a table like no other. Not one to save the fine china for fine events, Louise could make a special event out of a simple meal. A table complete with china and linen napkins, silver flatware with the various sizes of forks and spoons, each with their assigned designation—these wedding gifts were pleasures to Louise and reminders to both of us of happier days when our two lives had become one life. Now those days seemed a lifetime ago, so far away and yet so precious and so familiar. Homesickness swept in like a furious wind.

"To have and to hold, from this day forward, for better, for worse, for richer, for poorer, in sickness and in health, to love and to cherish, till death do us part, according to God's holy ordinance." Our vows had been spoken with both sincerity and naivete. Now they were being tested like silver in a furnace. And they would come out gleaming and stronger and more valuable—of this I was sure—not like the flimsy tin I held in my hand.

Yet this is what I have for now, I thought with renewed resolve. Gone were the dinners with Louise and friends and family, delicious food, and fulfilling fellowship. For now, I had this tin cup and watery soup that quieted the roaring of my hunger, yet brought the misery of diarrhea and constant nausea.

I rubbed the smooth metal once again and then pulled out the small stick I had picked up as I emptied the contents of my waste bucket weeks ago. With the stick I etched my initials into the thin metal: S. H.

It felt good to make my mark. I was here. This was the hand I had been dealt. This was my lot in life. I prayed I would one day return to the fine china of my beloved Louise, but even more, I prayed for the strength to return with honor. Return with honor. Yes, that was my highest goal. Alone with these thoughts and many others, I once again dipped my tin cup in the murky water bucket in the corner of my windowless, concrete cell. Never in my wildest dreams would I have imagined that my small tin cup would one day be featured in the National Museum of American History at the Smithsonian.

LOUISE 17

JULY 1964

I sat on the base-issued rattan sofa in the living room of the home I had once shared with Smitty.

Fourteen weeks, I thought. Fourteen weeks since I had heard his voice, fifteen since I had seen his face. I closed my eyes and allowed a rare moment of remembering. Scenes like an old movie reel flashed in my mind as I remembered my former life, which now seemed light-years ago.

Mustn't stay in that place long, I reminded myself as I opened my eyes and looked around the room. Most of its square footage was taken up by sealed cartons filled with our belongings, ready to be shipped back to the United States, where the children and I would be in a matter of days. Three suitcases that would fly back with us sat in the corner of the room. A wave of anxiety swept over me, and just as I had learned to do on the beaches of Panama City, Florida, as a young girl, I braced myself to stand against the waves and then recovered quickly to focus on the task at hand.

Mentally, I went over the day's plans, stoically omitting the emotional side of leaving–that is, until Shieko entered the room. So lost was I in my focused thoughts that I had not heard the kitchen doorknob as Shieko had entered our home for the last time it belonged to us. Another couple would soon move in, and Shieko would faithfully serve them as well, for that is what she had announced on the day we had moved in–"Hello, Okasan. My name Shieko. I come with house."

"Oh. Well, I will have to talk to my husband."

"No, I come with house." And so it was. And oh, what a blessing it was that we had selected this house, for Shieko's quiet servant's heart had been a balm to me from day one, especially in the dark days of the past two months. My eyes filled with grateful tears for this small, spunky, forty-something Japanese woman who had loved us well. I quickly squelched the emotion and stood to once again work side by side with Shieko.

Avoiding the emotion of the coming good-bye, we together set about completing the final tasks of preparation for the unknown journey ahead. Two hours later, all tasks were completed, and all was ready for departure. Since our car had been sold, Bill and Shirley Meyerholt and Patti and Ivy McCoy had volunteered to take us to the airport. Shirley and Patti were two of my best friends—family in every sense except blood. That was the hardest part—leaving my people. These friends, and many others, had gone above and beyond to comfort, help, and serve me and the children. From meals to babysitting to crying in their pillows through their late-night prayers on our behalf, these people embodied the essence of true friends.

The storm of dread once again churned in the pit of my stomach when I heard their car arrive. I was about to embark on a journey, trading in my known reality for a life of unknowns. My support system was intact here. We Air Force wives knew the complexities of this life of sacrifice we had all chosen. Back home, there were even greater complexities to come that I had not chosen. And as my mind traveled ahead, cataloging the options before me, I realized that returning to the U.S. meant I would be more than seven thousand miles further away from my Smitty and the life we had lived together.

I was also closing a door to information. Would I be apprised of the information, as I had been here? Claude Watkins was my casualty officer, the same Sergeant Watkins who taught Smitty the Tap Code, though we didn't realize the significance of this at the time. He went beyond the designated procedures of tending to this wife of an MIA. Unbeknownst to me at the time, Officer Watkins had an even greater role to play in our story, for he had been Smitty's instructor at Escape and Evasion school, who had by chance drawn out the grid for the Tap Code that Smitty had by this time begun to share with other POWs, who shared with others, who shared with others. If I had been privy to this information at the time, I might have been more confident in what lay ahead. With the poor health of Smitty's parents and the weak constitution of my own mother, I knew I must be the strong one. I must be the one to decide what life my children would experience in the coming months, maybe years. Even so, I applied my mustard seed of trust and faith and walked forward into an unknown life.

Officially, Smitty was still MIA—Missing in Action. I was constantly reminded by officials that they had very little information. But I knew. I knew he was alive, and I knew he would one day come home. I just wasn't sure when that would be and where he would find us.

When the suitcases were loaded, Shieko walked with us to the car. The emotions that I had successfully held back thus far began to force their heavy weight beyond what I could bear. Tears filled my eyes as I saw Shieko's own tears silently fall when she hugged four-and-a-half-year-old Robin and three-year-old Carolyn. She hugged them tightly and then patted their blonde hair, which contrasted greatly with her own ebony strands salted with the grays of middle age. She then reached for six-week-old Lyle and quietly held him, as if they were the only two in the world. Soon she returned him to my arms and leaned in to share a long embrace with me. Tears threatened to overflow, and my voice shook with emotion as I spoke in her ear.

"Thank you, Shieko. For everything. I love you," I said.

"I love you too, Okasan."

"I will try to get messages to you," I said hopefully.

"Not worry, Okasan. I will keep up with you."

We parted and both helped the children into the car. Patti held Robin; Shirley held Carolyn; and I entered last with Lyle in my arms. Bill and Ivy sat up front, and as Bill pulled away from the curb, I looked back through the window to see petite, precious Shieko waving her American family away to a new life. I never saw Shieko again, and though we exchanged messages through Bill and Shirley for a while, we eventually lost touch. But Shieko will forever be in my heart—a beautiful bright memory in my life's story.

The drive was subdued, and even the girls seemed to understand that this somber moment required soft and quiet tones. We drove to the base, where we would spend the night in a Quonset hut in a BOQ–Bachelor Officer Quarters–at the base. The girls' previous subdued behavior immediately was overturned when they saw the bunk beds in the hut. Patti and Shirley hugged the girls before leaving, promising to return the next day to drive us across the base to catch our flight home. In time, the girls settled down and quickly slipped into a sound sleep, as did Lyle. What a mercy that Lyle was an easy baby. I, however, did not sleep.

Questions flew across my thoughts in quick succession and then lined up to be repeated in random order throughout the long night. *What is ahead? Where will we live? A house? An apartment? How will everyone react? What will the trip home be like? How will Smitty's parents react to our homecoming without Smitty? They were not well. His father had cancer, which had been diagnosed before we left. Would he live to see Smitty's homecoming, which I was certain would one day come?*

I would soon find out that Smitty's determination to live was likely inherited from his father, who was also determined to live until he could see his son again. In the coming weeks, months, and years, he would constantly say to me, "I can't wait to see Smith come home." That sentiment seemed to improve his health more than any medication he took to combat his cancer. He held off his heavenly homecoming until his eyes had once again beheld his son. He died seven months after Smitty returned home.

The next morning, Bill, Shirley, Patti, and Ivy returned as promised to once again load our suitcases into their blue sedan and take us on the final leg of our Japanese journey. We approached the giant aircraft that had already begun the low rumbling of its engines, preparing for takeoff. The wind blew the girls' blonde hair across their faces, and Shirley held it back as she hugged them and kissed their soft cheeks. Patti lifted the girls one at a time, knowing her pregnant belly would not allow her to kneel gracefully before them as Shirley had. Patti hugged them each tightly, while their little legs fell straight before her, much like the tears falling down Patti's cheeks.

Telling these friends good-bye was one of the hardest parts of leaving. My stomach wrenched, and my heart felt as if it were breaking, but I didn't cry in front of them. Smiling, I said, "It's all going to be fine. I will be good," trying to convince myself as much as them. I hugged them both tightly as I told them I would miss them and that I loved them dearly.

Standing outside the big plane, Bill said, "Louise, I will go with you," just as he had said many times before.

"I will be fine," I repeated my parrot-like response.

Another officer about to board the plane overheard the exchange and offered to sit with us and take responsibility for the girls. I declined. My children needed me. And that knowledge was what gave me the strength to climb the steep metal steps with my children in tow. I stopped at the top of the portable steps and then turned back and waved to my dear friends. It would be many years before I saw them again, and just as I knew at the time, they turned out to be lifelong friends through every future season. I then took a deep breath and entered the plane. I settled the girls into a three-seat section and took my seat by the aisle, with Lyle contentedly resting in my arms. I forced a smile on my face, wanting to encourage the girls and assure them all would be well. I wanted to believe that myself. I didn't look out the window, so focused was my illusion of cheerfulness, but if I had, I would have seen my dearest friends waving to the plane, with tears streaming down their cheeks.

As the plane roared and the landing gear retracted within the belly of the plane, I dispersed snacks and new coloring books and spoke to the girls of the exciting adventures we would embark on as soon as we landed in the United States. More than any other time, I finally realized it truly was the home of the brave, and I was determined to be counted among those brave ones.

LOUISE 18

Thirty-three hours, forty-three minutes. That's how long the plane rides were from Okinawa to Andrews Air Force Base in Prince George's County, Maryland. Looking back, the plane rides were a bit of a blur. I do recall passing out many snacks and complimenting many newly colored creations. I also recall praying for a long stretch of sleeping time for all of the children. The Lord must have heard my cry for mercy, as my prayer was answered and the girls and Lyle slept soundly for hours at a time. I, on the other hand, slept only stretches of a few minutes.

By the time our plane landed, exhaustion had begun to break through my cheerful illusion. A second wind of energy came as we neared the base. We were minutes away from seeing Smitty's parents and my mother. I knew the reunion would be emotional, filled with unspoken words of grief and the unmistakable joy of seeing their grandchildren, including a grandson they had never met. The comfort of seeing familiar faces came inching up my stoic resolve, and I began to feel great excitement as we came closer and closer to our loved ones.

As was the standard procedure, my first encounter when we landed was with an apple-cheeked, young second lieutenant, who was to serve as my initial stateside casualty officer. He introduced himself, and as I inquired how he came to be in his current position, he promptly announced, "Well, I didn't want to fight in the war."

As the wife of an MIA Air Force pilot, who had just traveled half-way around the world with three small children, his insensitive reply nearly put me over the edge of decorum. Luckily, I saw our parents near the plane, which prevented a different type of war from ensuing. At my prompting, the girls ran to greet their grandparents, and the potentially sad occasion became a joyful reunion filled with the innocent squeals of young girls who were thrilled to have exited the big aircraft. The three grandparents immediately scooped up the girls and took them to the Harris home on the eastern shore of Maryland, about an hour's drive away, while Lyle and I remained behind to meet with the casualty officer.

The inexperienced and reluctant officer was assigned to drive me and Lyle to join the family after a short debriefing session. Our fairly uneventful plane ride seemed particularly easy compared to the next hurdle I had to cross. I was informed by the young lieutenant that the Secretary of the Air Force had decided that I would only receive $350 per month of Smitty's pay, and the rest of the money would be placed in a savings account until his return. Of course, with Smitty's MIA status, the absurdity of this decision was magnified even more in my exhausted mind. The battle that had been averted earlier was about to be ignited.

"What are you talking about?" I asked incredulously.

"Um, well, the Secretary of the Air Force has decided that your husband's pay will go into an Air Force program that will offer 10 percent interest."

"And when was this decision made?" I asked as anger began to creep up my arms and neck until my face felt hot and red.

"Just recently. You, um, are the first MIA spouse to return to the States."

At this time, Smitty was still the only member of the squadron who was MIA. He was the first officer with a family to be shot down. I was the first Air Force wife to return home without my husband. And therefore I was the first one in the system to have the newly established, untested procedures applied.

"Wait just a minute. I have power of attorney, and I am to get full pay to take care of our children. I certainly can't do that on $350 per month. My husband signed the Casualty Information Card, which stated that I, his wife, would get everything—his pay and his allowances—in the event of him becoming a casualty of war, which he obviously is, or I wouldn't be sitting here with you."

"I'm sorry, ma'am, this is coming directly from the Secretary of the Air Force."

"Well, get the Secretary on the phone," I stated emphatically.

"Ma'am, I can't call the Secretary of the Air Force," he said nervously.

"You do the dialing, and I will do the talking. But first, take me to my family."

The hour-long drive was tense, to say the least. Any threatening tears had long dried up, and what was left was a seething anger and a determination to fight for what I knew Smitty wanted. When we arrived at Smitty's childhood home in Maryland, the grandparents took one look at my face and knew that their best course of action was to keep the girls occupied.

I sat on the antique fainting couch in the Harrises' den, with Lyle sleeping in my arms. The young lieutenant was the one who looked as if he might faint when I demanded once again that he call the Secretary of the Air Force.

"Ma'am, I can't call the Secretary of the Air Force," he repeated once again.

"Oh, yes you can. Tell them that you are with the wife of the MIA, Captain Carlyle Smith Harris, who insists that she talk to the Secretary of the Air Force. Tell them she is very upset and is threatening to call a news conference."

He obliged without further argument, and as the call was put through, he quickly handed the phone to me before the Secretary answered.

"Mr. Secretary, this is Louise Harris, and I want you to know that I have a general power of attorney. Before my husband was shot down, he allotted me 100 percent of his pay. I have been receiving this for the past fourteen weeks, and I intend to continue receiving it. I have three babies, ages four and a half, three, and six weeks old, and I cannot support them on $350 a month. My husband intends for me to take care of his children. He is doing what he has to do, and I will do what I have to do. I am a former legal secretary—a smart woman—and I know my rights. I will not settle for one penny less. I intend to have every cent."

"Ma'am, we are just thinking about your husband," he replied.

"Well, you better think about his children. I am furious; I am tired; and I will absolutely call a press conference if need be."

"I will have to think about this."

"Absolutely not. I have just flown across the world with three young children. I am very tired. I need rest, and I can't get it if I have to think about this. I expect to hear back from you by close of business day, which is five o'clock. No later than five."

"Mrs. Harris, I need . . ."

"I don't care what *you* need. I am telling you what *I* need. I had everything going smoothly until now, and I will not put up with it. This is what my husband intended, and this is what I will have."

"Well, Mrs. Harris, I will get back to you," the Secretary said.

"By five," I replied. I then hung up the phone and looked up at the young casualty officer. His eyes were wide and scared, but he did not say another word about the matter. Later that day, I got the rest I needed—and I got the money I demanded.

AUGUST 1965

On August 29, after dark, Shu and I rolled up our mats and were taken to a vehicle in the main courtyard. We were blindfolded and climbed in to join Ron Storz, Scotty Morgan, and a small Asian prisoner we learned later was from Thailand.

Ron started a coughing fit that had me worried until I found it was a signal to other men in HBH that he was leaving camp via auto. *Where were we going? Who knew?* We could never outguess the Vietnamese— perhaps because they never seemed to have a plan and moved prisoners around for no rational reason.

An interrogator had told me we would be sent to a new camp in the hills, away from the city. Conditions would be very good there. He was right about the hills at least. Briarpatch, as Scotty Morgan named it, was thirty-five to forty miles west of Hanoi. As there was no electricity, it was hard to tell what the camp would be like when we were pushed into tiny cells in the middle of the night. When the guard left with his kerosene lantern, my cell was utterly black. Only with difficulty could I see the single barred window with closed louvered shutters on the outside.

With no visual references, my other senses were sharpened to discover and explore my new environment. I was in a whole new world. There was no evidence of people or civilization—only nature. The smell was fresh and invigorating. I could barely discern the urine odor that had permeated my other cells. It was overpowered by the smell of freshly cut grass and of the outdoors I had loved as a boy.

Mosquitoes buzzed in my ears; a cricket sounded outside; a night bird trilled; a rat or some small animal scurried overhead—sounds that would not even be heard in Hanoi where vehicles, guards walking on a brick walkway, voices, hammering in a nearby shop or plant, and other man-made noises dominated the senses.

I was struck by the contradiction that the absence of sound in this hill camp merely revealed new sounds hitherto unnoticed. I felt stark naked and alone in a wilderness, without the comfort and security of civilization; yet I felt God's presence. How revealing! At times when I was in pain, rejected, abused by society, or alone, I was always comforted and assured that God cared. When I was most alone, I was most close to an all-just Supreme Being who would someday right all wrongs.

"O God, please help me. Accept my penance . . ." I prayed and then drifted off into a fitful sleep. Those damned mosquitoes! *Tomorrow I will be able to string up my mosquito net,* I thought, trying to cheer myself. Little did I know that mosquitoes were not the only pest I would be dealing with. The buildings were infested with rats, ants, and roaches as well.

"Hey, Smitty, are you there?" Scotty Morgan's voice came from somewhere—but where?

"Yes. Where are you?"

"Shu, Ron, you, and I are all in the same building." I had been the last one removed from the vehicle the previous night and had not known where the rest had been taken. A guard's voice barked at us from nearby as he banged my shutters with his rifle butt.

We went to the walls. In a short time, by tapping, we found that we were in a brick building divided into four small cells. Each cell was almost identical, with room for two wooden bunks and a narrow aisle. There were no stocks at the end of the beds! What a relief. I hated even looking at those medieval torture machines that were a constant reminder of our sadistic captors.

At midmorning, food and water were brought. I couldn't believe my eyes. The guard gave me a loaf of bread and a container of scrambled eggs! Real, fresh eggs. There must have been four or five eggs in this one serving. Little did I know that those would be the last eggs and bread we would see at Briarpatch. Our subsequent meals were mostly rice. We also received some watery soup and sometimes fish heads mixed with cooked bananas or a few small pieces of tough chicken.

Our captors chopped up a chicken into half-inch pieces with an ax or some other heavy implement. The result was smashed splintery bones with a little bit of tough meat attached. One scrawny chicken could probably be distributed in this manner to twenty or more captives.

The shutters over our windows were generally left open, depending on the mood of the guards. However, when any of us were taken out of our cells to dump our buckets in a large container, the shutters were closed. The enemy went to great lengths to keep one American from seeing another American, but we were allowed to see the Asian prisoner at work outside. Tim, as we called him, used a "chogie pole" on his shoulder from which would be suspended two large, heavy cans of water or two cans of our refuse that he carried off to dump someplace. He kept a two-foot concrete cistern outside each cell filled with water, with which we bathed and washed our eating utensils.

The drinking water was boiled but murky and very greasy due to the pork fat and greasy pumpkin soup residue left in our bowls. The water in our cisterns soon became stagnant and sometimes had water bugs swimming in it, but it was the best we had in this camp without running water or electricity. Usually following two or three days of griping and fussing about the condition of the water, we would be allowed to drain our cistern and scrape the green mold from its sides and bottom.

Diarrhea was a constant problem. There was one poorly trained medic for the camp who passed out some pills that helped a little, but the poor sanitary conditions soon brought on repeated attacks. Had there been a real medical emergency, the medic would have been unable to cope with it.

On the third day I was at Briarpatch, a guard opened my cell to let me bathe. He had a small basin and some rough soap for me to use. I stripped down to the nude and stepped just outside my cell door to bathe. Two guards with rifles and bayonets attached stood in a charge position with the tips of their bayonets less than a yard from my bare body.

I was probably the first American they had seen, and I am sure their superiors had briefed them that we were the most despicable, dangerous criminals alive. Somehow the ridiculousness of the situation touched my funny bone. I could not have been less prepared to harm them or even to attempt to escape. I filled the basin with water and dumped it over my body, trying to control my mirth. As I began to soap my body, I couldn't restrain myself any longer. I broke out laughing, with soap suds sputtering on my wet lips.

The two young soldiers—almost boys—looked a little nonplussed and confused. They saw nothing funny and didn't know how to react to this obviously deranged criminal. I completed my bath and was locked again in my cell. From then on, when I was allowed to bathe, one soldier would stand discreetly nearby with his rifle slung on his shoulder. The turnkey, who did not usually carry a firearm, would also look away to give me some privacy.

Each POW was taken out of the prison at night and led to the guards' quarters on the top of the hill. There the camp commander would interrogate us and then spend an hour or more simply practicing his English.

After a few days, I began to hope that our interrogations had ended. Sitting on a hard stool for an hour or more while some Vietnamese practiced his English and heaped verbal abuse on us and our country was no fun. However, compared to what would come later at this camp, this interrogation was mild. We had heard their arguments and distorted version of history so many times that we could finish verbatim many of their government-provided clichés.

Bob Shumaker was the first to be called out to a stool session. A young Vietnamese officer, whom we called "Rabbit," acted as interrogator. He later became known to almost all American POWs as a sadistic enemy who enjoyed mistreating Americans.

The setting was a small room illuminated with one kerosene lamp. Rabbit spoke at length with the usual drivel but at the end tried to satisfy his own curiosity about Shu. *Time* magazine had carried a story about Shu when he was shot down. It mentioned the fact that his father was a successful lawyer in Pennsylvania.

Rabbit spoke. "Your father owns a large home, doesn't he?"

"Yes."

"He also owns his own car?"

"Yes."

"He has a radio and electrical appliances?"

"Yes."

Then Rabbit concluded, "Your father is indeed a very wealthy man."

It struck Shu how distorted a view of America our captors had. Here in Vietnam, no one owned a private car. Some high officials were provided one by their government, but almost everything was owned by the government. A bicycle, radio, and wristwatch were almost ultimate status symbols of affluence in their society, and it was inconceivable that most American families could possess those very things that so impressed Rabbit about the wealth of Shu's father.

While we hated to be taken out for interrogations, they did provide a break in the monotony of our daily POW life. But each time a turnkey unlocked our cell door at any but routine times, we immediately tensed up, not knowing what would ensue. Most times, we were taken to an interrogation room and endured the current effort by the North Vietnamese to indoctrinate us and try to get us to provide them with some kind of propaganda statement or other compliance to their demands.

Sometimes this led to brutal beatings or torture when we refused to cooperate. As a prelude to worse torture techniques, we were often tied to stools, unable to defend ourselves as we were beaten with sticks and fists. But more often at this point in captivity, we were just giving our interrogators a chance to practice their English.

As with Rabbit's distorted view of Shu's father's great wealth, in these long sessions we learned a great deal about the North Vietnamese culture and history. We also learned that the North Vietnamese people did not enjoy freedoms like dissenting opinions that accompany free speech—freedoms that Americans are guaranteed by our Constitution.

Our move to the Briarpatch was short-lived, and we learned another facet of their decision making. It was never well thought out. Changes were made for no apparent reason but often resulted in some advantage to POWs. Camps opened and closed. POWs were shifted between camps and often moved to different parts of the same camps. This provided (through our communication ability) the knowledge from new shoot-downs of happenings at home and the names and location of all POWs. But most important, it provided our POW leadership with the ability to set policy and direction for all of us.

LOUISE 20

A week after we arrived back in the States, the children and I moved to Tupelo, Mississippi, to live near my sister, Janice, and her family.

Tupelo was a sleepy little community where friends were like family and "do unto others" was a motto to live by. Everyone attended church, which was the social hub of the community. Janice and her family were members of the Episcopal Church, but the children and I began attending St. James Catholic. St. James was founded in 1914, but they did not get their first priest until 1919. Father Robert Reitmeier was an amiable man who served thirty-three years in Tupelo and its surrounding areas.

The original church had been built downtown at the corner of Green Street and Magazine Street. It had survived the great tornado of 1936, and the building contained many memories of worship until 1960, when the expanded congregation outgrew the building. As was the custom, its wooden walls were torn down, for "once a church, always a church," and it could never be used for anything else. The new brick church was built on Gloster Street and expanded back to Lakeshire Drive, and has served the community well ever since.

Members of this church prayed many a prayer on our behalf and were a help and comfort to me and the children over the years. Though we later transferred our membership to First United Methodist, those years of attending Mass at St. James somehow made me feel closer to Smitty. While listening to Rev. Clarence Meyer, my mind would often wander back in time to a peaceful memory of sitting next to Smitty

94

during a worship service in our small church in Okinawa. It was a modest chapel that served all the different denominations represented on the base.

A bittersweet memory often surfaced of me standing alone before the priest in Okinawa as he baptized Lyle. It was an emotional time as I committed Lyle to God without Smitty there to participate in that monumental event. Thankfully, I wasn't totally alone. A small group of loyal friends had showed up to support me. Patti and Ivy were named as Lyle's godparents, and Shirley and Bill, the Shirmans, and Smitty's wing commander, Col. Robert Cardenas, all came to support me. And Shieko was there too. Sweet Shieko. Oh, how I missed her!

For the first six weeks, we lived with Janice and her husband, Dick, as well as their teenage children, Rick and Deb. During this time, I was anxiously awaiting the freedom that having my own car would bring. I had sold our Oldsmobile in Okinawa and while there had selected a Chevrolet station wagon and paid for it in full, emphasizing that it should be shipped to the port of New Orleans, the closest port to Tupelo. The car prices offered to GIs returning from overseas were well below dealer cost, so to avoid dealer involvement, the cars had to be picked up at a U.S. port. My plan was to ask Janice to keep my children for a day while I took the bus to New Orleans and then drove my new car back to Tupelo.

Though I had been adamant about the need for the vehicle to arrive in New Orleans, I received a notice that my car had been shipped to the port of Baltimore. I was blindsided, knowing it would take days to ride the bus to Maryland and return home. I did not intend to be away from my children for that long during this difficult time of adjustment.

What should I do? I wondered. I was constantly making decisions on behalf of myself and my children. I knew I would serve Smitty well by overseeing our family affairs with strength and dignity. Remembering my success with the Secretary of the Air Force, I decided to call the president of the General Motors Company in Detroit. I called the operator and requested for a call to be placed to Mr. Estes, the current president of General Motors—collect, no less. As she patched me through and requested the acceptance of the long-distance charges,

I began to speak to him, above the operator, telling him my situation. He finally agreed to accept the call, and I repeated my request.

"Mr. Estes, this is Louise Harris. I am the wife of Captain Smitty Harris, who was shot down and is MIA in North Vietnam. I, in good faith, ordered and paid for a new station wagon before I left Okinawa and was very clear about my need to have it delivered to the port of New Orleans. I have three young children—ages four, three and a half, and nine weeks—and I cannot leave them for the time needed to get to Baltimore, where my car is now. I need my car to be in New Orleans. How can you help me?"

"Well, Mrs. Harris, first let me tell you how sorry I am for your circumstances. Let me think just a minute." He paused as he considered my situation. "I don't know Tupelo, Mrs. Harris. Is there a General Motors dealership there?"

"Why, yes there is. It's not far from my sister's house, where I am staying."

"I'll tell you what I can do for you. I am going to give you a code. You can go down to the General Motors dealership, give them this code, explain your situation to them, and tell them if there is any problem, they can call me personally. I want you to pick out any car you would like on their lot."

"What should I do if there is a price difference between what they have and what I have paid?"

"Pick out any car you would like on that lot," he repeated.

"I don't mind paying the difference, Mr. Estes."

"You tell them it is fully paid for. You go pick out any car, and I want you to enjoy it. And I hope you get good news about your husband soon."

"Thank you, Mr. Estes," I said with relief. "You have really helped me."

"The pleasure is mine, Mrs. Harris," he replied.

An hour later, I was at the Tupelo General Motors car lot. Nervously, I told my story to George Ruff, the owner of the dealership. He just laughed. He led me straight to the only station wagon on his lot. The fully loaded yellow Buick had all the bells and whistles—leather seats, air-conditioning, and three rows of seats, including a flexible bunk seat in the back. As I drove back to Janice's house in my new car, I was filled with relief and gratitude for the good people God had brought to help me. Robin and Carolyn came flying out the door when I pulled up, squealing the happy cry of little girls, excited to see their new, bright yellow car. Once again, I hoped this would make Smitty proud.

● ● ●

Later that month, I found myself once again in a new home. I remember sitting on the couch looking at the cardboard boxes stacked in the corner of the room and feeling a wave of exhaustion. The house was quiet, as I had successfully gotten all three children to bed early. The days were still long and hot, and I hoped the curtains in the bedroom would block out the light still shining that evening. I knew I had to take advantage of the time I had without children underfoot, so I took a deep breath, forced myself off the couch, and headed to the mountain of boxes. This was the third time I had moved since I had been in Tupelo. While I appreciated the roof over our heads, I longed for the comfort of my own home. Renting and moving, renting and moving, renting and moving–this was not the stability I had intended for my children.

Maybe in time I can find a way to buy a small place of my own–a place to make memories with the children, a place for Smitty to come home to, I thought wistfully.

As I opened box after box, organizing the contents of each, I thought of Smitty. He would never have allowed me to move the heavy boxes alone had he been there. I loved how he seemed to have the perfect balance of being protective and taking care of me, while at the same time trusting me to be capable and independent. That's probably why I could handle the situation so well.

Janice had been a lifesaver. Almost daily, we went to her house on Madison Street. The children played in the massive backyard, while Janice and I had a cup of coffee. Robin and Carolyn had become fast friends with the Hall children who lived next door. I had also gotten close to this sweet family, as we shared a common bond. Sam's brother, George Hall, was also flying missions in RF-101s during bomb damage assessments after previous strikes in Vietnam.

Janice was always ready with a kind word but also quick with a witty observation to make me laugh. She was a lot like Smitty in that way. She and Smitty had a unique relationship, which to an outsider may have seemed a bit confrontational. They loved to tease each other, and no matter what one dished out, the other would send right back. The first day they met was no exception.

Smitty and I had driven to Aliceville, Alabama, where Janice and Dick lived early in their marriage. Janice was seven years older than I was, and at age eighteen she had announced her engagement to Dick, much to the consternation of my grandparents and my mother. They wanted her to go to college. However, as usual, Janice was right, and they were well suited for a wonderful marriage that lasted more than five decades until they were parted by death. Janice's personality was bigger than life, and she was intent on a relentless testing of my new boyfriend, Carlyle Smith Harris. The first time they met, she was confrontational, and he gave it right back. Half in jest and half serious, she was determined to find out who he was.

"So you're the guy who thinks he can date my sister," she said with raised eyebrows.

"Yes, isn't she the lucky one?" he quipped.

It was a rather awkward drive as we headed to Columbus Air Force Base, where Smitty had secured dinner reservations for the four of us. After enjoying a delicious steak dinner while serenaded by a well-known pianist, Janice finally gave her stamp of approval. But while they loved each other, the ribbing between Janice and Smitty never stopped. I loved that about them, and I missed those funny moments.

LOUISE 21

Six weeks later, I found myself repacking the cardboard boxes for the fourth time in six months. We were moving next door to Janice in the house that Sam and Pat Hall had rented. Though I was happy to be next door to Janice, Dick, and their children, the reason for the availability of the house brought a great familiar sadness.

Two weeks prior, I was busy preparing dinner when the phone rang. It was Janice, and I immediately knew something was wrong.

"Louise, I have some sad news. Sam's brother, George, has been reported KIA. They are devastated."

"I'll be right there," I quickly replied.

After dropping off the children at Janice's house, I slowly walked across the yard. Scenes from my own experience filled my mind as I imagined what they must be feeling. I knocked on the door, and Pat answered. I didn't say a word; I just hugged her. She led me into the den where Sam was, and the three of us sat together, heavy with emotion.

"Do not give up hope," I said with conviction.

"The casualty officer said they saw his plane in flames and didn't see a chute," Sam answered dejectedly.

"Do not give up hope, Sam," I repeated. "They didn't give me much hope at first either."

"You're right. We won't give up hope. But they've just told my mom and dad that their son has been killed in action. We need to be near them, so we have already made the decision to move back to Hattiesburg. Do you want to move next door to Janice?"

And so it was. We moved into 732 North Madison, right next door to Janice's house at 734 North Madison. Our two backyards became one big playground for Robin, Carolyn, and Lyle.

I could now get our swing set out of storage. Smitty had built the swing set when were stationed in Wichita and had it shipped to Okinawa. When I returned to the States, I couldn't bear to leave it behind and had it shipped back. In this way, Smitty had a small part in their everyday play. We often told the story of how Daddy had made this for them because he loved them so much. We talked of Smitty as if he would walk through the door at any moment. As children are so miraculously capable of, they filled their young lives with laughter and play.

Our house was built in 1951 and was a red brick, ranch-style cottage with heart pine floors and a floor furnace for heating. There were four bedrooms and three bathrooms, and given what we had been renting, I felt we were now living in a palace. I had barely unpacked when I had another huge decision to make concerning our home life.

When I answered the phone, I once again knew that Janice must have stressful news to share. Funny how sisters know each other so well that great amounts of information can be gleaned from a single word.

Janice, as usual, got straight to the point. "Louise, I just got a phone call from your landlord," she said.

"Is there a problem? I mailed the rent check before it was due," I replied.

"Well, the problem is that they no longer want to rent the house. They want to sell it. He didn't have the heart to call you, given your situation, but he wanted me to ask you if you would be interested in buying the house."

"Buy the house? I don't know if I'm prepared to buy a house," I said as my stress level rose with every word.

"But, Louise, if you don't buy it, you will have to move. Again."

"Oh, I don't want to move. The kids are finally settled, and it is such a comfort to be next door to you and Dick. I guess I better think about it," I replied. *And pray about it*, I thought as I hung up the phone.

A week later, I had a plan. "I will use a VA loan. I have Smitty's power of attorney, so there should be no problem," I told Janice, a bit more confidently than I felt.

When I called the VA office in Jackson, Mississippi, I did not get the response I had hoped for.

"You can't use your loan because you need your husband's signature," the man told me.

"If I could have his signature, I wouldn't need the loan because I would be with him. I have full power of attorney."

"I'm sorry, that won't help. The signature has to be specific to this house," he replied unsympathetically as he quickly ended the conversation.

I was incensed. *Here we go again*, I thought.

I picked up the phone and called U.S. Senator John C. Stennis. Stennis was a very senior senator, and he was head of the Senate's Armed Services Committee. He was also a wonderful Southern gentleman from Mississippi.

The operator gave me the phone number to his office in Washington, D.C., and surprisingly, he took my call straight away. I quickly explained my situation.

"Senator Stennis, I have a general power of attorney for my husband, Captain Carlyle Smith Harris, who has been confirmed as being held in a POW camp in North Vietnam. My credit is good. Please, sir, I have moved my children four times in the past six months, and I don't want to move them again."

In his deep Southern voice he said, "Well, Mrs. Louise, we will see what we can do about this. Just sit tight, and you will be hearing from someone soon."

The next day, there was a knock at the door and when I answered, I found the head of the VA standing on my doorstep. He had driven three hours up from Jackson, and he said, "I'm here to help you get your VA loan."

"Well, that's good, because I intend to have one. You must have talked to Senator Stennis," I replied.

A month later I was sitting at a long table with my attorney at the Bank of Mississippi, signing thirty pages of documents that secured the rate guaranteed by the VA. I walked out with the legal papers declaring my ownership of 732 North Madison in Tupelo, Mississippi.

By now, I was getting accustomed to living in Tupelo. Though we had only lived there a couple of months, I already knew I could not have picked a better spot to raise my children. With a population of 17,000, everyone knew everyone, and in the hospitable Southern way, the town quickly welcomed me and the children warmly and without question. While other POW wives were experiencing the negative effects of antiwar activists, I was experiencing the open arms of acceptance and support.

My casualty officer at this time was still Claude Watkins. He called to check on me and the children often. Each time, he asked if I was experiencing harassment. POW wives in other states had reported episodes of vandalized homes and yards, as well as fierce verbal attacks. I knew nothing of such behavior. When Watkins came to Tupelo for the first time, his plane was hours late arriving, without his checked baggage. He commented, "Now I see why you're not being bothered by the activists—they can't find you here in Tupelo." Maybe he was right.

The idyllic north Mississippi town, with its picturesque tree-lined streets, was first established in 1867. Its claim to fame now is being the birthplace of Elvis Presley, and Tupelo Hardware is still visited by Elvis fans as they travel far and wide to see where he bought his first guitar. When Elvis was a baby in April 1936, he was a survivor of the Tupelo tornado, one of the deadliest storms in U.S. history. Striking at night, the tornado leveled forty-eight city blocks and claimed the lives of 233 people and injured more than seven hundred. But from these ruins, Tupelo rose in determination and strength to rebuild itself into a beautiful, loving, and caring community. I, too, felt that a storm had swept through my life, destroying what I had known and cherished before. But the warm reception from the people of Tupelo helped carry my burden as I raised the children alone and provided, despite our circumstances, what all three would describe as a happy childhood.

As I settled into my new home, I fluctuated between being grateful and overwhelmed. It was tough navigating so many changes without Smitty's help and support, but not knowing how he was faring was simply terrible. One day, around four in the afternoon, I received a call from the local postmaster, Banks Livingston. I answered the phone, and he quickly got straight to the point.

"Mrs. Harris, I think I have a letter for you from your husband," he said all in one breath.

"You have what?" I practically screamed in the phone.

"I think I have a letter from your husband. It is addressed to Louise Harris, Tupelo, Mississippi. There's no street address on it. In the top left corner, it says Carlyle Smith Harris."

"Oh, Mr. Livingston! Where are you and how can I get it?"

"I'll meet you at the back door of the post office," he quickly replied.

I called to my niece, Deb, to please watch the children, and I hopped into my car and practically flew to the post office. True to his word, Mr. Livingston was waiting at the back door. He handed me the letter, and with one look I exclaimed, "It's from him! I recognize the handwriting!" My name and Smitty's name were definitely in his handwriting, though the partial address was in a different script. Overcome with joy, I threw my arms around a startled Mr. Livingston. He seemed as excited as I was, and he hugged me right back.

I immediately took the letter home, intent on opening it with the children, wanting to share this moment, this precious memory, with them. I ran into the house, and Deb helped me gather all three around me on the couch. With shaking hands, I opened the envelope and unfolded the paper that Smitty's hands had also held. It was dated Friday, June 25, 1965. Careful to keep my emotions in check, I read the letter aloud.

Dearest Louise,
Words cannot express my love and concern for you and the girls and our new baby boy. My thoughts and prayers are with you constantly. The people here found out and advised me of the birth of our son and that you both were OK. I have never had

happier news. Because of you and the kids, I can still say I am the luckiest man on earth.

Louise—please don't worry about me because it is completely unnecessary. I am uninjured, healthy, in good spirits, and well taken care of. I am living with other American pilots, and we get plenty of good food, clothes, medical care if required, and adequate living and hygiene facilities.

I paused slightly wondering if this part was true. I knew Smitty might try to paint a better picture so that I wouldn't worry, and I had been informed that if he sent letters, it might include some propaganda—information that the North Vietnamese wanted portrayed. I could not dwell on that thought long, as the children were antsy to hear more.

I have started daily exercises and am sure that when I am released, I can get a job on TV with an exercise program and be the idol of 1,000,000 American women—what do you think of that?

Now that sounds like my Smitty, I thought as I laughed out loud. The children didn't understand what I was laughing about, but they joined in anyway.

I know that Mother, bless her heart, is very upset over my capture. Please help her, and Dad and Mary too, to understand that I am just fine and it is just a matter of time until I am released. Give them my love and tell them I demand that they not worry and that if they do, I will fuss with them when I get home.

On a serious vein, Louise—I am convinced that there is a reason for all of this. Perhaps we are being given an opportunity to strengthen our faith to merit some very special graces in the future. Whatever the reason, I am sure we can use this time to become emotionally and spiritually stronger. We are separated, but we still have our love and will have years and years together after I am released. So we are really losing nothing important, and I am sure will gain in other ways.

Louise, I know the big responsibilities you suddenly are facing at a time when you are having to take care of the almost constant demands of a new baby. I have absolute faith in your good judgment and your ability to take care of all of this and still maintain your sense of humor and composure, and remain your own lovely, lovely self. I will never understand how I was lucky enough to fall in love with and marry the most wonderful girl in the world.

I am addressing this to Tallahassee because I imagine that you will be or are in the States now. My guess is that you will spend some time with both our families and perhaps stay with one until I am released. Later on, you may want to get a place of your own. In any event, please get a maid to help you with the kids and to give you some free time to entertain, go to parties, etc. See how much fun you can have, and I am sure the time will pass quickly until we are together again.

I am anxious to hear from you and get all the news about our little boy, also to hear about the latest doings of Robin and Carolyn. You might try regular mail, a peace organization, or a U.S. Senator as a means of getting me a letter.

Give Robin and Carolyn a big hug and kiss for me and tell them I love them very much. They are such good and sweet little girls, and their daddy misses them very, very much. I am popping all my buttons with pride over our little boy. Give him an extra hug for me too.

Louise, I must repeat, I am in excellent health and spirits. I keep mentally and physically busy so the time passes quickly. In retrospect I am sure this separation will seem short. I love you with every ounce of my heart and soul. Please take care of yourself.

All my love,
Smitty

When I finished reading the letter, I refolded it, placed it back in the envelope, and held it close to my heart. I scooped my three children in my arms and hugged them closely. As tears began to form in my eyes, I dismissed myself so they would not see my emotion. Such bittersweet words of comfort and encouragement!

About that time, Janice wheeled into the carport and ran into the house. Deb had called her at her real estate office when I went to the post office, and she had rushed home as soon as she could. I reread the letter to her and laughed and cried all at once. I then picked up the phone to call Smitty's parents. I knew they would be just as happy as I was to know that he was alive and well. I only wished we could read it together in person. Tears fell freely on both ends of the telephone as I read the letter aloud to them. When I hung up, I placed a call to my mother and then my grandmother, and then I had one more call to make. I called the Pentagon. They had given me a special number to call after hours, and someone answered immediately.

When I explained that I had received a letter from my POW husband, their first response was, "Please send the letter to the Pentagon right away."

"Well, yes—but I need to make you a copy," I stammered.

"We need to see the original one, ma'am," was the reply.

"Well, I will still need to get a copy for myself," I said.

"There must be some place you can get a copy made tonight?"

"I live in a small town, sir. I will see what I can do. But I need the original letter back," I replied.

"We will get it back to you, Mrs. Harris. I promise. But we will need to keep it for at least a week."

"Do not damage my letter," I said firmly.

"We will take good care of it."

I hung up the phone, and Janice and I headed back to her office to make copies of the letter. I made copies for myself and Smitty's parents. By that time, it was too late to mail the letter to the Pentagon, but the next morning it was headed to Washington via registered mail with a return receipt requested.

Years later, I found out how the letter came to find me in Tupelo. The letter had been written in June 1965 when Smitty briefly shared a cell with Phil Butler, Bob Peel, and Bob Shumaker. A visiting delegation of diplomats who were investigating to see if the North Vietnamese were following the rules of the Geneva Convention was scheduled to arrive, and the POWs' captors wanted them to see these letters as a propaganda piece, proving that they were allowing the POWs to write and receive letters, in adherence with the Geneva Convention.

Knowing this might be the case, Smitty and the others wrote the letters, believing they would have a better chance of being delivered if there were positive words concerning their circumstances. The North Vietnamese had no intention of delivering any of the letters, but when the Vietnamese hosts briefly left the room, the diplomat from Great Britain slipped one of the letters in her purse. When she returned to England, she mailed the letter to a contact in the States, who mailed it to me in Tupelo.

SMITTY 22

Vietnamese had no intention of delivering any of the letters, but when

SEPTEMBER 1965
BRIARPATCH

With no running water or electricity, Briarpatch was the most primitive of all the prison camps. It was also the only camp in North Vietnam where true malnutrition existed because of the extremely poor diet. Many of my fellow POWs contracted beriberi, as well as injured feet and impaired eyesight. Briarpatch, also known as "Country Club," was located west of Hanoi near Xom Ap Lo. The actual briar patch from which we derived its name was located on the east side of the hill.

Briarpatch had been built as a prison. Each of the nine buildings was surrounded by a wall that formed a pattern much like a tic-tac-toe game, with one high wall surrounding the complex. As a few new POWs were brought to the camp, they were put in solitary confinement in adjacent buildings. The inside walls of the cells were dabbed with concrete and then painted over with muddy water. This decorative plan gave the cells a true cave-like appearance.

The sanitary conditions were also very primitive. Our toilets consisted of uncovered metal buckets that we called "Bos"—the American spelling of the Vietnamese word. Once a day, we were instructed to empty the Bos into a barrel that was located between "A" and "B" huts. I was in hut "A," and the smell of the waste barrel was at first a nuisance, at best. Thankfully, the olfactory sense is the first to acclimate, and soon I barely noticed the smell.

The opening of this new camp was the first time that military guards were utilized, although there was no organization among the guards, mainly due to a lack of supervision. This resulted in daily confusion each day when we emptied the Bos. One of the guards was nicknamed "Freckles" and later known as "Pox." He was obviously mentally unstable and was often seen talking to himself. None of the guards spoke English.

Knowing that if we had visual contact with other Americans, we could communicate with them, the Vietnamese hastily added three to four feet of matting to the tops of the inner walls. Buildings were situated twenty to thirty feet from any wall, so covert communication within the camp was virtually impossible. Nevertheless, we watched the guards carefully to learn their habits and routines.

When we thought there were no guards in the complex, we talked through our windows loudly enough that men in adjacent buildings could hear. Invariably this brought armed soldiers into the complex, but they did not know who had talked and were unable to effectively stop our communication. We kept constantly abreast of who was in the camp and the new information brought into the camp. From some later shoot-downs I found that four of my squadron mates from Okinawa were now POWs, including my squadron commander, Lt. Col. Robinson Risner. Word was soon passed to me from them that Louise had given birth to our son. I was overjoyed!

Each morning, one by one, all of us were permitted to carry our buckets to be dumped in the container near my building. As we walked from one walled area to another, we tried to pass as close to another hut as the guards would permit. Often the guards were so inattentive that loud whispers could be exchanged without their knowledge. We also used the ruse that we were saying something to the guard, knowing he could not understand English.

With the help of a nail, I had been able to make a small hole in my shutter and watch everyone as they entered the small compound surrounding my hut. At HBH, I had caught a glimpse of Navy Lt. J. B. McKamey. Knowing that some new POWs had been brought in the previous night, I was watching carefully as the men dumped their buckets. I immediately recognized McKamey as he walked directly toward my window.

The guard seemed unconcerned until J. B. spoke in a loud voice not more than two feet from me. "Tell Smitty Harris that his wife got his letter."

Little did J. B. know that he shouted the message almost in my ear; all four of us in the hut could hear him clearly. The guard reacted quickly by running over to vehemently protest, in Vietnamese, J. B.'s transgression. J. B. ignored him and calmly emptied his bucket.

J. B. had been held in HBH, where Rudolph was still the turnkey. In his own slow-witted way, Rudolph was learning more English words. J. B. pointed to his eyes and repeated over and over until Rudolph could copy the sound "I'm." Then he repeated the process, pointing to his ear and saying, "Crazy." For the next few days the men in HBH laughed as Rudolph walked around the camp audibly practicing, "I'm crazy," as he pointed to his own eyes and ear.

Although Rudolph was probably not plagued with mental illness, in his childlike way he was interested in everything these strange Americans did. When the men in HBH bathed in cell number eight, he often brought in a chair, placed it on the end of one of the concrete bunks, and sat on his throne as he watched the proceedings. At Briarpatch, we also laughed at the joke J. B. had played on Rudolph.

● ● ●

We often heard aircraft while we were at Briarpatch and sometimes saw F-105s fly over at altitude. On September 8, we observed a strike at close hand. Less than two miles from our camp, we learned later, was a Vietnamese supply dump. I heard the aircraft approach and jumped to my window to see if I could spot them. Fortunately, my window faced the strike area, and I was able to see the whole action.

When the first 750-pound bombs impacted, even from this distance there was a terrific blast. I quickly ducked down away from the window, really frightened. Within moments, I realized the camp was not in danger and resumed my watch. The F-105s were beautiful. Though a huge aircraft weighs more than fifty thousand pounds fully loaded, in flight it looks like a slick dart. The bombs raised a large black column of smoke, and there were smaller puffs of smoke at altitude from the antiaircraft guns. We could hear them, as well as the smaller automatic weapons, clearly. Some of the guards in our compound shot futilely with their own automatic weapons at the aircraft that were hopelessly out of range. I could imagine the fear of the men in the target area, for here the noise and blast caused many of our guards to duck down and seek shelter.

The raids on the supply area continued almost daily for ten days. Usually, from eight to twelve aircraft were involved in a raid. Invariably, between a half hour and two hours after a raid, a single RF-101 reconnaissance aircraft would fly over the area to take battle damage pictures. The Vietnamese knew this too and were waiting. As soon as the RF-101 came within range, all guns would open up. I gained new respect for the men who flew this mission.

As the aircraft flew its steady course over the target, from my window I could see the puffs of smoke that looked so harmless but were deadly antiaircraft bursts. Fortunately, the Vietnamese were not leading their target sufficiently, and the puffs of smoke would follow behind the aircraft as it zoomed across the target.

Each night at dusk, we could hear trucks rumbling in the distance. They continued until morning throughout the raids. We surmised that they were bringing in antiaircraft guns and taking away supplies, for each day there was a noticeable increase in the number of guns used when our aircraft flew in.

All truck activity was quiet during daylight because the Vietnamese knew that moving trucks were a sought-after target for our aircraft. At an interrogation, Rabbit told me that the Yankee aggressor pilots were bombing a dam that would cause hundreds of innocent women, old folk, and children to die if it broke and also would cause starvation in the area when the peasants were unable to irrigate their crops. I knew he was lying, and this was confirmed when I talked later to men who had been on the raid. No American aircraft were shot down in this series of raids, though some of them had battle damage when they returned to their bases in Thailand. These lies were meant to manipulate our emotions, confuse our loyalties, and weaken our resolve. They missed their mark by a long shot. Instead, they strengthened our resolve to adhere to our assigned Code of Conduct.

An executive order signed in 1955 by President Dwight Eisenhower, "Code of Conduct for Members of the Armed Forces of the United States," had its origins in response to the brainwashing tactics of Communists, as well as to a small number of defectors during the Korean War. It was decided that more guidance was necessary for Americans held by enemies in times of war, in order to ensure correct conduct in times of extreme hardship. The Code of Conduct was memorized by every serviceman and, unless otherwise directed by the Senior Ranking Officer, was the go-to for behavior among the POWs. The Code of Conduct included six basic articles:

I

I am an American fighting man. I serve in the forces
which guard my country and our way of life. I am
prepared to give my life in their defense.

II

I will never surrender of my own free will. If in command I will never
surrender my men while they still have the means to resist.

III

If I am captured I will continue to resist by all means available.
I will make every effort to escape and aid others to escape. I will
accept neither parole nor special favors from the enemy.

IV

If I become a prisoner of war, I will keep faith with my fellow
prisoners. I will give no information nor take part in any
action which might be harmful to my comrades. If I am senior,
I will take command. If not, I will obey the lawful orders of those
appointed over me and will back them up in every way.

V

When questioned, should I become a prisoner of war, I am
bound to give only name, rank, service number, and date of
birth. I will evade answering further questions to the utmost
of my ability. I will make no oral or written statements disloyal
to my country and its allies or harmful to their cause.

VI

I will never forget that I am an American fighting man, responsible for
my actions, and dedicated to the principles which made my country
free. I will trust in my God and in the United States of America.*

The Code of Conduct became our goal. We were intent on returning with honor, having adhered to the Code.

---

* "Code of Conduct for Members of the Armed Forces of the United States," Executive
Order 10631, August 17, 1955, President Dwight D. Eisenhower, www.loc.gov/rr/frd/Military
_Law/pdf/POW-code-of-conduct.pdf.

SEPTEMBER 1965
THE ZOO

On September 20, after barely more than three weeks at Briar-patch, we were loaded into trucks after dark. As in all camp moves, we were blindfolded. and we traveled at night. There were now fifteen POWs in our group. The Vietnamese must have thought the camp might be a target for American aircraft to close it so soon after it was opened. What next? We always felt some apprehension when moved from familiar surroundings.

September in Hanoi is hot. Very hot. The oppressive heat mim-icked the internal hell we all experienced. Guards led us from the truck to our new cells. When blindfolds were removed, four of us were in a large lighted room, perhaps eighteen by thirty feet, which was divided in the middle by an arched doorway. Phil Butler, Hayden Lockhart, Bob Shumaker, and I were together—all old friends by now.

The cell was empty, so we put our grass mats on the floor to get some sleep. As tired as we were, sleep was almost impossible due to the swarms of hungry mosquitoes that tormented us. We tried doubling up our mosquito nets to place over us. Although this provided some protection from the mosquitoes, the extra layers of netting made the heat almost unbearable.

Morning finally came. Still sweating and fatigued, we surveyed our new surroundings. We were not in a prison. There were no bars in the windows, and the door to our new cell was a lightweight louvered wooden one that would have provided little security against a deter-mined effort to break out. The windows were covered with louvered shutters with boards nailed across them on the outside. Through cracks we could see other similar buildings and a swimming pool in the center of an open area. We soon discovered it was currently being used for raising fish. We were sure we were in Hanoi because we could hear a streetcar, vehicles, and other noises of the city. Escape became the foremost topic of conversation in this minimum security camp. If we were going to do it, now was the time, for security would surely tighten.

We could come up with no good ideas that would provide even a minimal probability of successful evasion once out of camp. Our size, skin color, clothes, speech, and lack of local knowledge would make recapture almost certain in this densely populated area.

Perhaps we could get some outside help by cultivating or bribing a guard or a worker in the camp? Perhaps we could find the location of an embassy that would give us asylum? Perhaps . . .

Tap, tap, tap tap, tap—to the meter of "shave and a haircut"—sounded from the next cell. This standard call-up told us that Americans were trying to contact us.

Instead of tapping back, we spoke softly through our louvered window. "Who is there?"

"Red Berg and Pop Keirn. Who are you?"

Within a short time, we had the complete lineup of all the men who had moved from Briarpatch. We were all in similar cells in the same building. A wooden board covered a two-foot-square hole between Red and Pop's cell and ours. Within fifteen or twenty minutes, we had pulled it loose and were able to shake hands and talk directly to our friends. Hearing guards approach, we quickly replaced the board, pushing the nails that had held it into their previous holes.

Directly in front of our building was a small ditch. Two Vietnamese began building a fire and bringing in some large pots and utensils. While we watched through cracks in our shutters, our first meal was prepared at the Zoo, as our new camp came to be called. It was very apparent that almost no preparations had been made for our move.

The Zoo was located approximately five kilometers southwest of downtown Hanoi, on the outskirts of the city. Apparently, it was a former movie studio, as movie posters and film cans were found at various places around the camp. The buildings were concrete and were topped with tile roofs. Initially, the Zoo served as a temporary encampment to house the prisoners from Briarpatch, which had continued to be under fire. And though the cellblocks were sturdy, they were initially unsuited for prison use. That would quickly change.

We had almost no interrogations now, except to be threatened and harangued when we were caught communicating with our fellow POWs. However, Pop Keirn was taken to an interrogation room, where he found Rabbit and a Frenchman who was introduced as a writer.

At the end of a short interrogation, the Frenchman gave Pop a book titled *Wing Leader* by Group Captain J. E. Johnson of the Royal Air Force. He told Pop he could keep it for two or three days. For the next few days, Pop, Red, and the four of us in my cell took turns reading the book. Someone was reading it twenty-four hours a day except when we were interrupted by guards opening our cell doors. For almost six months, I had had nothing to read except a couple of propaganda pamphlets from our captors. My mind was like a dry sponge, yearning to soak up knowledge of any kind.

The book was particularly interesting to us because it was a personal story of a fighter pilot in World War II. The interest of the enemy in the book was apparent also. The entire book had been reviewed carefully, and all references to tactics used by fighter pilots were underlined in red ink. Someone was trying to learn lessons that would be of benefit to North Vietnamese pilots who were flying Russian-built MiG aircraft. We passed the book back and forth through the board-covered hole until everyone had read it—and just in time, for true to his promise, Rabbit made Pop give back the book.

New POWs began to arrive in camp. Through our communication system, we found that one of them was Alvarez. We were elated. Not only had Alvy been in solitary confinement for over a year, but he had also been completely isolated from other POWs. We all had experienced some isolation and knew how terrible it could be—especially when there was no other American with whom to communicate. Alvy seemed no worse for the experience. He was mentally sharp, had strongly resisted all enemy propaganda efforts, and was in good spirits.

He was a real inspiration to all of us and epitomized the indomitable spirit we must try to emulate.

Camp security tightened. Workers came in and began bricking up our windows, leaving out a couple of bricks near the top so we would have some air. The heat was oppressive. Our doors were replaced with very heavy cell doors, with the usual barred peepholes at eye level so that guards could observe us. A high wall topped with barbed wire was begun around the perimeter of the camp.

While construction was in process, POWs were moved from building to building. Shu, Phil, Hayden, and I were moved to a building with the old rickety doors. By pushing out on the bottom of the door, we could produce a crack large enough to observe all activity in the camp. We now had no communication with other POWs, but we could watch them as they emptied their buckets or picked up their food. After just two days in the new cell, while Shu was pushing out on the door, the clasp holding our lock broke loose and the cell door flew open. Some guards standing nearby got excited and shouted in Vietnamese while they trained their guns on us.

Shu was taken to interrogation and accused of an escape attempt. When he returned, the guards with him took each of us to a new cell for solitary confinement.

My new cell was almost airless. There were two bed boards, supported by sawhorses, in the cell. By placing one sawhorse on my bed, I could climb up to look out a brick-sized hole that had been left at the top of the former window. Fortunately, the hole faced the end of another building where there was a small toilet. With the door open, I could see the only sit-down type commode, without a seat, that I had observed in North Vietnam. Many of the POWs in the camp emptied their buckets here, so I was able to see and occasionally pass a word or two to the men when they were not guarded closely.

Mosquitoes were unbelievably thick in my new cell. The only openings for them to enter were small holes at the top of my bricked-over windows. The bare light that burned constantly in my cell must have attracted them. Each morning, I spent an hour or more swatting them with a rubber sandal, particularly under the bed boards. I kept count of the ones I killed—never fewer than one hundred per day and often twice that number.

Scotty Morgan and Ron Storz moved into the cell next to me. We tapped to each other, but a better method of communication seemed possible. A doorway between the two cells had recently been bricked up. The Vietnamese had used such a poor mixture of concrete that it was not difficult to dig it out with a sharp tool. I broke off a piece of metal strap used with our food dishes and went to work. Within a day I had made a hole almost an inch across through the concrete. Now we could talk directly to each other. To prevent the guards from finding the hole, we used it only after our cell doors had been locked for the night.

Before we went to bed, we put a plug in the hole made from a chunk of loose concrete broken from the sloppy concrete job on our windows. Rubbing a similar piece of concrete on the floor produced a powder, which when mixed with a few drops of water made a paste that covered up the cracks around the plug. Our efforts at communication not only kept our minds busy and morale up but also occupied many hours of time. It was important that we not succumb to the debilitating effects of complete boredom and inactivity.

Ron Storz was a hard-nosed resister who continually gave the Vietnamese a hard time. When guards entered our cell, we were supposed to stand at attention. None of us did, although we did stand up slowly and take a slouchy posture. This usually satisfied the guards, but Ron's attitude and lack of cooperation would often infuriate them. One entered his cell and demanded by gestures that Ron put his heels together. Ron refused or pretended not to understand. The angered guard struck Ron in the shins with his bayonet, but still Ron did not put his heels together. I could hear Scotty Morgan telling Ron, "Don't lose your head and hit him."

We all knew that attacking a guard was not smart. Though in pain, Ron maintained his composure. The guard left but came back soon with help to take Ron away. Within a day or two, we found out that he had been terribly beaten. His arm was injured and useless, and he was on half rations in solitary confinement.

Seeing and hearing friends suffer was almost as excruciating as suffering myself. Moans, groans, and sometimes screams often poured out of my brothers, though we all tried to stifle the misery as best as we could. The horror of the sounds of suffering around me was especially disturbing at the beginning of my captivity. And I hated to see the suffering of my cellmates when they came back from a torture session bruised and broken, both literally and figuratively. The lack of medical attention for our injuries after a torture session was an additional torture. Often, when we were already injured, the guards would manipulate the injury, adding even more excruciating pain. My broken shoulder was manipulated numerous times until it finally healed.

We tended to each other as best we could, not only physically but also emotionally. When our brothers were able, we also encouraged them to give us as much information about their torture session as possible, including the questions asked during the session. We would then tap this on to the Senior Ranking Officer (SRO), thus making all of us better prepared for our torture session, which we all knew would eventually come.

Though we didn't have much to offer our suffering brothers, prayer was our greatest medicine. Our suffering did make us stronger, and now, so many years later, the sting of its memory has faded. But I will never completely forget the misery I witnessed.

OCTOBER 1965

Throughout my years as a POW, our biggest obstacle and constant effort proved to be communication. It was of utmost importance for many reasons. First and foremost, it was a great morale booster, and it helped us maintain our sanity. If a POW felt totally alone, without any communication with those who were experiencing the same tragic existence, his mental and emotional capabilities were severely vulnerable.

Communication also helped us order our ranks within the camp. Through tapping or whispering, we were able to discern who was in top command of our POWs. We still adhered to the order of command, which often helped us resist the enemy as a united force. The effectiveness of our united front through the directives of the SRO—Senior Ranking Officer—was aided or hindered by our level of communication.

Our first SRO at the Zoo was Robbie Risner. When Jerry Denton came to the Zoo, he teamed up with Risner. Together they wrote a list of directives for all the POWs on a scrap of paper with a hidden pencil. The directives were then passed to George Hall, who whispered them aloud to the men in the buildings known as the Pigsty and the Stable.

The directives began with the obvious: follow the Code of Conduct. Next, we were directed to communicate by every means available. This was our lifeline, and this was what occupied the majority of the time in our endless, monotonous days. We were also told to refrain from antagonizing the guards and were instructed not to try to escape unless there was obvious outside help.

Another directive was an important one for unity—to learn all the names of the POWs and their locations. This was difficult to say the least, as we were kept away from each other and moved frequently.

We were told to collect and save any matches, wire, rope, nails, and paper we might find. We were instructed to complain at each interrogation about food, clothing, lack of exercise, and lack of church services. We were urged to always keep a listening watch. We were directed to sleep when the Vietnamese slept so we would not miss any vital observation. This was an important directive, lest we sleep away the hours of boredom and depressing day-to-day routine.

Despite our isolation from each other, we were also encouraged to participate in church services to be held in unison each Sunday morning. The signal to begin was the whistling of "God Bless America." When we heard the whistle, we all joined in. Then, separately yet corporately, we would at the minimum say the Lord's Prayer and the Pledge of Allegiance. Often, our church services would continue through tapping Bible verses and prayers. These Sunday worship services were a great source of unity for our group as a whole, as well as a source of strength for me personally.

With these directives from our commanding officer, we had our orders. This gave purpose and mission to our otherwise bleak and miserable existence. It also gave all of us a bond together and the hope-giving encouragement that we were not alone.

Larry Guarino, in particular, was surprised at the risk being taken by having these in writing, and he encouraged Hall to destroy the paper.

"Dump that paper in the Bo, Hall," Larry whispered. If found, the consequences would be swift and certainly devastating for Risner, Denton, and all of the POWs.

Hesitant to destroy the written directives of a Senior Officer, Hall instead passed the paper on to Shumaker, who was my cellmate at that time. On October 24, 1965, the Vietnamese found the note of directives written by our SRO, as well as the holes in the wall, and proceeded with a thorough search of each cell, which revealed many contraband items. Risner was transferred to "Heartbreak Hotel," and Denton, the next in line, covertly took his place.

Many of us were also punished for making the holes in the wall and for communicating with each other, but that did not stop us. I still remember the pain of the iron shackles at the foot of my concrete bed tightly snapped at my ankles, limiting motion and causing pain whenever I moved. I lay for many days in this position. For some of us, in addition to these leg shackles, a heavy iron pipe—an inch in diameter and six feet long—was put through the shackles, the weight of which lay heavy on our shins, causing excruciating pain every time we moved. With hands tied behind us, we were unable to adjust the bar or the shackles and simply lay there in agony. During times of torture, I prayed for the pain to end. But even more than that, I prayed to remain an honorable soldier.

One of our fellow POWs admitted to communicating but refused to tell the Vietnamese what was said or who it was said to, and therefore he was punished by limiting his food to a small piece of salted bread and one cup of water twice daily for eight days.

After finding the note, as well as the other contraband, the guards began to crack down on security and discipline. They conducted frequent cell searches and thoroughly punished POWs who were caught communicating. More guards and turnkeys were assigned to each cellblock; they unsuccessfully tried to make us salute them and bow to them. They also decreased our already inadequate food and threatened us with a pretrial for war crimes, which one of our group had to endure. Though they went to great lengths to eliminate communication, which hindered our ability to hear from our new Senior Ranking Officer, we continued to operate within the guidelines of our previous directives.

A few days after the discovery of the directives document, the North Vietnamese wrote their own set of directives for us. These were pasted with sticky rice glue to the walls of every cell.

In accordance with the prevailing situation in the camp and following the recent educational program of the criminals about the policy toward them based on the provisions of detaining the blackest criminals in the DRV, the American criminals must strictly follow and abide by the following provisions:

1. The criminals are under an obligation to give full and clear written or oral answers to all questions raised by the camp authorities. All attempts and tricks intended to evade answering further questions and acts directed to opposition by refusing to answer any questions will be considered as manifestations of obstinacy and antagonism that deserve strict punishment.

2. The criminals must absolutely abide by and seriously obey all orders and instructions from the Vietnamese officers and guards in the camp.

3. The criminals must demonstrate a cautious and polite attitude toward the officers and guards in the camp and must render greetings when met by them in a manner already determined by the camp authorities. When the Vietnamese officers and guards come in their rooms for inspection or when they are required by the camp officer to come to the office room, the criminals must carefully and neatly put on their clothes, stand at attention, bow a greeting, and await further orders. They may sit down only when permission is granted.

4. The criminals must maintain silence in the detention rooms and not make any loud noises that can be heard outside. All schemes and attempts to gain information and achieve communication with the criminals living next door by intentionally talking loudly, tapping the walls, or by any other means will be strictly punished.

5. If any criminal desires to ask a question, he is allowed to say softly only the words "bao cao." The guard will report this to the officer in charge.

6. The criminals are not allowed to bring into the room and keep in their rooms anything that has not been so approved by the camp.

7. The criminals must keep their rooms clean and must take care of everything given to them by the camp authorities.

8. The criminals must go to bed and arise in accordance with the orders signaled by the gong.

9. When allowed outside his room for any reasons, each criminal is expected to walk only in the area as limited by the guard-in-charge and seriously follow all his instructions.

10. Any obstinacy or opposition, violation of the preceding provisions, or any scheme or attempt to get out of the detention camp without permission are all punishable. On the other hand, any criminal who strictly obeys the camp regulations and shows his true submission and repentance by his practical acts will be allowed to enjoy the humane treatment he deserves.

11. Anyone so imbued with a sense of preventing violations and who reveals the identity of those who attempt to act in violation of the foregoing provisions will be properly rewarded. However, if any criminal is aware of any violation and deliberately tries to cover it up, he will be strictly punished when this is discovered.

12. In order to assure the proper execution of the regulations, all the criminals in any detention room must be held responsible for any and all violations of the regulations committed in their room.

13. It is forbidden to talk or make any writing on the walls in the bathrooms or communicate with criminals in other bathrooms by any means.

These directives became the new law of the camp. Of course, they couldn't stop the Tap Code, which we all had become adept at using through any means of noise making, whether tapping walls, sweeping, or knocking on our buckets. Still, with the renewed efforts at prohibiting our communication, we had to be even more diligent and careful in our covert communication.

A new era in our captivity was beginning. The propaganda efforts of the Vietnamese had been futile. No American had written any statements, and our enemy had been able to get no useful information from us. Our morale and resistance were high. Frustrated in their efforts to exploit us, the Vietnamese turned to gross mistreatment to achieve their ends.

We heard from new captives that from the very beginning they were tortured when they refused to answer questions. There was a decided change in the attitude of our guards. The atmosphere was hostile.

● ● ●

After about three weeks in solitary confinement, my cell door opened and in walked Bob Shumaker. Shu had good news for me from Robbie Risner, my former squadron commander. They had been held in the same building, and by means of the Tap Code, Shu had pumped Robbie for information, knowing he might be moved back with me.

Among other things, Louise had been an inspiration to other squadron wives. She had held up very well after hearing the news of my shoot-down. Both she and my new son were doing fine. She had named him Carlyle S. Harris Jr. and called him Lyle. Our home and car were both sold, and Louise had left Okinawa for the States, well in control of the situation. I choked with emotion.

Communication between buildings at the Zoo was very difficult. Through cracks we tried to keep track of guards so we could talk from one building to another when they were out of the area. The Vietnamese provided us with one of the best sources. They often moved men from one cell to another—between buildings—for no apparent reason. Voice or tapping provided good communication within buildings. Each night, someone would be required to pick up buckets that were left outside cell doors to be dumped. While making the rounds with the buckets, often it was possible to pass a few words at the cell door.

While I was so engaged one night, we stopped at Commander Denton's door. His bucket was not outside, so the turnkey with me opened his door. Denton had been in solitary confinement for about four months. On an impulse, I brushed by the guard, walked in, and shook the startled Commander's hand.

I said, "Hi, Commander Denton. I'm Smitty Harris."

He responded, "Are you my new cellmate?"

I could see the disappointment on Denton's face as the guard gathered his wits and ushered me quickly from the cell. The guard was angered and spoke harshly, but nothing came of the incident. I'm sure the guard told no one because it was his own negligence that permitted me to enter the cell. Also, he should not even have opened the door in my presence because we still were not permitted to see other Americans.

One of our guards was particularly lax. We called him "Sweet Pea" because of his mild ways and mannerisms. When Sweet Pea was our turnkey, we could get away with more communication than with any other guard. He often made the mistake of letting us see and talk to other POWs when we were getting food, going for our baths, or emptying buckets.

One Sunday morning, he forgot to lock our cell door after we had been given our food. When he was safely out of the area, I pushed the door open and walked out. Escape entered my mind, but in broad daylight there would be no chance to get far enough away from the prison to avoid immediate recapture. Instead, I entered the other empty cells in the building to see if there was a trapdoor in any of the ceilings. There was one in our cell. The ceilings were very high, but it might be possible to climb up through the trapdoor at night and exit through another in an empty cell that wasn't locked. No such luck.

I did, however, chat with Commander Denton, who was on the opposite end of our building, and with Morgan and Storz. I had been careful to watch the area for guards as I sneaked around the building, but someone saw me. There was loud shouting. Within minutes, five armed guards were ushering me back into my cell with Shu. Sweet Pea was in charge. His face was livid. He shook his finger in my face, sputtered, and fumed in Vietnamese. I fully expected a beating, solitary confinement, or worse. Instead, nothing happened. A few days later, in an interrogation, Shu was told that Sweet Pea would no longer be a turnkey. I was amazed that the blame was put where it belonged but disappointed that Sweet Pea would no longer be an unwitting aid to our communications.

SMITTY 25

It was 1859, and Genevan businessman Henry Dunant was horrified at the gruesome scene before his eyes. He had traveled to Emperor Napoleon III's headquarters in Italy to ask for land rights for a new business venture. He came away with more than land rights, however, when he witnessed the aftermath of the Battle of Solferino, an excessively gory battle in the Second War of Italian Independence. What he saw greatly impacted his life, and he wrote his account in a book called *A Memory of Solferino*, in which he described the grisly scenes of war and posed the question, "Would it not be possible, in time of peace and quiet, to form relief societies for the purpose of having care given to the wounded in wartime by zealous, devoted and thoroughly qualified volunteers?"*

A man of action, Dunant didn't just write about this concept; he also proposed a solution, which suggested that all nations come together to create volunteer relief groups that could serve as impartial humanitarians to assist the wounded and those affected by wars. A committee was formed that included Dunant, and in 1864, the first Geneva Convention was held in Switzerland. Twelve nations signed an agreement for the nonpartisan care for the sick and wounded by war. They also proposed an international emblem to identify the personnel and their supplies so that their safety would be assured from both sides of war. The emblem

---

* J. Henry Dunant, *Un Souvenir de Solferino* (Geneva: Imprimerie Jules-Guillaume Fick, 1862); English version, *A Memory of Solferino* (Philadelphia: American Red Cross, 1939, 1959, reprinted by the International Committee of the Red Cross in 1994), 115, www.icrc.org/en/doc/assets/files/publications/icrc-002-0361.pdf.

was a red cross on a white background, chosen in honor of Dunant's nationality; it was the reverse of the Swiss flag. Thus, the Red Cross was born. In 1901, Dunant received the Nobel Peace Prize.

In 1906, thirty-five nations met to update the rules of the First Geneva Convention. These updates included additional protections for the wounded and those captured in battle. After World War I ended, it was clear to all that more updates were needed to ensure the humane treatment of prisoners of war. In 1929, those updates were made in another Geneva Convention. These new updates insisted that all prisoners of war must be treated compassionately and humanely; this included the living conditions of said prisoners. After World War II, it was clear that the Convention of 1929 did not prevent horrific acts from being carried out inside the prison camps and concentration camps. The Geneva Convention of 1949 addressed these issues, which included expanded protections for prisoners of war, including the following areas of protection:

- They must not be tortured or mistreated.
- They are required to give only their name, rank, birth date, and serial number when captured.
- They must receive suitable housing and adequate amounts of food.
- They must not be discriminated against for any reason.
- They have the right to correspond with family and receive care packages.
- The Red Cross has the right to visit them and examine their living conditions.

Every member of the armed forces knew the articles of the Geneva Convention. In fact, each member also carried a Geneva Convention Identification Card. This was a requirement of the Geneva Convention, which stated:

Each Party to a conflict is required to furnish the persons under its jurisdiction who are liable to become prisoners of war, with an identity card showing the owner's surname, first names, rank, army, regimental, personal or serial number or equivalent information, and date of birth. The identity card may, furthermore, bear the signature or the fingerprints, or both, of the owner, and may bear, as well, any other information the Party to the conflict may wish to add concerning persons belonging to its armed forces. As far as possible the card shall measure 6.5 x 10 cm. and shall be issued in duplicate. The identity card shall be shown by the prisoner of war upon demand, but may in no case be taken away from him.*

Not only did every member of the military know their rights as provided by the Geneva Convention, but they also knew that North Vietnam was one of the 195 countries that had ratified the articles of the Geneva Convention of 1949. It was in this knowledge that the early POWs had hoped that their treatment would be fair and humane. We quickly found the opposite to be true.

In order to justify their unlawful and unethical treatment toward us, the North Vietnamese refused to refer to us as prisoners of war and instead continually used the words "criminals of war." They went to great lengths to propagate the illusion that we had committed war crimes and thereby did not merit the safety measures laid out in the Geneva Convention.

We were constantly inflicted with painful punishments in an effort to extract a written or taped statement that we were being treated fairly and humanely. We might be forced to kneel on the rough concrete floor or sit on a stool with irons locked around our ankles and our hands cuffed behind our backs. If the weather was cold, the guards would throw cold water on us and then open the shutters so the freezing wind would blow across our wounded bodies. Often we were kept in these positions all night, and some of us were worn down to the point of experiencing hallucinations. The irony of the statements they wanted us to write would have been laughable had the treatment not been so miserable.

----- • • • -----

* "Questioning of Prisoners," Geneva Convention (III), August 12, 1949, https://ihl-databases.icrc.org/applic/ihl/ihl.nsf/Article.xsp.

It was now November 1965. Shu and I were moved to the first building we had entered two months earlier. In our absence, the large cells had been divided into two smaller cells. We were on the end of the building. The cell immediately behind us had been converted to a bath. Water oozed under the newly partitioned wall, keeping our cell damp, but we were pleased that we could have contact with most of the men in camp who used this bath.

We stayed busy tapping with them and passing information we had obtained. Shu and I could keep an accurate count of the number of men in camp because we now washed all the eating utensils in this bath, twice daily. We also had voice contact with men who dumped their buckets in the toilet next to the bath. The window in the bath had not been bricked up, but iron bars were installed and the louvered shutters retained. Through cracks we could usually keep track of the guard and had time for a few whispered comments when the men entered or left the toilet.

In keeping with the changed attitude of our captors, the Vietnamese demanded that we bow whenever a guard entered our cell or we saw one outside. This was a most onerous requirement for Americans, and we refused. At first, the guards got angry, reported us to the interrogators, and by threats tried to obtain compliance with the new regulation. They also implemented a "no bow, no chow" policy, which led to many hungry POWs. Usually, the food was withheld for a few hours, but some POWs were deprived of food and water for up to three days.

When this failed, they resorted to cruel punishment. A refusal resulted in a beating, half rations, or other punishment. Their favorite tool was a truck fan belt, with which they beat our buttocks and back while we were held prone on the floor by other guards. Sometimes they banged our arms and backs with the butt of a rifle.

Slowly, we all learned to grudgingly comply. We were supposed to bend down about sixty degrees from the waist, but generally got away with little more than a nod of the head. To help our own self-esteem when showing deference to these barbaric captors, Shu and I began uttering an oath at each guard as we reluctantly made some pretense at bowing. We knew the guard did not understand us when we nodded and audibly said, "F–you," but it helped our morale immensely.

DECEMBER 1965
THE ZOO

I had known Bob Purcell when he was in a sister squadron at Kadena Air Base in Okinawa. Percy, as we called him, was extremely active and gregarious. The prison environment, especially solitary confinement, would be particularly difficult for someone like Percy to adjust to. How would he channel his almost boundless energy? As might be expected, he became a key to his building's communication network. There was a trapdoor in his twelve-foot-high ceiling, but somehow Percy was able to climb up through it, crawl to the end of the building, and talk to men in an adjacent building through a louvered roof eave.

Some of the men in Percy's building were on half rations or worse, so he decided to see if he could help them. He found there was a hole in each ceiling through which the electric light wire passed. By scraping and chipping away at these holes, he was able to enlarge them so he could drop pieces of bread down to the men. Percy divided up his own meager portion of bread and passed it out in this manner to the men being punished. He realized that if he were caught, he would be punished even worse than those he was helping, but providentially, the Vietnamese never discovered his actions.

Shu and I moved to the same building with Percy in the next cell. We tapped to him, but he instructed us to place a tin cup at a designated spot on the wall and to place our ear tightly against the bottom of the cup.

I was very surprised to hear Percy's voice very clearly. He explained that he had wrapped his cup with a blanket and with the remainder had made a doughnut-shaped circle around his head. By pressing the end of his cup to the wall and speaking into it, we could hear him, but the blanket muffled the sound enough that it would be difficult for a guard passing by outside to hear him talking. Cup talk was great. We had all become very proficient with the Tap Code, but it was still a slow way to communicate. Percy talked a great deal with us.

Since he and I were both Catholic, we tried to help each other remember some prayers and the Rosary we had learned as children. This time for reflection had helped all of us sort out the really important things in life, and I believe, without exception, we all found a new relationship with our God.

How could two people cooped up together for days, months, and even years find things to talk about? Seemingly without real effort, Shu and I always found something. When nothing else seemed interesting or informative, our minds wandered to new areas. We started building things. It might be a building, a picnic table with a built-in Lazy Susan, a game, or an educational aid. Though the only building taking place was in our minds, it was a wonderful way to keep sharp and occupied.

We would explain our current project in detail—right down to the nuts, bolts, and measurements of every component. We exchanged recommendations for improvement and often argued over the best approach. We did not, however, quarrel. Though of different temperaments, we enjoyed a great deal of mutual respect and knew we had only one real adversary—the enemy, our captors.

Time weighed heavily on POWs in North Vietnam. We all came to appreciate what a valuable commodity time is and the frustration of having almost nothing to do. Days, weeks, and months were slipping by. We were missing important periods of time with our families. Anniversaries, birthdays, graduations, christenings, and all the important dates that are cherished for a lifetime were gone, never to be recreated.

What an awful waste! We could not even occupy our minds or find entertainment because our captors would not permit us to have books, paper and pencil, games, or anything else with which to utilize our time. We painstakingly made cards and chess sets from the rough brown toilet paper. Mashing rice with a little water produced a paste with which we could stick layers of paper together for stiffness. Regular inspections of our cells usually turned up our creations, and they were confiscated with threats of what would happen if we did it again.

We all had a regular exercise program. Though our diets were meager, it was amazing how well our bodies adapted and became strong, even if underweight. Our exercises served the dual purpose of some gainful use of time while our bodies became tough for whatever demands might accrue in the future. We talked and planned for that future.

Shu had had some musical training that he began to impart to me. With burnt matches, I drew up a full-sized piano keyboard on toilet paper. We also drew up sheets of music. I practiced daily, hitting the paper notes on my piano with the proper timing. The music was written for exercise only, and I often wondered how it would sound if it were played on a real instrument. One day we were permitted to visit the reading room for about an hour. Here the Vietnamese kept their propaganda material that we occasionally were forced to read.

One of the pamphlets had the Vietnamese national anthem, with musical score printed in it. I tore it out and hid it to take back to my cell. I now could play real music on my "piano." Shu said it sounded better than his composition. We hid our music sheets, as well as some math problems Shu was working on, between the louvered shutter and the bricked-up window. Using a string taken from a blanket, we reached through the hole at the top of the window and tied one end of the string to a protruding piece of concrete and the other to our secret possessions. In this manner, our packet of papers survived several inspections.

We were moved to the other side of the building with no time to retrieve our work. We heard some loud banging by workers and were told through the communication net that the bricked-up window in our old cell was being knocked out. Our hidden items were found. Surely we would be punished, particularly for tearing out a page from one of the propaganda books, but nothing happened. The workers in the camp were almost friendly when they saw us and undoubtedly did not turn us in.

Commander Denton had tried on several occasions to make some friendly overtures to one of the workers he saw when he was out of his cell. We still were interested in pursuing any opportunity to cultivate outside help for a possible escape attempt. Just obtaining some old clothes would be a big help. Denton made the Catholic sign of the cross when he saw the worker, hoping he was Catholic and would be receptive. The next day when Denton was out of his cell to bathe, the worker slipped a crudely carved crucifix onto his bed.

Although in this police state we could never obtain outside assistance, we found evidence that these people were much like people everywhere. They had compassion and cared for others. We found too that theirs was a very disciplined society in which the state had a remarkable ability to control the thoughts and emotions of its people. Our guards were told that we were criminals and should be treated as such. They blindly followed their instructions.

The weather was getting cold. Although the temperature rarely gets down to freezing in Hanoi, we had insufficient blankets and clothing to be comfortable in our unheated cells. At night, our wooden bed boards made us as cold on both the bottom and top, so we tried wrapping up in our two cotton blankets. We kept track of the date and knew Christmas was coming.

Our thoughts turned more and more to our loved ones on the other side of the earth. What kind of Christmas would this be for them? At least we knew they would be warm and safe, but we also knew this separation was in many ways more difficult for them than for us. We were comforted by the fact that they were safe, but they had no assurances about our welfare, and in many cases they didn't even know if we were alive. If only the Vietnamese would permit us to write and receive letters. I had been lucky to write one.

On December 10, Shu and I were taken to interrogation with Dog. He talked about Christmas and what it would mean to us. I thought he was trying to torment us. He mentioned that we might receive letters from home. When the guards came to take us to our cell, Shu left, but I stayed for a few final words with Dog. Dog accused me of being disrespectful and having a bad attitude. He was right about my attitude toward him.

He thought I should preface everything I said to him with "Sir." Because I had not, I would not get a letter at Christmas. He was true to his word. Although I could perceive no difference in Shu's attitude from mine, I was sure Dog wanted to make a point with us. Although I was almost as pleased as Shu when he got his letter from his wife, Lorraine, a few days later, I was sure I would in no way change my demeanor or attitude toward our cruel, heartless captors.

SMITTY 27

1965
THE ZOO

Shu had been out of the cell on a clean-up detail. He returned, grinning, with a quiz for me. He said, "Smitty, select one of the following:

A. I just saw a Red Cross vehicle filled with packages for us.
B. I just saw a naked woman.
C. I just saw an American officer in uniform in camp.
D. All of the above.
E. None of the above."

I thought for a moment and selected E. Shu laughed. "No, you are wrong. The correct answer is B." I couldn't believe it. But Shu explained that he had to go into the bath to get a bucket of water, and sure enough, a Vietnamese woman (one of the workers) was stark naked a few feet from him when he entered.

I should explain. There was a great deal of work going on in camp. The outer walls had been completed, but now walls were being constructed around each building for security and to keep us from seeing and communicating with our friends. More than half of the workers were women. They dressed in rags with patches over patches on their pajama-style clothes. They seemed to do the very hardest kind of work—unloading trucks, carrying heavy baskets of bricks, and digging ditches. The men did the construction—laying bricks—and directing the women. We even saw one woman in advanced pregnancy toting bricks around. By government edict, all Vietnamese workers, both men and women, are equal. The Vietnamese version of women's liberation appeared to have some undesirable side effects.

In April 1966, a new POW was moved into the cell next to ours. He did not respond to the Tap Code, so we attempted to obtain voice contact with him. While one of us looked through the crack under our cell door to scout for guards, the other tried to talk to our new neighbor. He responded in very broken English. We found out he was a sergeant from Thailand who had been a crew chief on a C-47 aircraft. He had been shot down about one week earlier.

He asked, "How long have you been prisoners?"

We answered, "Since February and April of 1965."

We could hear him gasp and almost sob. "Oh no! So long?"

When we asked him if he was married, he answered, "Yes, I have one wife."

In Thailand, men have a number one wife and can have as many others as they can afford and desire. Ty, as we named him, soon moved in with the other Thai we had named Tim. We often saw them sweeping and working outside. We envied their being permitted the luxury of being outside their cells during the day but were glad they weren't locked in their cells, except for brief minutes each day. No prisoner had an easy experience in the camps, but those from the United States seemed to be targeted to even greater degrees.

Propaganda efforts were being intensified over the speakers in our cells. Not only did we hear the radio program for American fighting men in the south, but the camp authorities were also reading other propaganda directed specifically to us. Over and over we heard that we were criminals and would be tried for our crimes. The guards became even more hostile and tried to enforce the bowing regulation more strictly.

It was impossible for the Vietnamese to enforce all these regulations, but they tried. Men who had attitudes that were perceived to be bad were put in isolation cells. These were special cells separated from other POWs where communication was almost impossible. They were small, dark, hot, and dirty.

At the height of the increased propaganda and concerted effort to enforce camp regulations, I was taken to interrogation on July 6, 1966. The guards were hostile and as demanding as possible. They grumbled and tried to hurry me to get fully dressed. In our cells we wore shorts but had to put on long-sleeved shirts and pajama-like trousers for interrogation. I was sure this was going to be trouble. I had been accused many times of a bad attitude. Perhaps they would try again to get me to write something. Dog went right to the point.

"Here is a letter for you from your wife. Now you may return to your cell."

I was dumbfounded. The address was to me, and I recognized Louise's handwriting. There must be a trick, or perhaps the letter contained bad news. My heart pounded in anticipation as I walked back to my cell.

When I opened the letter, a picture fell out. There were Robin, Carolyn, and a smiling chubby little boy. Tears welled in my eyes. I turned away from Shu because I couldn't control my shaking, sobbing body. My little girls and my son!

I wiped my bleary eyes to see better. They were on a beach—in Clearwater, Florida, the letter said. I thought my emotions were completely inured because of my imprisonment and that I had absolute control, but I was blubbering like a child and embarrassed that Shu could see me so shaken up.

I read the letter, the first of many times. It was a happy one. They missed me and loved me. Lyle was born on May 14, 1965. Mother, Dad, my brother Joe, and Louise's family were doing well. All sent love. They prayed for my return. I read and reread the letter. I refused to go to the bath so I could look at my picture and letter. This had to be one of the happiest days of my life, though short-lived, as other events were about to unfold.

By coincidence, Louise had moved next door to her sister's home in Tupelo, Mississippi, where Captain George Hall's brother had lived—the same George who was now a POW with me at the Zoo and who had helped pass the directive to follow the Code among the POWs. I never found out how George knew of the arrangement, but he had been waiting for an opportunity to share this information and boldly took a chance. As he was dumping his bucket, he said, "Tell Smitty Harris that his wife is next door to Janice and Dick Blake in Tupelo, Mississippi."

The guards did their best to stop communication but simply could not cope with an unexpected bold move by an American. They were so startled by George's statement, which they did not understand, that they merely fussed and fumed. Perhaps he was not communicating, only uttering an oath or extraneous remark. If they turned him in, it would be a reflection of their own inability to control the Americans. At any rate, I got the message, and George was not punished.

I was extremely pleased that Louise had chosen Tupelo as her new home. Janice and Dick were super fine people, and I knew Dick would do everything possible to be a foster father for the children. It was a great consolation to know where they were and to picture their activities in Tupelo.

I had been in the home that Louise bought and had liked it. Heretofore I had no idea where my family was, but this scrap of information provided a solid base for my thoughts. They were near family and friends, and someone would be able to help them when needed.

JULY 1966
THE ZOO AND THE HANOI MARCH

A guard came and took away one of our long-sleeved pajama tops. Through peepholes and tapping, we found that one shirt had been taken from each POW. As always, when anything out of the ordinary routine occurred, there was a great deal of speculation among us.

An hour or so later when the shirts were returned, a large stenciled number was on each one. We were sure this was for the benefit of someone outside of camp—to make us look more like criminals. There were almost as many ideas as there were POWs about when, where, and for whom we would be displayed.

In the late afternoon, guards directed us to put on our long clothes, and then we were blindfolded and led to a truck. Shu and I were hand-cuffed to each other, as were other pairs of POWs. We traveled only about fifteen minutes in the trucks until we disembarked and waited. Finally, guards lined us up in some kind of formation as we started walking. We halted.

Rabbit had a megaphone. He said we should all keep our heads bowed so the people would not get angry, and we must not try to communicate. We still had no idea what was going on. Guards removed our blindfolds as Rabbit said, "Now the walk begins. You will see the indignation of the Vietnamese people."

We had heard the noises of a lot of people, but we weren't prepared for the huge multitude we saw as we walked a block and entered a very large square in the city. By now it was almost dark, but the square was lit with streetlights and very large spotlights carried on trucks.

A roar of noise greeted us in the square. Loudspeakers blared. People screamed and chanted. I shuddered as I remembered my parade in Thanh Hóa. At least here, the people were being kept separated from us. Movie cameras and other cameras of all types were recording our march. English speakers continuously reminded us to keep our heads bowed.

Just as in Thanh Hóa, the authorities began losing control of the thousands of people they had intentionally brought to a fevered pitch of hatred. As we left the square in a long file of twos, the mob began closing in on the guards and army men who walked beside us. Sticks and rocks were thrown. Men were being hit and kicked. Jeremiah Denton was knocked stunned to his knees. Bob Peel literally dragged him to his feet and kept him moving as the crowd closed in for the kill. They wanted blood. All of us were hit, and most were bleeding when we finally arrived at a stadium. Two or three hundred people were milling around the gate as guards and POWs tried to push through them to enter. The last fifty feet were the toughest.

Angry fists struck at us. Some landed. We were kicked and struck by thrown objects. Somehow we managed to push through to the gate and enter the stadium. What a relief—the guards and army men had been able to keep all but a handful of the mob outside. I was truly worried. Shu and I had been near the front of the formation of fifty to sixty POWs, but the men behind us probably were feeling the brunt of the mob's violence, which had increased throughout the march. I could picture the mob knocking someone to the ground, and in their frenzy, there would be little chance for his survival. Miraculously, my fears were ill-founded, and no one was killed.

In the unlit stadium we sat on the ground, waiting to be moved. Lt. Chuck Boyd was handcuffed to Lt. Cole Black, who had been shot down just a few days previously. Chuck was trying desperately to teach Cole the Tap Code whenever they could exchange a few words. There was so much noise, activity, and shock from the harrowing march that Cole was not able to comprehend what Chuck was trying to teach him. Finally, Cole turned to Chuck and, still wide-eyed over what he had been through, asked, "Do they do this very often?" Chuck knew there was no use trying to keep going on this occasion to teach Cole the Tap Code. Trucks carried us back to the Zoo.

We heard cell doors open and close. Guards barked orders—some men were moved. We felt like caged animals because we knew there was trouble in camp. The arrogant, abrupt manner of the guards revealed some new instructions that had been given them by their superiors. Through our communication system, we heard that some men had been seen chained to trees in the courtyard. In the morning we heard from Pop Keirn that he had been tied between two trees and whipped with a strip of rubber from an old tire. He had been randomly picked, and I knew my turn was coming. That was all part of the mental torture we were enduring.

Apparently, the Hanoi March was the culmination of a program to rile up the hatred of the Vietnamese populace against American POWs in preparation for our trials. We were to be exploited. The North Vietnamese were going to try to obtain some propaganda advantage from us.

Starting immediately after the march, a torture program was initiated to force American POWs to write statements that would be of benefit to the DRV. They wanted letters written to antiwar congressmen, confessions, and statements against our government. Ironically, they tortured us to obtain statements that their treatment of Americans was generous, kind, and humane.

The torture included creating intense pain with tight ropes; leg and arm irons being tightened down; beatings; manipulating broken arms, shoulders, and legs; and other methods that would not leave too many obvious scars. Usually the most intense pain was induced after a POW had been worn down by being forced to kneel for hours or days, being chained to a stool, and/or being denied food and water. Their purpose was to intimidate, extract propaganda statements, and gain compliance with their wishes. They failed. They got some useless statements and temporary satisfaction.

In retrospect, their torture was a big mistake, and we gained from that mistake. Once grossly mistreated, no POW was ever again fooled by their propaganda, brainwashing, or lies. Never could our captors let the International Red Cross or other unbiased outsiders visit and report on our good treatment—the propaganda they desperately desired. Their mistreatment hardened us, and as we fought back, we developed a great pride in ourselves, our leaders, and the others who after each torture session vowed to try harder next time. Our unity and steadfast resistance gave us strength and singleness of purpose that some believe is the main reason we came home without the kinds of emotional and mental problems that were expected from our ordeal.

Much later we found out from new shoot-downs that world public opinion and outrage at the Hanoi March had forced Ho Chi Minh to assure several important national leaders that American POWs would not be tried as criminals. This foiled their plan to use us as public hate objects in trials around their country. It did not, however, stop them from trying to exploit us by attempting to extract propaganda statements. On the contrary, it probably caused them to increase their efforts in the latter program.

For the next few days, a number of men were moved out of their cells. On July 11, guards opened our cell door and motioned to Shu and me to roll up our gear for a move. As we sat on a concrete curb, blindfolded, waiting to board a truck, I tried to peek under my blindfold to see what was happening. Fortunately, looking down, I saw my letter from Louise lying loose on the ground. My most prized possession! I've always been a very lucky person—or perhaps Someone was looking out for me.

Years later, I learned that my Louise knew more about the Hanoi March than I realized. A few weeks after the torturous march, she received a call from Claude Watkins, her casualty officer and the man who had taught me the Tap Code, informing her that he was coming to Tupelo from Washington, D.C. He had classified information in his possession he was sure she would want to see. Shortly afterward, Claude was knocking on the door of the Madison Street house, and Louise nervously invited him in. He got right to the point and explained about the Hanoi March, what we had endured, and how a Japanese reporter had relayed the information and smuggled out

143

photographs. Watkins then pulled out a black-and-white photograph and gave it to Louise.

"Louise, tell me if you recognize anyone," he said as he put the photo in her trembling hand.

She looked for a moment and replied, "No, I don't think I do."

"Look closer," he said.

She pulled the photo closer to examine each face. Then she saw them. My cheekbones were the giveaway, though they were now more prominent because of the weight loss.

"Smitty," she said with mixed emotions. Her heart sank because the photo revealed how painfully thin I was, and then her heart soared because it was the first proof she had that I was alive.

"You can show your sister if you'd like," Watkins said with compassion. He knew that if something happened to Louise, Janice would be the children's guardian, so she was included on most of the communication, including this classified photo. Later, Louise was also allowed to call my parents and tell them about the photo. All of them had the same reaction—a mix of emotions in opposite extremes. They hated to see me and the other men in such terrible circumstances, but it was great reassurance that we had survived thus far.

That photo, now quite recognizable, showed Pop Keirn on the front left of the scene; his normal 250 pounds had dropped by around fifty pounds. Redheaded Kyle Berg and Shu were beside me, and Larry Guarino and Ron Byrne were behind us. We were all emaciated, but all alive—at least for now.

SMITTY 29

JULY–NOVEMBER 1966
BRIARPATCH

Our new destination was a familiar one. In July 1966, I found myself back at Briarpatch. If I had thought that my first experience there was difficult, I was about to be in for a rude awakening. We were the last group of POWs to arrive at the Briarpatch, and we brought with us stories of torture that had started after the Hanoi March, which quickly moved to Briarpatch, as the guards launched into extreme harassment of all POWs that was uncontrolled and sadistic. A man we named "Frenchie" announced that many of the guards had lost relatives in the previous bombing raids, and he was therefore not responsible for their actions.

Bowing became the most degrading initiative. Lessons in bowing were given to the POWs, and when we were uncooperative, we were slapped and beaten with fists, which soon progressed to rifle butts and sticks. Initially, the SRO gave the order—"Do not bow." This order was rescinded, but due to poor communication, many POWs did not know. Therefore, abuse continued and eventually became so violent that several POWs were permanently maimed.

Guards would harass the POWs through the barred windows by beating or stabbing us with long sticks. Being outside was a particular torture, and soon the once-oppressive cell became a sanctuary to many of us. However, this sanctuary became hellish when the guards sealed the windows closed, forming an individual steam bath for each POW. Food rations were cut, and due to no salt in the diet, boils were common.

After the Hanoi March, an intensive program called "Two Choices" began over the PA system and continued in the violent interrogation sessions. The first choice was to change over to the Vietnamese side and help end the war. In return for agreeing to this choice, POWs would get the privilege of continued "humane and lenient policy" toward them. The POWs were instructed to show that they had chosen this option by writing or taping propaganda statements.

The second choice was to continue in our loyalty to the United States and resistance to the Vietnamese. Selecting this choice led to threats of dying the death of the "blackest criminal." Approximately forty POWs were at Briarpatch during this time, and all forty of us chose to support and remain loyal to the United States of America.

In early August 1966, a civilian we nicknamed "Doc" came to Briarpatch, along with an officer we called "Louie the Rat." I would encounter him later at Son Tay. Doc began his "quizzes" with a few POWs, apparently trying to find willing writers to make propaganda statements, which we later felt were intended for the Bertrand Russell "International War Crimes Tribunal." This tribunal was funded by many sources, including a large donation by North Vietnam, after a request was made by Russell to Ho Chi Minh, the infamous revolutionary leader of the Vietnamese Communist Party. When the POWs refused, the torture began.

A POW would be moved with all his meager gear to a quiz room and told what to write. After refusing, we were beaten, threatened, and made to sit on the stool for days on end, without sleep. After continuing to refuse to write, we were given the twisted cuff treatment. This was a form of torture in which our arms were tied behind us, and handcuffs with accompanying ratchets were applied to our arms. The sickening click, click, click sound indicated the tightening of the cuff until the two bones bent together as one. This torture continued until some form of statement was written. It was a depressing and disappointing moment for all POWs when they reached their breaking point and could no longer withstand the pain of torture. To be forced to write or say during recorded video the opposite of what one believed created an added burden of guilt.

Time and time again, the Vietnamese "won" this game of torture. However, one final layer of defiance lay within the heart of each man.

When forced to write, we took advantage of their lack of understanding of the idioms and jargon of American language. Because the Vietnamese often dictated what to write in their unrefined English, it was possible to write in a way that sounded suspicious and ridiculous to an American, thus announcing the coercion and redeeming the guilt of the forced scribe.

Jeremiah Denton was forced to record a 1966 televised propaganda interview, which was broadcast in the United States. His words were calmly expressed as he falsely stated that he was being given adequate food, clothing, and medical care. However, he feigned trouble with the television lights and was seen blinking in an unnatural way. In reality, Denton was blinking in Morse code. His message? T-O-R-T-U-R-E. Naval Intelligence was able to decipher his blinking message, and this was the first solid evidence the outside world had received of our deplorable situation.

Early after my return to Briarpatch, we observed the Vietnamese digging a series of six-foot-deep trenches at various places around the camp. We were told that these trenches were dug to save the lives of the POWs if the U.S. were to bomb the camp. In reality, a much more sinister plan was in place. During this time of torture, we continued our communication as best we could through the use of the Tap Code. These short messages were communicated by tapping in various ways, including using anything that made a sound, such as bumping the Bos when they were being emptied, shaking our clothing, or whistling the Tap Code.

Soon there was an attempted communication purge, and new forms of torture were added. Some of the men were bound, blindfolded, and thrown into the newly dug trenches for many days and then removed and taken immediately to receive the twisted cuff treatment. Others were forced to sit in small caves throughout the day, blindfolded and situated in forced, cramped positions. Still others were forced to run blindfolded and barefoot while being dragged by a noose around their necks. This form of torture seemed like a game to the Vietnamese, which they thoroughly enjoyed. It was not uncommon to hear men crying out in pain and anguish at all hours of the day and night. Every man seemed to have a breaking point, and after two and a half months of continuous torture, the Vietnamese had the "confessions" they wanted, although these were full of ridiculous statements and outright lies.

One example was a statement that Nels Tanner, a Navy pilot, was tortured into writing. The North Vietnamese wanted to get a statement that U.S. pilots were antiwar and would refuse to follow orders. After painful torture, Nels wrote that two antiwar pilots in his squadron had influenced his squadron to refuse combat missions. The Vietnamese really liked his statement and sent it to Bertrand Russell at the International War Crimes Tribunal, where Russell read it to attendees. There were two problems with the paper: (1) How did Nels Tanner get shot down if his squadron refused to fly combat missions? (2) Nels had gone to great efforts to name the two squadron mates—Dick Tracy and Clark Kent. Apparently, the North Vietnamese had not heard of the famed comic strip characters. Nels paid dearly for this embarrassment but was proud of his deception.

When the Vietnamese selected men to read their propaganda over the camp PA system, the recently tortured men complied. However, they still managed to covertly defy the Vietnamese by making the material sound ridiculous through the use of mispronunciations and exaggerated accents. An exaggerated Southern accent was a favorite among the men. The limited ability of the Vietnamese to speak and understand English gave the POWs a small victory. We often said, "They have beaten us physically, but we can fight them with our minds."

By the fall of 1966, we experienced another malady when our feet became so hot and painful at night that it was excruciating to touch them. We found temporary relief by running in place on the cold concrete floor. It wasn't until our release in 1973 that this malady was diagnosed as beriberi, caused by a thiamine deficiency. Our poor diets were the cause of this debilitating illness.

Toward the end of November 1966, the season of torture came to an end. As Thanksgiving approached, I was thankful that we had a temporary reprieve. On Thanksgiving Day, I was one of two people in one of the isolation huts, which had four cells. The other occupant was Ron Storz, who had been captured on April 28, 1965, less than a month after I had been shot down. Ron was a tough resister and was continually as defiant as was humanly possible. Having been together on several occasions, we knew each other fairly well. During that time at Briarpatch, our hands were continually tied behind our backs. We were untied only long enough to eat our morning and evening meals.

On this Thanksgiving morning, with hands tied, I backed up to the wall that connected our two cells and began tapping, describing in detail an imaginary Thanksgiving dinner. It did not take Ron long at all to chime in. He tapped back his favorite holiday foods, complete with the perfect pairing of wine. After several hours of exhausting all of our ideas for the perfect Thanksgiving meal, I tapped a final message to Ron: "Ron, now that we've concocted this great meal together, why don't you come on over?"

Without missing a beat, Ron replied by tapping, "I would, Smitty, but I'm all tied up today."

Maintaining a sense of humor, despite our horrific circumstances, was a balm to my weary soul.

Ron Storz went on to be a part of the Alcatraz Gang, one of the eleven bullish POWs who endured much at the Alcatraz Camp, where the North Vietnamese deemed them as troublemakers. Known also as the Alcatraz Eleven, these American servicemen maintained a stance of defiant resistance that ultimately cost Ron his life. In an effort to defy the North Vietnamese, he refused to do what he was told, including eating what was placed before him. His fellow POWs tried to get him to eat, but he refused. Weak and unable to walk, Ron was carried away by the North Vietnamese and was never seen again. Later, it was reported by the Vietnamese that he was one of the POWs who died in captivity. The Alcatraz Eleven returned with only ten.

Years later, at one of our POW reunions, I noticed a tall young lady whose name tag showed Storz as her maiden name. I walked up to her and said, "I know who you are. I knew about you when you were a little girl." I told her about that memorable Thanksgiving Day, and we were both overwhelmed with the connection of a shared love for her father. It meant so much to her—and to me—as she had not heard anything about his years in captivity.

THROUGH THE MIDDLE YEARS

From the start, the people of Tupelo were welcoming, supportive, and kind to me, and they soon became like family. They often respectfully–almost tentatively–asked for updates on Smitty. It was almost as if he was *their* POW, not just mine, even though they had never met him. There were no protests in our little town, and the people were very protective of my young family. Janice and her family became even closer as they helped me raise Robin, Carolyn, and Lyle.

I received a total of fourteen letters from Smitty over the almost eight years of captivity–an average of one or two a year. The days when letters arrived were filled with joy! The children would get so excited and share the news with everyone they would see. One day, after the children had already gone to school, I saw Mrs. Blue, the traffic guard, when I arrived at the school for a PTA meeting. She was beaming with excitement.

"I hear we got a letter!" she said.

We. That word sums up my experience with the people of Tupelo. They took us in and shared our burdens–and our joys. It was a wonderful place to raise our children and gave me a great sense of belonging and security. Even so, I was adamant about the safety of my children and very protective of each of them. Being solely responsible for everything in their world was a great responsibility and a challenging aspect of those years. However, God always provided the help and support I needed.

I tried to keep our lives as normal as possible, and the children and I lived as if Smitty were about to walk through the door at any moment.

Each summer, we took a trip to see our family. With frequent stops at Stuckey's, with their famed pitched roof, teal shingles, and decadent Pecan Log Roll and Pecan Divinity, the children and I traveled almost five hundred miles in the station wagon from Tupelo to Asheville, North Carolina, where we met my mother and her best friends, Ruth and Charlie McCary. We would spend a week there and then travel another five-hundred-plus miles to the eastern shore of Maryland to visit Smitty's parents for two weeks before making the trek back to Tupelo. In all, we would be gone for nearly a month.

We also took a trip each year to Florida, visiting Clearwater and Panama City, as well as Tallahassee, where my mother and grandmother lived. Both Smitty's parents and my mother would vacation together, and I was grateful that both sides of the family got along beautifully. I cherished these vacations and our time with our families, but by the end of the summer, I was always ready for the routine of the school year.

Our days were full and busy. I was invited to be a member of Junior Auxiliary, an active women's community service group that helped me meet and serve even more citizens of Tupelo. I also volunteered as a den mother for several years, leading twenty-two Brownie Scouts. I often joked that my children wore a sign around their necks that read, "My Mother Can Do It," as they volunteered me for every task. And I loved it all! Being busy and involved kept me focused and purposeful and, more importantly, kept my mind off myself and my situation. I have always believed that the best remedy for carrying a weighty burden is to help others with their burdens. And I was afforded many opportunities to do so.

Saturday mornings were a bit more relaxed. I allowed the children to watch the classic favorites of that era, *The Archies*, *H. R. Pufnstuf*, and *Bugs Bunny*. Together we enjoyed watching *Gilligan's Island*, *The Brady Bunch*, *The Carol Burnett Show*, and the old reruns of *Tarzan*. Whenever *Tarzan* came on, I always thought of Smitty. Back in the late fifties when we had just started dating, Smitty had invited me to attend a party at the Air Force base. When he ran into an old friend, he turned to introduce me and famously said, "This is my girlfriend, Jane." *Jane? Who was Jane?* But I didn't miss a beat and quickly replied,

"Well, Tarzan, you at least need to get my name straight." I think that is when Smitty fell in love. He liked my spunky side, and that would prove to be a characteristic that would serve me well during his years away. He always lovingly called me Jane after that night. Oh, how I missed our shared laughs and inside jokes!

Smitty and I had been extremely frugal in our years together, a habit I continued in his absence. But by now, I realized it could be many more years before Smitty returned home, so I set out to make the house a true home for the children. About two years after I bought the house, I turned the attached garage into a huge den, updated the kitchen, and took advantage of the high-pitched ceiling in the attic to create two bedrooms for the girls. Lyle's bedroom was downstairs near mine. What began as a rental house with three bedrooms and two baths ended up being a four-bedroom, three-bath, 3,800-square-foot home. The best improvement was adding central heat and air, which helped accommodate our fickle Southern temperatures.

Around 1968, the State Department informed the wives of the detainees and MIA wives that the North Vietnamese had decreed that we would be allowed to send a small package to our husbands—which we learned later they rarely received. We were given the address and specifications. A favorite activity was our monthly trip to TKE Drug Store on the corner across from Reed's department store. There was an old-fashioned soda fountain where the children could sit at the counter and order a Coke float or milkshake while I planned and plotted what would be most helpful to send to Smitty. Gene DeBow, the pharmacist there, would help me pick out the best vitamins and most effective toothpaste, given Smitty's meager meals and lack of dental care. The package was restricted to a four-inch by six-inch box, which I skillfully fit as much into as I possibly could. Each box would contain vitamins, toothbrush, toothpaste, hard candy, a T-shirt, underwear, soap, and photos of the children. In every package, I selected something I thought he might use creatively if he should attempt escape. One such item was an aluminum comb, which I selected when I remembered how he had once made a key for my antique corner cabinet out of a similar aluminum comb.

On occasion, I was given the privilege of sending something covert to help the POWs. Claude Watkins would call and tell me he would be traveling to Tupelo to give me something. I knew not to ask questions. One such item was a special tube of toothpaste, which I found out later contained microfilm hidden in the tube. On another occasion, he brought a small wooden cribbage board with pegs. I didn't realize at the time that there was a transmitter hidden inside, but I was confident there was something covertly hidden that could help Smitty. I felt proud to be a part of anything that might help him and the other POWs.

When Smitty returned home, I learned he had only received two of the approximately one hundred packages I sent over the years. I suppose there were many Vietnamese enjoying tubes of Colgate and Fruit of the Loom skivvies, but sending those monthly packages made me feel closer to Smitty.

THROUGH THE MIDDLE YEARS

Looking back, the middle years of my captivity seem like an endless movie reel that plays over and over. We were transferred from one camp to another, where our living conditions were always primitive– usually a seven-by-seven-foot cell with two heavy board or concrete bunks, often with leg stocks at the end. A thin straw mat was our mattress. There was never any heating or cooling, and the oppressive heat or freezing cold marked the changing seasons year after year.

A waste bucket was provided in each cell. Using this effectively while chained to a stool or clamped to the hard bed with both legs in stocks was humiliating and extremely difficult.

A hinged door, about ten by ten inches, was in each heavy wooden or metal cell door so that the guards could look in. We were usually fed two times a day with rice or bread and some watery soup. We received very little protein, and many of us suffered at least once from beriberi, a vitamin deficiency. Most lost about 20 percent of their normal weight. We were not allowed outside our cells to exercise or to mingle with other POWs. We spent countless hours chained to stools or forced onto our knees, and we endured endless hours of propaganda, coercion, and ultimately torture. Then, for unknown reasons, we were blindfolded, loaded in trucks at night, and hauled away to the next location, where the endless movie replayed itself yet again.

When times were really bad–and especially during those times when I feared I might not survive–I prayed frequently and fervently because I had nowhere else to turn. I knew I needed help. And help came. No, I didn't experience a personal miracle. The torture didn't stop. I wasn't free and back home. But I gained more than I even knew to pray for. After prayer, I knew I was no longer alone. Prayer gave me renewed strength to continue resisting a brutal enemy. And all those miracles I prayed for came true—just not on my timetable, but on God's. Now I feel that I have everything I could have ever wanted. Through the difficulty of my years of captivity, I found a renewed belief in a Supreme Being—God, my Father—who looked after me then and still does today.

During my years of captivity, I spent time in eight different prison camps. The first—and last—was the infamous Hanoi Hilton. Its real name was Hoa Lo Prison complex, and it was located across from the North Vietnamese Ministry of Justice, which is ironic, given the injustice we endured.

Next I was moved to Briarpatch, west of Hanoi, and then back to the outskirts of Hanoi to the Zoo. After the Zoo, I was moved back to Briarpatch and later back to the Zoo Annex. The Zoo Annex was adjacent to the Zoo. Its main purpose was to isolate junior POWs from those more senior. It was adjacent to the southwest wall of the Zoo and was surrounded by a ten-foot wall. May 1969 would prove to be a miserable turning point in the lives of all POWs. Two POWs escaped from the Zoo Annex, provoking wrath that spread like wildfire from the Zoo Annex to the Zoo and throughout every one of the prison camps.

I also spent time in Son Tay, Camp Faith, Camp Unity, and Dogpatch. Each camp was unique, but the overall experience was similar, with the ebb and flow of hope and despair, misery made bearable by camaraderie.

Despite the deplorable conditions, we experienced occasional moments of lighthearted fun, especially when we were placed with a cellmate. Chuck Boyd was my cellmate at Son Tay. We frequently took turns peeking under our door into the hallway just to see if we could get a glimpse of what was going on with others in the camp. We often saw a very small Vietnamese woman carrying a chogie pole, which they used to carry balanced buckets on either side. These buckets could contain anything from bricks or other construction material to waste materials to be emptied. This small, shapeless, unattractive woman

155

looked old and miserable, but she carried those loads as instructed. We nicknamed her Gravel Gerty.

One day, I was looking under our door and saw her carrying the chogie pole laboriously. She was an awful sight. I looked and looked and finally turned back to Chuck and said, "Chuck, I think I've been a POW for too long."

"Why, Smitty?" he responded.

"Because Gravel Gerty is starting to look good to me."

We had a good laugh that day, despite our circumstances.

<hr/>

During the middle years, our communication gained momentum from that providential meeting of four friends in 1965, when I first taught them the Tap Code. It was a little slow at first, but we eventually used the code successfully. Soon the others in the cellblock were using the code, and extraordinary efforts were made to see that every POW knew the Tap Code. Soon, tapping on a cell wall was not the only way the Tap Code was transmitted. Almost any sound the POWs could make was in Tap Code. Sweeping a cell corridor, chopping wood, hoeing down weeds, snapping a towel, and coughing were all in code. These noises would be carried from one building to another without our captors being aware that any communication was happening.

We tapped about anything and everything. Any special talents— from music to chess to Scripture memory—were passed from cell to cell through the Tap Code. The North Vietnamese always became incensed when they finally realized how well we were communicating. They went to almost insane efforts to stop it, including torture. But they were never successful. We could send the Tap Code silently with a hand or a note on a piece of paper through the cracks under our cell doors. We used rough toilet paper and makeshift pens to write out notes that were hidden in a commonly used wash area.

We developed our own mute code, using one hand to form letters. It was similar to American sign language but modified so that we could speak with only one hand. If we could crawl up to a barred window that could be seen from another cellblock up to fifty or seventy-five feet away, we could communicate silently and swiftly, one hand forming the code, the other grasping the bars tightly. Much of each day was spent either in the role of communicator or in the role of lookout while my brothers made efforts to communicate. Whenever our captors tried to stop one form of communication, we just developed another more secure method.

The importance of communication between POWs cannot be overstated. It boosted morale. It provided a vehicle for the chain of command to be utilized. It shared information to counter the efforts of the enemy to divide the POWs and helped POWs form a common resistance to their aims. It provided information from friends and family back home and in our units as later shoot-downs joined our ranks. It provided educational opportunities from a wealth of knowledge.

All POWs needed to make some productive use of time spent in prison, and we achieved this through our covert communication methods. Communicating, watching for guards, and all efforts to assist the communication process (not just the Tap Code) helped pass the time. Through the Tap Code, POWs gained the strength of unity. Shared information of torture and mistreatment created peer pressure for every POW to resist to the best of his ability. When POWs were depressed from recent torture or isolation, the Tap Code provided a means of group support. Under difficult circumstances, we operated as an effective organization to counter our captors' efforts to exploit us. Communication helped us to come home with honor, knowing that in the end, we had prevailed over a brutal enemy.

Through the Tap Code, we helped each other. Sometimes it was in the normalcy of lighthearted communication. If someone tapped GNST—Good Night, Sleep Tight—we would, of course, respond by tapping DLTBBB—Don't Let the Bed Bugs Bite. While this may have been a common expression for parents in their nighttime routine with their children, for us it was much more literal. We all had experienced the misery of bed bugs! However, our most frequent sign-off had much more significance for each of us.

We each had terrible experiences of being forcefully taken out of our cells and led to the interrogation rooms. There we experienced untold misery through sadistic torture methods—sometimes for days at a time. When we finally returned to our cells—broken and beaten physically, mentally, and emotionally—within minutes of the turnkey throwing us in our cells and locking us in, we would hear Tap tap, tap tap—G. Tap, tap tap—B. Tap tap tap tap, tap tap tap tap tap—U. GBU—God Bless You. Those three words became a symbol of strength and understanding for us. Tapping GBU not only meant we wished the blessings of our Creator on our brother; it also meant we understood. It meant we were not alone. It meant that no matter what we had just endured, men on the other side of the wall were praying for us, rooting for us, and believing we could endure. And somehow that helped us endure.

Little was I to know that the Tap Code would become the standard talk throughout all the survival schools in all the services for covert communication. Even now, the Navy introduces it as the Smitty Harris Tap Code. For that contribution, I can only credit my curious mind and the providence of a loving God.

1969
SON TAY CAMP

In 1969, I found myself at yet another prison camp. This one was called Son Tay. It was originally called Camp Hope, but my time there was anything but hopeful. Camp life was typical of the previous camps in which I had lived. There were purges sparked by our continued communications, and there were continued interrogations to extract written statements. Hope was, however, inching its way into our thoughts and spirits, as we had survived the horrific season of torture after the Hanoi March. That feeling was not to last long, however.

On May 10, 1969, two POWs executed an escape, which they had planned in detail for over a year. John Dramesi and Ed Atterberry were bold resisters, and Dramesi, in particular, was a huge risk-taker. Knowing that the path of escape was difficult and highly unlikely to be successful, the current Senior Ranking Officer, Konrad Trautman, resisted their request to try their escape. Many of the POWs were against the plan and objected vehemently to it through the Tap Code, stating that even if the two could get over the wall, there was zero chance that two Caucasians would go undetected in the densely populated area where the Zoo Annex was located.

There were a few sympathizers among the POWs who acknowledged that if they succeeded, Dramesi and Atterberry could expose the inhumane treatment we were all enduring. These sympathizers also recognized that escape was part of the Code of Conduct that called for escape if at all possible. Senior Ranking Officer Trautman knew that if their attempt failed, their punishment would be horrendous and the repercussions would be felt by all of the POWs.

However, the tap, tap, tapping continued from cell to cell, ultimately reaching Trautman day in and day out. Dramesi and Atterberry also used the silent hand code to send messages to POWs they encountered, which would then be passed from prisoner to prisoner until the message reached Trautman. Finally, he gave the directive in the following way: "I won't tell you that you cannot go." This was not a command to go, but permission to proceed. And proceed they did. Under the cover of night, Dramesi and Atterbury began their escape. They dressed in peasant clothes they had made from hoarded scraps and hidden until the infamous night. Once outside, there was no turning back. They made it over the ten-foot wall and headed toward the river. Disoriented, they lost track of time, and fearing sunrise fast approaching, they hid in a dense thicket. Sadly, by morning, they had both been caught, and their escape plan was thwarted.

Once back at camp, their punishment began. Both were brutally tortured, and Atterbury did not survive. He finally received his ultimate freedom and his heavenly homegoing, though the bridge of beating he inevitably crossed would have been indescribable. Dramesi suffered greatly. Though short of death, Dramesi's torturous punishment included thirty-two days in irons and fifteen episodes of rope torture.

The punishment for the failed escape did not stop with the torture of the two escapees. As suspected, this punishment extended to all POWs, starting in the Zoo Annex where the escape attempt had originated, extending to the Zoo, and in time to all of the prison camps, including Son Tay. The Vietnamese believed that the peasant costumes, as well as a handmade knife, indicated a well-laid plan and suspected a network of escape plans among all the POWs. This, of course, was untrue, but what came to pass was perhaps the most brutal season of torture throughout the long years of captivity. Summer of 1969 became known as the "Summer of Horror." This season of torture quickly made its way to Son Tay.

Son Tay was located approximately thirty-five kilometers northwest of Hanoi, near the town of Son Tay in Ha Tay province. It lay two kilometers west of Song Con, the small river that Dramesi and Atterberry had tried to reach. The prison was a walled compound that at its beginning in 1968 held twenty POWs. It reached its maximum capacity of fifty-five in December 1969. Our accommodations, of course, left much to be desired. POWs were housed in a long building made of thick masonry and brick, which we called the "Opium Den." Thankfully, I was assigned a two-man cell, and Chuck Boyd became my roommate.

Our cell had no windows and only a small barred transom over the door for ventilation, which was partially blocked in each cell by a PA system speaker. All the cell doors opened to a narrow hallway that had openings to the courtyard. Thus, our cells backed up to cells facing the opposite hallway. This arrangement provided us three walls to use for communication with other cells.

In addition to the horror of torture in the summer of 1969, we encountered another formidable enemy—the heat. Typical summer temperatures were in the mid-nineties; however, our lack of ventilation caused the temperature in our cell to rise to an estimated 120 degrees. We were allowed to go outside for a maximum of ten to fifteen minutes. This time was a welcome reprieve from the oppressive heat, though we never knew what new sadistic tactic might befall us.

In the bathhouse, water was piped to a large tank and had to be carried by bucket to the sinks. Our baths were accomplished by pouring the cold water over ourselves with a bucket or our drinking cups. Though primitive, the cool water was a soothing balm to our hot and dirty skin.

Our encouragement at Son Tay was, of course, communication. Because of the layout of the building, communication happened easily and without much detection. Tapping on the walls was our main mode of communication.

Our food was similar to other camps. Greens, pumpkins, and cabbage were our primary vegetables. Bread was our staple, and rice or noodles became an occasional treat. We received very little protein the entire time I was at Son Tay, which created various medical issues for many of the POWs. I was soon to encounter my biggest health crisis, and it all began one night in June 1969.

Diarrhea was a common occurrence for all of us, but on this particular night, I knew that something was wrong. The cramping and ferocious explosion in my gut wiped me out and nearly cost me my life. This sickness continued for months, and as I struggled to walk to empty my bucket, I knew I was throwing away pound after pound of any semblance of healthy weight. At the time of my capture, I weighed 160 pounds, with minimal body fat. As the weeks turned into miserable months, my bones began to protrude, barely covered by my ghostly pale skin. Continuous questions were tapped to my roommate, Chuck Boyd. "How's Smitty?" they asked.

Boyd's response was of equal concern, as he witnessed me losing strength almost to the point of lifelessness. I had energy only to lie on my cot. I tried to eat but couldn't retain any food. The only activity I could manage was the forced chore of emptying my waste bucket. This misery went on for months. I continually lost weight, but just when I thought it couldn't get any worse, my symptoms became even more severe. Not only was I dealing with continuous diarrhea, but nausea became my constant companion, followed quickly by forceful vomiting.

Over and over, Boyd and I requested medical help but were denied. That was the standard mode of operation at Son Tay. No medical attention was received unless the Vietnamese thought death was imminent. We knew this to be true from other POWs who were left to die but lingered on. If they thought the POW might die, only then would the Vietnamese intervene. At least we were more valuable alive than dead.

Three or four months into my ordeal, other POWs spotted me through a crack under their door and guessed my weight to be under ninety pounds. By this time, along with the dysentery and added nausea and vomiting, I could not sit up without graying out, except for the excruciating required journey to empty my bucket. Getting up took three or four different moves and constant prayer that I wouldn't pass out. My thighs became smaller than my knees.

Fearing my death was near, the tap, tap, tapping of my brothers on my behalf reached Render Crayton, the Senior Ranking Officer, who passed the word, using the Tap Code, that all POWs would take every opportunity to tell any English-speaking Vietnamese this message:

"If something isn't done for Harris soon, there will be such a revolt at Son Tay that superior officers in Hanoi will be very upset."

It was a hollow threat, but this camp-wide insistence lasted for three days and resulted in a visit to my cell by the Vietnamese medic, dressed in a white jacket. After examining me, they decided on their course of action. They took me out that night and made me walk to and climb into the back of a truck, while blindfolded, and carrying my own bucket. We drove thirty minutes with a guard to the site of a medical aid station. They forced me to walk in but quickly realized I would never make it without help. Inside, they gave me eight ounces of a white, chalky substance, which I miraculously kept down long enough for the exam. They took me back to the truck, where I asked the interpreter what my diagnosis was.

"Your intestinal track is inflamed," was the reply. This, of course, I already knew and could have diagnosed myself. However, back in my cell, White Jacket appeared with my turnkey and gave me an injection of vitamins and an antibiotic every day for a week.

Because all my fellow POWs stood up for me, my life was spared. It was, however, to their great peril, because in doing so, they revealed how extensive our communication was between the prisoners. They knew there would be severe repercussions. Many of my brothers were tortured to explain our communication system. Many more were punished and tortured for the very act of communicating. Each man who demanded medical help for me knew this would happen, but they did it anyway.

In time I was able to keep my food down, and in six months, my weight was up to "normal" weight, 115 pounds—forty-five pounds less than my pre-capture weight. The ordeal lasted almost a year.

Indirectly, the Tap Code saved my life. But it was Render Crayton and all the other POWs in the camp who accepted certain torture by exposing our communication ability who were the heroes. They were willing to risk it all to save one of their own.

SMITTY 33

It was well into 1970 before I regained my full strength. But once the worst of the illness had passed, I was no longer given medical attention and fell back in line with the continued crackdown due to the failed escape attempt. Though the hellish cruelty had lessened, the Vietnamese at Son Tay were infamous for looking for ways to punish us—and they were not past framing us to have that opportunity. Because they were closely watched, the guards and turnkeys felt they had to justify punishments, even creating false scenarios.

Chuck Boyd and I were still cellmates, and together we left our cell one fateful day to bathe. We were gone approximately fifteen minutes, and when we returned and were once again locked in our cell, we noticed some bits of loose concrete on the floor. A few minutes later, guards entered our cell for a random room inspection and "just happened" to have a ladder with them. The guard climbed the ladder to check the bars on the transom above our door. He "discovered" that some concrete and mortar had been chipped from one of the bars— thus the reason for the loose bits we had noticed. Obviously, the guard had entered our cell while we were gone and loosened the mortar as a setup. We were immediately accused of trying to escape.

Boyd and I were hauled off separately and taken to the interrogation rooms. They wanted us to confess to an escape plan, which we refused to do. As a result, we were told we would be punished until we told the "truth."

The guards forced me to my knees on the concrete floor and kept me in that position all day and night. I still remember the brightness of the cell throughout the night, as the single bulb of the ceiling light was never extinguished. This was common for us by now, but in that miserable position, it seemed even more bothersome. At least I could see to brace myself as the guard struck me with the flat side of his bayonet in the head repeatedly throughout the night.

At one point, I looked down and my knees looked like elephant feet, as the kneecap was flattened and the swelling from fluid buildup spread the sides of my knees out in a large, awkward, and obviously excruciating position. We were often tortured by sitting on a stool or on the floor for days on end and weren't allowed to lie down. Guards would leave us there for hours until we yelled, "Bao cao," which meant "I give." I put off those demoralizing words for as long as I possibly could, as did all POWs. Inevitably, though, everyone reached their breaking point. Recovery from that punishment took a few days; however, that was mild compared to what was to come.

The longest recovery was from the rope trick, followed closely by the handcuff torture. Before the Vietnamese began the worst tortures, they first tried the process of weakening us and wearing us down by less invasive practices, such as shortened food rations or chaining us to a stool for two or three days. Inevitably, this led to something much worse.

The Vietnamese rope trick was one of the most brutal methods of torture we endured. This method involved binding our arms behind our backs with rough rope, then rotating our aching arms upward until our shoulders popped out of their sockets. After this excruciating torture, the Vietnamese would take torture to the next level by hanging us in this position from a meat hook in the ceiling. Particularly sadistic guards would beat us further as we hung in this hellish state.

—•—•—

As 1969 neared its end, the cool winds of winter blew in a calmer setting at Son Tay. Torture punishment sessions lessened, although the opportunities to use us for propaganda continued in new—and creative—ways. On December 10, 1969, I was one of a small group of POWs blindfolded and forced into a truck. We drove about thirty minutes, and our heightened sense of hearing detected the sounds of city life. Soon we discovered we were back at the Zoo.

Two weeks later, we were once again blindfolded and forced into a truck. We drove a short distance and then stopped abruptly. As our blindfolds were removed, we discovered we had parked in front of a Catholic church. Further inspection revealed that all of those who had been forced into the truck were Catholic, including all the POWs from Son Tay who had recently moved to the Zoo.

We were led inside the church and discovered that prisoners from other prison camps were already there. All of them were Catholic. Photographers surrounded the perimeter of the church, snapping our photos as we experienced a Catholic service. We all knew we were being used. Those photos were intended to "prove" to the world that the POWs were being treated in a lenient and humane manner, which, of course, was untrue. Nonetheless, despite the reason, when the priest offered us the bread and wine of the Holy Communion, I felt a peace that passed all understanding. I knew I was not alone, for the One who came to earth to rescue me was alive and well. His power was not diminished. His love was everlasting. He came to set the prisoners free, and though we returned to the Zoo immediately after the service and I was once again locked up as a prisoner of war, I knew my spirit—and my soul—were already free.

My experience at the Zoo this time was slightly improved. We were granted a little more freedom than we had experienced in previous years. Interrogations had declined, and extreme torture had ceased. Bricks that had covered the windows of the cells were taken out of the upper third section of each window. This provided more air circulation and allowed light into the cells. POWs received a normal-sized towel instead of the hand towel we had previously been given. We were allowed more outdoor time, which provided guarded communication, as well as exercise and fresh air. Games of cards, chess, and checkers were allowed, which offered a welcome reprieve from the constant boredom.

I was told by other POWs that the reversal of treatment began six weeks after the death of Ho Chi Minh. Ho Chi Minh was the despised Communist revolutionary and the prime minister and president of the Democratic Republic of Vietnam. We had often been forced by torture to speak well of him on the PA systems throughout the camps. Though we read the statements we were forced to read, we restored our dignity by reading these absurd statements with incorrect pronunciations, thereby announcing throughout the camp our coercion and indignation at reading the statements. Ho Chi Minh became known as "Horseshit Men" to all the POWs through clever defiance of the announcers. The Vietnamese could not understand English well enough to detect the difference.

When Ho Chi Minh died on September 2, 1969, no one knew how this would affect our miserable situation. There was still harassment and threats; however, these were not followed up with action. The last interrogation at the Zoo took place on October 16, 1969. My fellow POWs told me that the next morning the Vietnamese came to each building with bread and a small plate of sugar for breakfast. This seemed to mark a positive change in POW treatment. Since Ho Chi Minh had died only six weeks prior, many felt that our horrific treatment was from his direct command. Once he died, the Vietnamese leaders had the freedom to change the harsh policies. Others speculated that it was political diplomatic pressure resulting from the Paris peace talks. No matter why, we were all thankful for the more bearable situation.

By this time, I had been a prisoner for almost five years. While I appreciated the new atmosphere, I suspected it was another propaganda ploy. I longed for the means of recreation I had previously enjoyed, and I continually thought of what I would be experiencing if I were back home. By now, Robin was well into her ninth year, and Carolyn was eight and a half. *What did they enjoy? Piano? Art?* And Lyle, the son I had never met, was five years old. *What was he like?* I often wondered. *Did he like sports? Could he read yet? Would he enjoy the pilot memorabilia I had collected over the years?* Though I had acclimated to my new foreign life, it still was a miserable one made worse by thoughts such as these. I longed for home.

Meanwhile, back at Son Tay Camp, my brothers also experienced improved circumstances. These would not last long, however, as Son Tay's use as a prison camp was quickly coming to an end. Throughout the stay at Son Tay, the POWs often dealt with water shortages. It was difficult to determine the reason for the shortage, for the events did not seem to line up with a dry spell in the weather. Nonetheless, it was a problem we endured periodically. When water was short, the POWs imposed their own water rationing systems, including limiting bathing to just a few cups of water.

In the summer of 1970, there was another water shortage, which limited the POWs' daily baths that were crucial in the oppressive heat. As a result, the Vietnamese asked the POWs to help dig the well to a deeper level, hoping for more water. Many refused, but some participated, citing the SRO's directive to help the Vietnamese only if it was something that would benefit the POWs. More water would definitely benefit the POWs, so some participated in the work and increased the depth of the well from twenty-two feet to thirty-two feet. This did slightly increase the amount of water, but not enough to make a difference.

On July 13, 1970, several vehicles arrived at the camp, and the POWs silently observed as camp equipment such as the PA system and the kitchen equipment were taken down and loaded onto trucks. That night, soon after dark, all POWs in Son Tay were loaded onto buses. Son Tay prison camp had come to its end.

On November 21, 1970, we heard fighter aircraft and bombing in the distance. News filtered in from the guards that the attack was a raid at Son Tay by the Americans, who were sent to set the prisoners there free. Sadly, their intel did not include the forced move of all the Son Tay prisoners because of the water shortage. Shortly afterward, the Vietnamese strengthened their defense at the Zoo by constructing additions to each corner of the buildings, which were large enough for a guard with his weapon to hide behind in case of an attack. Thankfully, however, the more positive attitude of the Vietnamese toward the POWs did not change.

SMITTY 34

NOVEMBER 21, 1970
SON TAY RAID

During my years of captivity, as well as throughout the war, the U.S. Department of Defense was perhaps the most important and busiest department of our government. The Department of Defense includes a small group of the highest-ranking individuals from each branch of the military—Army, Navy, Marine Corps, Air Force, and Coast Guard. The Army National Guard and the Air National Guard are the reserve forces that operate under the authority of each state. From these groups come the Joint Chiefs of Staff, appointed by the President of the United States and made up of representatives of the various branches of the military.

Underneath this important group is another team of individuals— the Operations Deputies—who assist the Joint Chiefs and confer in matters of lesser importance or review matters of greatest importance before they reach the Joint Chiefs of Staff. In May 1970, these Operations Deputies assigned to the Joint Chiefs of Staff met on the first floor of the Pentagon in offices under twenty-four-hour guard. It began as a routine review of the POW situation, but this meeting brought forth the mustard-seed idea that would blossom into what would go down in history as the Son Tay Raid.

Two months later, on July 10, 1970, the proposal was presented to the Joint Chiefs of Staff. The feeling was unanimous. All the chiefs agreed that the plan was worth the great risk it would require. The objective was clear: rescue as many POWs as possible. The planning continued through the channels of the Pentagon, and in August 1970, it was time to bring in military leaders. The first call was made to Air Force Brig. Gen. Leroy J. Manor. He was in his office at Eglin Air Force base when he received a call requesting that he immediately report to the Pentagon. He asked no questions, but simply made arrangements to go. The next call was to Col. Arthur Simons, who also made immediate plans to go to Washington. When questioned later about the mission, Manor said, "I considered it a humanitarian effort of the highest order." Those in the military had been extremely frustrated that they had been unable to do something to help the POWs in Vietnam. Now was their chance.

The rest of the team members were selected for their various strengths and experiences. None of the team members knew what they were preparing for, as the mission was top secret. Any leak would not only thwart the mission but could also create an ambush scenario if the North Vietnamese had any hint of their plan. Despite not knowing where they were going or exactly what they were going to do, the men threw themselves wholeheartedly into their training.

As time went on, the training became more specific, and most knew deep down the gist of what was planned, though they did not speak of it. They understood the high priority for secrecy. There were fifteen officers and eighty-two enlisted men on the mission team, and all of them were volunteers. Eglin Air Force Base in Florida became their new home for several months as they went through extensive training.

Son Tay had been selected as the camp they would raid, as it was outside of Hanoi and the terrain gave them a better chance of success than at the other camps. Intel was extremely hard to come by, but air photos showed that it was an active camp, and POWs had been sighted. Since the POWs were not regularly allowed outside, it was harder to ascertain how many were there. A mock-up of Son Tay had been erected at Eglin, and by the time the mission took place, the men felt confident in their objective and abilities. They were trained in every aspect of the mission, including how to deal with physical injuries or illnesses of the POWs, the mental disorientation that might occur from the sudden artillery, and the effects of months and years of isolation. A doctor, Lt. Col. Joseph Cataldo, would also be included on the mission team. After a month of intense training, the first list of the ground team was chosen, and the rest of the men would serve as the backup team, though they had many other responsibilities in their supportive role.

On November 18, 1970, a secret meeting was held at the White House, resulting in the authorization of the mission by the Commander in Chief, President Richard Nixon. The mission was a go, and November 21 was the day.

The team flew to Udorn, Thailand, as the time drew near. The men still did not know their exact mission. Up to this point, they had only speculated. On the day of the raid, Col. Simons addressed the group and officially told the men what their objective was—that they would be raiding a heavily defended prison camp outside Hanoi in order to free American prisoners of war from a camp called Son Tay. This was the first time they had heard the name of the location of their mission.

Simons spoke simply and plainly. This was an extremely dangerous mission that could lead to death or the possibility of becoming a POW like the men they were trying to rescue. He reiterated that this was a volunteer mission and that there would be no court martials if anyone should choose to drop out. No one moved. Simons looked for signs of nervousness among the chosen men and saw none.

Simons, also known as "Bull," put into words his perspective of the situation. He said, "I feel that we are all part of the same family, and that these people [the POWs] should not feel that they have been abandoned by their military family. No man should feel that way. That's why we are going in and getting them."

In the silence that followed, Simons turned to walk from the room when suddenly all the men stood and applauded with thunderous approval of their mission. Simons ended the meeting with these parting words: "If, in fact, we have walked into a trap, we will simply make it as costly for the enemy as we can. There's no walking out of North Vietnam."

A few hours later, all the men were dressed in combat fatigues, ready to go free their brothers. When the raiders arrived by chopper at Son Tay, they found resistance by the Vietnamese soldiers but were able to take out that problem. Out of all the scenarios they imagined, the thought of there being no POWs at Son Tay had never entered their minds. The disappointment cut deeply into every one of the men as they cut the locks from every cell and found no one.

Two days later, Brig. Gen. Manor and Col. Simons represented the team at a special press conference. North Vietnam took advantage of the failed raid with a relentless outpouring of false information, including the deceptive propaganda that American POWs had been injured during the raid. The reactions were fierce. But in the end, history recounts the story of the Son Tay raid not so much as a failed mission but as a mission of courage and compassion in which men were willing to lay down their lives for their brothers in captivity.

LOUISE 35

In 1970, the press was overrun with stories of antiwar protests, led by the famous actress Jane Fonda. To put it as politely as I can, I was not fond of Fonda. The protests were hard to watch and harder to understand. But despite the loud, raging voices on many college campuses, there was another side to the story—a quieter side that wanted to support U.S. troops in Vietnam without being involved in the controversial riots and protests. And it all began with two college students, Carol Bates Brown and Kay Hunter. The two friends met through their involvement in the Los Angeles–based student group, VIVA–Voices in Vital America. Bob Dornan, a television personality in the 1960s, introduced Brown and Hunter to three wives of missing pilots, who allowed the students to brainstorm with them about ways to muster support for U.S. soldiers without becoming enmeshed in the controversies of the war itself.

At the time, Bob Dornan wore a bracelet he had purchased in Vietnam that he said reminded him of the suffering of the war. Brown and Hunter wanted to create similar bracelets to remember the U.S. POWs. Naively, they initially thought of traveling to Vietnam for the bracelets—an idea quickly nixed by their parents. They pursued other avenues for making the bracelets and eventually found an engraver in Santa Monica who agreed to make ten sample bracelets. This number was eventually raised to 1,200 when the husband of Carol Coppin, the adult adviser of the student group, bought enough brass and copper for the initial run.

They decided to put the name, rank, and date of loss on the bracelets, and they soon had the interest of the families of the POWs, as well as free advertising from Bob Dornan through his television talk show. The price was set to match the cost of a student movie ticket–$2.50 for a nickel-plated bracelet or three dollars for a copper bracelet. By tradition, people would wear these bracelets with the name of POWs engraved on them until the POW returned and then give it to the POWs upon their homecoming.

On November 11, 1970–Veterans Day–they launched their program with a press conference from the Universal Sheraton Hotel. Public response grew quickly. In the next few years, VIVA distributed millions of bracelets, as well as other promotional items such as bumper stickers and buttons.

The bracelets were available to anyone through mail order or community civic groups. I had my own stash for friends who wanted to purchase them. It was such a lovely experience to see people sporting metal bracelets with my dear Smitty's name engraved on them. It was a balm to know that, though the protesters were loud and boisterous, there was a giant population who rallied around us and our men with a quiet strength and daily display of support.

One day, I led my children through the double mahogany doors of Reed's department store on Main Street in downtown Tupelo. Reed's was (and still is) a staple of Tupelo and had been for decades. Founded in 1905, Reed's provides clothing and gift items for adults and children alike. They also carry the required uniforms for Boy Scouts and Girl Scouts, of which I was a leader.

As we entered the store and headed toward the grand staircase that led to the children's department, a shiny object on the wrist of a fellow patron caught my eye. I paused just a moment and walked over to the owner of the bracelet. I did not know her, and she did not know me. She did not know that the name on the bracelet she wore was that of my beloved husband. I felt the sting of hidden tears as I approached her. Determined to never get emotional in front of the children, I simply said, "Thank you for supporting our boys." She never knew my name, and I never knew hers. But I remember her many decades later.

This same story played out in different locations all over Tupelo. Friends and strangers alike supported me and my children, as well as my POW husband, through the persistent choice to place the metal bracelets on their wrists each day. Our grandchildren, now around the age of Carol Bates Brown and Kay Hunter when they conceived the idea, are often spotted wearing remnants of that trend. Almost fifty years later, we still receive letters that begin with "You don't know me, but I wore your bracelet." What a blessing that people remembered the POWs then and still do today.

For Smitty's eighty-ninth birthday, our daughter Carolyn presented him with an exact replica of the bracelet made of sterling silver. When I see it, I am reminded of the refining fire a silversmith uses to produce the finest, purest silver. In the same way, we endured a refining fire of sorts, and it has produced in me, Smitty, and our family a refined character and a pure love. And for that I am very grateful.

SMITTY

36

SMITTY

The mind is an incredible tool. Researchers believe that the more we use our brains, the better the brain function we have. My experience in captivity has proven this to be true. Many times, we came to a crossroads—we were either going to lose our minds or make use of them in ways we never imagined. Some of my brothers lost the battle of the mind at that crossroads. But the majority of us were spared a mental breakdown and instead spent our days pushing our minds to the outer reaches of our intelligence.

Howard Rutledge stated in his book *In the Presence of Mine Enemies*, "This computer-like miracle between our ears seems so strong a proof of a loving Father behind creation."* I agree. We were able to miraculously recall song lyrics, Scriptures, hymns, and even details of people and places we thought were long gone from our memories. We all experienced this to some degree or another as we turned to our Creator for help and comfort. Forgotten words of Scripture—often unbidden from our memory since childhood—became a balm to our souls. I knew not one atheist among the POWs, for in the midst of our troubles we sought the mercy of One higher than we are, and as a whole we were gifted with a measure of grace.

For me and many others, one of the most difficult things to deal with was time wasted. It was very discouraging to see four dirty walls most of the day. Therefore, I would assign myself projects. Mind projects.

---

* Howard and Phyllis Rutledge, *In the Presence of Mine Enemies, 1965–1973: A Prisoner of War* (Old Tappan, NJ, 1973), 71.

Sometimes I would get so caught up in my mind projects that I was excited to wake up the next day to continue my project of thinking.

One such project began, surprisingly, after I was summoned to the interrogation room. Sometimes the interrogation room was about propaganda rather than torture—the age-old good cop/bad cop routine. We were withheld the pleasure of reading, unless it was reading their propaganda material. In one such book, I thumbed through and saw a listing of the dates of TET for the previous ten years. TET, the North Vietnamese New Year, is based on a lunar calendar rather than on the Gregorian calendar we use. From this list I understood that some of the years had twelve months and some had thirteen.

When I knew the date of each TET, I could figure out whether it was a twelve- or thirteen-month year. With the information I read, I could figure out the phases of the moon and the time between lunar phases in days. I found out that the moon comes up fifty-four minutes later each day. Keeping track of the phases and knowing the date, I could figure where in the sky the moon should be. When taken out of my cell, day or night, by seeing the moon, I could figure the time accurately to about thirty minutes. This was helpful as a regular exercise, given our lack of clocks and calendars.

We all had some mental project we were working on. We didn't will ourselves to do it; we just became interested in something and couldn't wait to wake up the next day to think about it again. And all without pencil and paper. One such project was a group effort when we were being held in Camp Unity, a section of the Hanoi Hilton. There we were housed together in large groups and were free to communicate.

A good friend began the project of tackling the value of pi. He rallied helpers, and I was recruited to help. Eventually, we figured out pi up to fifteen digits. For some reason, we wanted an accurate measurement. As we got further out, we had to do huge multiplications, and mental math was not possible. We used our coarse toilet paper and a homemade pen for our calculations. Sometimes we found a random piece of roofing from the slate roofs and used that to write on the floors of the large cells. With hours upon hours of unplanned, unentertained time, the mental projects were a wonderful way to stay occupied, purposeful, and mentally sharp.

——— • • • ———

In the fall of 1970, I spent my days in Camp Faith, located approximately twenty miles southwest of Hanoi and about ten miles from Son Tay. On November 24, 1970, we witnessed heavily armed and nervous guards gathering any movable property of the camp. An hour or so later, we were instructed to gather all movable objects from our cells, including buckets, brooms, and our tin cups. An hour after that, 221 other POWs and I were moved from Camp Faith to Camp Unity. This was three days after the Son Tay raid, so we surmised that the North Vietnamese feared another U.S. plan to liberate the POWs at any of the outlying camps, including Camp Faith. Vietnamese prisoners were unloaded at Camp Faith as we were loaded up to be taken to Camp Unity, so it appeared that a prisoner exchange was in place between camps.

——— • • • ———

By December 1970, our hardship of isolation had come to an end. In a move clearly prompted by the Son Tay Raid and the fear of additional raids in outlying camps, all known United States POWs in North Vietnam were moved to Camp Unity, a section of the Hoa Lo—the Hanoi Hilton—located on the northwest side of the prison camp. There were seven large open cells approximately twenty-four feet by fifty-five feet. We were placed in cells one through four, and the remaining three cells were quickly filled by prisoners from other camps.

Though the cells were large, more than fifty POWs occupied each cell, and conditions were crowded. A long concrete slab that ran down the middle of the cell became our bed. We lined up on the slab and slept side by side. Inevitably, there was not enough room for all to sleep on the slab, so some slept on the floor of the four-foot aisle or at the end of the entrance that was eight feet wide.

Communication was now possible face-to-face, although the Tap Code and other covert means of communication were still utilized between cells. Some information and names of other POWs that had been scrambled through Tap Code were now fully sorted out. Organization of the men through ranking was established, and policies were memorized through assigned "memory banks" in each cell. These policies were followed throughout our time at Camp Unity and continued when we were once again moved to other camps.

During this time in Camp Unity, the Senior Ranking Officer and others in leadership were moving toward standardizing directives that would apply to the POWs in Camp Unity and would remain applicable if the POWs were once again separated into other camps. POWs were held in other wars—World War I, World War II, and the Korean War—and we were the fourth group of POWs. We called ourselves the Fourth Allied POW Wing.

A wing is the organizational step that includes several squadrons in the Air Force structure. Since then, this has been standard title. The Fourth Allied POW Wing policies were called "PLUMS." This name was selected randomly in order to throw off the Vietnamese. If the guards overheard us referring to PLUMS, they would hear an irrelevant term unlinked to the important policies the word referenced. Their limited English would instead assume we were referring to the fruit.

When the PLUMS came to our room—room three—and its roughly fifty occupants, we lined up to help interpret the directives. The "receiver" would interpret the hand code given from another room and speak it aloud. The first man in line would listen to the first three sentences and memorize every word of his assigned part. He would transcribe his sentences on the floor and then later make sure the markings were erased. The next man in line would go through the same process, memorizing and transcribing his assigned sentences. This process continued until we had received every one of the PLUMS, word for word. Another scribe would then write these sentences in one document on toilet paper, using his diarrhea pill mixed with water as ink. This written version of the PLUMS was hidden carefully from the guards but shared with all the POWs until each man had memorized every word.

These PLUMS governed the POWs from 1971 to 1973 and included things like Command Authority and POW Conduct. Wing Policy #2 included objectives we were to gain from the Vietnamese, such as POW status—versus War Criminal status—so that the rules of the Geneva Convention would be applied. Other objectives included gaining the opportunity for more and better food, more outside time, and educational materials.

Wing Policy #4 included Resistance Conditions. These were a listing of planned disobedience to the Vietnamese as a means of protesting various injustices. The SRO knew that the Vietnamese could possibly react with an anti-riot response and therefore cautioned the POWs to execute any resistance tactics with caution. The Resistance Conditions were called RESCONS, which was taken from DEFCON, the US military's five states of alert. There were five levels of RESCON, with RESCON 5 being the normal state of RESCON and going up to RESCON 1, the highest level of resistance. The RESCON states of resistance included the following:

RESCON 5: Stance
This resistance was our normal state of RESCON. The POWs were always instructed to act like officers and gentlemen. We were instructed to maintain discipline, order, and composure and to show reserved civility toward the Vietnamese. This normal state was a low-risk but highly erosive resistance. Our insistence on maintaining a soldier stance irritated the Vietnamese and silently shouted our status as soldiers captured as prisoners of war rather than war criminals.

RESCON 4: Stir
RESCON 4 involved lessening the cooperation with the Vietnamese in day-to-day tasks, while making sure they knew why the POWs were not cooperating. This involved being a military man at all times and only doing what the North Vietnamese forced us to do. In this way, we could constantly "stir the pot"

without overt defiance. The POWs were instructed to maintain discipline and order in this act of defiance and to avoid personal confrontations that could lead to one POW being taken out to be tortured or put in isolation.

RESCON 3: Soldier

This RESCON type of resistance involved using military formation in all outside activities. This RESCON showed the Vietnamese that the U.S. troops were still organized and unified, despite their current surroundings. The POWs were encouraged to be creative in the execution of RESCON 3.

RESCON 2: Squat

This RESCON involved resisting the Vietnamese through self-denial of what they offered, especially expressed through food. If RESCON 2 was implemented, the POWs would follow a food restriction for one to two weeks. The POWs were to send back half of the food given, while making sure the Vietnamese knew why this was being done. The sick and wounded were excluded from the food restriction.

Another RESCON 2 tactic included going outside only for medical treatment, interrogations, or a duty assigned to the POW by the SRO. This self-denial form of defiance drove the Vietnamese crazy, especially as they were now trying to save face by fattening up the POWs in the event of release. For years, the Vietnamese had claimed they had treated the prisoners humanely. Now they feared the world would soon discover their ruse.

RESCON 1: Sing

    a. Sing "The Star-Spangled Banner." The WCO—the Wing Commanding Officer—would initiate this by a sending a message to the others through singing the Notre Dame Fight Song. This let the other POWs know they were about to sing the national anthem.

    b. As simple as this initiative sounded, it was an incredible act of defiance, since the Vietnamese had serious restrictions against noise and especially against patriotism toward the

United States. The overarching goal throughout the years in captivity was to try to convince the POWs—and the rest of the world through their propaganda—that the United States was an evil empire. So to sing aloud the national anthem of a supposed "evil empire" was an incredible statement of resistance. It would demonstrate that our hearts were not beaten and that our loyalty remained true. And it would poke a hole in their propaganda lies.

    c. Sing "The Star-Spangled Banner" as well as other songs of choice, and repeat the singing for two days. This singing session would be initiated by the WCO by message or by the singing of "Roll Out the Barrel."

Other Wing Policies were defined to not only help us maintain a united front but also to prepare us to know how to respond as day-to-day conflict ensued. Wing Policies 5 and 6 were the ones we most looked forward to implementing, as they involved the united front we would maintain at the time of our release. We were instructed to have an attitude of pride in and loyalty to our country at the time of release. We were also reminded that a man's most prized procession is his reputation. We were to guard our reputation and act with discretion toward the reputation of others in our post-release behavior. While much of the content of Wing Policy 6 dealt with our post-release, one particular line stands out in my memory: "This principle of military and Christian behavior applies here while we are still POWs." All of these policies were learned and memorized through our "memory banks" in each cell.

Another policy assigned in the "memory banks" included the secret coding embedded in the letters we were occasionally allowed to write and send home.* When we got a letter from home, the form we were permitted to use was issued from an antiwar activist group—the only group the North Vietnamese would work with. If we wanted to have any hope of getting a letter through, this particular letter form was

---

* This once classified information has been approved by the Department of Defense.

what we had to use. This was a small card that allowed up to seven lines of text on each card. North Vietnam provided the form to the group and other antiwar groups, and they in turn would issue the letters to us and from us. In this way, the North Vietnamese had control of all communication from the United States.

When we got letters from home, we were called into the interrogation room to receive them. It may have been two years or more since we had received any mail, so it was a big event. We would be handed two to three letters at a time and given about ten minutes to read them. We then had to give the letters back to the Vietnamese. Oh, how we longed to keep those treasures from home! We knew the letters were being processed from our loved ones through the Pentagon, and we therefore surmised it was highly possible that a coded message might be embedded in a letter from home. This was later confirmed by Louise.

The long process began when Louise would write a short letter in longhand and send it to the Pentagon. They would rewrite it in code, while at the same time keeping the spirit of what she had written. They would then send the letter back to Louise, and she would rewrite it in longhand on the prescribed form. These then would be mailed to North Vietnam, which didn't know about the secret strategy. It was a complicated code, and only a select few had been taught how to do it in survival training. Shumaker was one who had learned the coded letter system. Just as I taught him the Tap Code, he taught me the Letter Code.

The cells in Camp Unity were organized much like squadrons. The Senior Ranking Officer was the commander, and the next-ranking POW was the operations officer. We then had four or five flights, assigned according to rank. In these flights, duties—such as serving the food, washing dishes, and sweeping—rotated among the POWs. There were also officers in charge of various areas of concern, such as security, communications, entertainment, education, sanitation, and sick call. We also had a chaplain.

My job at Camp Unity was in the area of education and involved teaching the fifty-plus men in my cell the embedded Letter Code, as no one else in the cell knew the code. I taught most of the men how to encode what they would send home, and I dictated their coded messages to be included in their letters. I would write out questions and information for the Department of Defense. This had to be concise, since there was only so much that could fit on a six- or seven-line letter form. I could include only about fifty coded characters, which amounted to approximately one or two short sentences embedded in the letter. I assigned portions of the text to different men, so if all the letters were read and three or four of the letters had the same portion, maybe one of the portions would get through. The content of the message was divided into parts, such as part A, B, C, or D. The Department of Defense would put them all together and read the parts in order.

We would tell of our inhumane treatment and include some of our escape plans. One question embedded in letters around Christmas 1972 involved the location of the Swiss Embassy. We thought if we could find the location of the Swiss Embassy, we might be able to incorporate that into an escape plan. Our guidance for these escape plans was directed by the SRO and always followed the mandate of "Do not try to escape unless you have outside help to escape." After the failed escape of John Dramesi and Ed Atterberry from the Zoo Annex, we had to be more careful than ever before. Our numerous escape plans never came to fruition, as outside help was never available.

As I taught other POWs and helped them write their own letters home with coded messages embedded, we were faced with complex problems that had the potential to thwart our efforts. The main problem we encountered was that it was extremely difficult to decipher the complex code in the ten-minute time frame we were allowed to see our letters. There were two methods of handling this problem.

The first method involved memorization, which was not as challenging as it may have been prior to our captivity, given our strenuous mental workouts through our mind projects. Some men memorized their letter and came back to the cell to rewrite it on toilet paper. It had to be verbatim, or the coded message would be lost.

The second method was an ongoing project during my time in Camp Unity. Since we shared a cell with more than fifty others and were free to communicate, I was intent on teaching the code as I had been taught. I would ask a couple of POWs who knew the code to write a letter with an encoded message. I would take that letter and give it to another POW who was learning the code, and he would try to decode it. This involved practice, practice, and more practice. It was very difficult, yet we continued with this process three or four times a day.

In time, we ended up with about six to eight men who were able to decode in their heads in the ten-minute time frame. When we got back to the United States and explained during our time of debriefing how we decoded our letters—and that they could decode as they were reading the letter—we were told it was absolutely impossible without a computer, or at least pencil and paper. So the men demonstrated their skill. Needless to say, the debriefers were astounded.

DECEMBER 1971
CAMP UNITY CHURCH SERVICE

Lt. Col. Robbie Risner, my squadron commander, arrived at Camp Unity on Saturday, December 26, 1970. He described in his book *The Passing of the Night: My Seven Years as a Prisoner of the North Vietnamese* the euphoric pandemonium when he walked into Cell 7 and was greeted by POW friends whom he had not seen or been in close contact with in years. It was like a grand family reunion, with laughing, shouting, and hugging—not unlike my own entrance into Camp Unity. Risner was respected by all as a strong leader and devout Christian who lived out his faith each day through his wise actions and attitudes. We all looked up to him. So it was not surprising that on the first day at Camp Unity, he was asked about leading a church service, now that so many were together. Risner agreed there would be no better way to begin their stay in Camp Unity than with a church service.

They quickly proceeded through the processes of planning, beginning with selecting a temporary chaplain, George Coker. The group was somewhat evenly divided between Catholics and Protestants, with a sprinkling of other faiths. All were united in their desire to participate as a unified group, even those who did not consider themselves very religious.

Once the idea took root, the determination and great desire to worship together spread with a decided purpose from man to man. Six men who had musical abilities were identified, and they quietly began to rehearse songs in a corner of the large cell. The chosen hymns were "The Old Rugged Cross," "In the Garden," and "America," and the lyrics were written out on toilet paper. The service was to be both religious and patriotic, and Col. Vern Liggon, the SRO, was asked to lead the Pledge of Allegiance.

The next day, Sunday, December 27, Liggon organized the men while the guards were at lunch. Some POWs formed a semicircle around the room, while many others stood on the concrete platform in the middle of the room. After the Pledge of Allegiance, another POW opened the service in prayer, and then the choir sang. This was followed by a Scripture "reading," though they did not have a Bible for reference. However, after years of mind projects, many were able to quote Scripture from memory. Then as a whole, the men recited the Twenty-third Psalm together. This psalm had become known as the Prisoner's Psalm and was given to almost everyone who had come through Heartbreak Hotel through Tap Code or whispered when the area was cleared of guards. After a short sermon by George Coker, the choir sang another song, and we all recited the Lord's Prayer in unison. Risner then gave the benediction.

Robbie Risner knew the Vietnamese would not be happy about our gathering, but felt it was important enough to risk the consequences. The first service brought a threat, which we all were used to by now— "How would you like to go back to the 1967 treatment?" Even with that threat, Cell 7 decided to continue with the church services, and many of the other cells joined in as well.

Though the threats continued and the Vietnamese camp commander, a man derogatorily called Bug, was livid, the POWs felt that worshiping together was worth the risk. The service was shortened to fifteen minutes, and the psalms, prayers, and Pledge of Allegiance were recited in lowered voices, but the Vietnamese still opposed the meeting.

On Sunday, February 7, the Vietnamese were ready to retaliate. The Hawk, one of the turnkeys, came and ordered the choir to stop singing, which they promptly ignored until they had sung the final stanza of the hymn. George Coker began his sermon and continued speaking, even after the Hawk told him to be quiet.

When he ordered the men to disperse and sit down, the POWs remained standing silently. The Hawk walked to the door to report to Bug as Howard Rutledge stepped forward to quote Scripture. The service was ending in the same way it had been planned, with Risner giving the benediction. Liggon then said, "Dismissed," which was the first directive the POWs had obeyed. This infuriated the Hawk. As the POWs began to disperse, the guards began to gather those who had participated in leading the service, including Risner, Rutledge, and Coker. As they walked out of the cell, Bug declared, "Now you will see that my hands are not tied!" We had not been tortured thus far during our time in Camp Unity. These brave men took the torture and isolation on behalf of all of us. I did not see Risner or the others again until our arrival back in the United States.

The guards lined up the men outside with their backs toward the building. A few seconds later, Major Bud Day began singing "The Star-Spangled Banner." It was a call to RESCON 1—the highest level of resistance. Immediately, all the men of Cell 7 joined in, singing as loudly as they could. This spread to other buildings, until all the POWs in Camp Unity were singing in unison. We hadn't heard "The Star-Spangled Banner" sung in all those years, yet here we were, raising our voices in unity and in resistance. As Risner later described, the sound could be heard throughout the camp, over the walls, and into the city of Hanoi. It was glorious! Risner and the others spent months in Heartbreak Hotel in isolation and enduring punishment as a result of this resistance, but they all felt it was worth it.

Later, when asked how he felt when he heard the POWs loudly singing their support and resistance, Risner famously replied, "I felt like I was nine feet tall and could go bear hunting with a switch." Thirty-one years later, a nine-foot-tall bronze statue of Risner, who had by then attained the rank of Brigadier General, was placed in the central plaza of the Air Force Academy (made possible by H. Ross Perot).

This memory-making church service built morale like never before. The resistance was ignited, and the POWs were emboldened. Other states of RESCON were also utilized during my stay at Camp Unity, including the use of military formation. Everywhere we went, we walked in formation, including during work detail and outside exercise. The Vietnamese were furious. Riot squads comprised of approximately fifty guards with helmets and tear gas grenades, joined our regular turnkeys in guarding us. Many of our leaders were taken out and put in leg irons, and still we resisted. Finally, the Vietnamese announced that our Sunday services were allowed. But by that time, we had made it clear we weren't waiting for their permission. Even while in isolation, the POWs who had been taken out continued with Sunday worship services, though they were conducted covertly. Rather than a choir, a whistling solo had to suffice each week. The Vietnamese referred to this time as "the riot," though in reality, it was only our enthusiastic singing and unified attitudes.

MY guards with balaces and rescues grenades joined our convoy

MAY 1972
DOGPATCH

On May 13, 1972, I was one of a group of 210 POWs to once again be blindfolded, loaded on trucks, and moved to yet another prison camp. In a convoy of sixteen trucks, we drove hours upon hours in extremely hot and uncomfortable conditions. We arrived around 2:00 a.m. on May 15. We had arrived at Dogpatch.

Dogpatch was the North Vietnamese camp located close to the Chinese border in an area of high karst—irregular "bowls" of eroded limestone. The bowl that housed the camp was fortified with automatic weapons and concrete bunkers. We observed lookouts on the high points of the karst. We were told we had been moved there for our own safety, which defied logic, since many POWs were left at Camp Unity. As usual, there was no rhyme or reason for our location changes.

We were placed in cells in buildings made of concrete and granite that were evidently bombproof. Obviously, this was a maximum security facility. The concrete roofs and walls provided a cold, damp, dark environment for our new home. The intent was apparently to hide us from U.S. bombers and rescue teams, as well as the local population, for the Vietnamese installed camouflage draping over the camp area and blinders in front of the buildings. The roofs were painted black, and an effort to camouflage them was seen in the bushes and vines that had been planted on top of them. Even the courtyards were camouflaged with large jungle plants placed on top of a bamboo framework, extending over the courtyards.

Living conditions took a nosedive compared to our conditions at Camp Unity. The cells were small and poorly ventilated, and eight to twenty prisoners were crammed into each one. There was no electricity, and the only light at night was from a kerosene lamp. We were allowed outside time, but it was limited to two hours in the morning and an hour and a half in the afternoon, six days a week. Water was provided by gravity from the surrounding ridges, which fed into a central water tank for each cell. Several of the buildings did not have enough water for bathing. The courtyards were small, and our regimen of exercise was difficult to maintain.

We did have playing cards, chess and checker sets, and even some educational materials, which was a step up from my early days of captivity. We were also given the opportunity to write home, though only once a month. We received some letters and some packages, but as always, the Vietnamese continued to cut open and sort through the contents.

Throughout the almost eight years of my captivity, I received only two packages. Those were great days! A guard would take me out of my cell and escort me to the interrogation room, where I would receive the package. I would then be escorted back to my cell. Once I was in the cell, I could take my time opening the package. Both of the packages I received were crumpled, broken, and practically empty by the time they reached my hands. I didn't really care though. I still had the joy of knowing that Louise's hands had touched the same package I now was holding. In one of the packages, I found a few pieces of broken candy, crushed soap, and a half-filled tube of toothpaste. Looking further still, I found a great treasure—a picture of Louise. She was in a big easy chair with a drink in her hand. I smiled, thankful that she was okay and looked happy.

Given my Escape and Evasion training—as well as my intense curiosity—I combed through each item, inspecting them closely. On a whim, I peeled back the seam of the toothpaste tube and much to my surprise and joy, I found a 3x4 microfilm. Further inspection revealed a bird's-eye view of a map of Hanoi. Obviously, Louise was working with the Pentagon to provide tools for escape. I was still under the directive to not try to escape unless I had outside help, so the map was never used. It did, however, provide endless fodder for dreaming of escape routes and plans. And it provided the wonderful, comforting knowledge that we were not forgotten.

I spent less than a year in Dogpatch. Though the accommodations left much to be desired, some aspects of our treatment improved. Our food was adequate and even included canned meat or fish on occasion. The torture had ended, but the propaganda remained. However, a poor PA system at Dogpatch helped to curb the constant blasting of taped propaganda, though we did occasionally have to endure statements by actress Jane Fonda and others speaking out against the war.

●―●・●―●

Jane Fonda, along with thousands of students and protesters, took over the University of Maryland mall in May 1970. From there, she became one of the most prominent faces of the antiwar movement. Though many activists may have begun with noble intentions, the false information and half-truths provided fuel to the fire that resulted in painful and infuriating propaganda used against the POWs—and our families—in countless ways.

In 1972, Fonda took her infamous trip to North Vietnam, which resulted in a disdain for the actress among the POWs and earned her the famed nickname "Hanoi Jane." Her trip to Hanoi in 1972 sealed her sordid reputation among many in the United States and especially among the POWs, who suffered the most from her propaganda with the North Vietnamese.

In Hanoi, Fonda met with seven POWs who had been housed separately from other POWs and given preferential treatment. They were well fed, well provided for, and never tortured, unlike the rest of us. Two of the POWs had led several young American shoot-downs to cooperate with the Vietnamese. Later, other POWs got word to the new POWs and informed them that they were being led by two turncoats. Thereafter, their attitudes toward and cooperation with the Vietnamese resembled the rest of ours. Though many of my fellow POWs were furious with the lot of them, the SRO determined that they were lost sheep who had come home. They too returned with honor. The two instigators, however, continued to be viewed as turncoats.

The action that most enraged the POWs, as well as all Vietnam veterans, was the infamous photo of Jane Fonda surrounded by North Vietnamese troops, posing happily as she sat on an antiaircraft gun—a gun that had most likely been used to shoot some of us down. To this day, it is hard for me to think kindly of Jane Fonda.

When we returned home and began sharing our stories of torture, Fonda called us "hypocrites and liars and pawns." After more than a decade of the repercussions of her Hanoi Jane reputation, she appeared to have a change of heart, though the half-apology she offered was incomplete and too little, too late. She told Barbara Walters in a 1988 interview:

> I would like to say something, not just to Vietnam veterans in New England, but to men who were in Vietnam, who I hurt, or whose pain I caused to deepen because of things that I said or did. I was trying to help end the killing and the war, but there were times when I was thoughtless and careless about it and I'm very sorry that I hurt them. And I want to apologize to them and their families . . . I will go to my grave regretting the photograph of me on an antiaircraft gun, which looks like I was trying to shoot at American planes. It hurt so many soldiers. It galvanized such hostility. It was the most horrible thing I could possibly have done. It was just thoughtless.*

Yes, she was thoughtless and so much more. In early 2000, she publicly declared that she had turned to Christianity, albeit mixed with Buddhist and Hindu practices. I do sincerely hope that she will find the redemption that Christianity offers. Though I and my fellow veterans will never forget, my faith compels me to seek to forgive.

---

* Quoted in Wikipedia's entry on Jane Fonda, https://en.wikipedia.org/wiki/Jane_Fonda.

In October 1972, there was a series of prisoner shufflings from cellblock to cellblock throughout the camp, the largest of which occurred on October 25. When we were all settled into our new cells, we slowly came to realize that we were now housed according to our shoot-down dates. This realization gave us great optimism toward an eventual release, and we sensed the winds of change blowing across the camp through subtle observations—such as better food and less restrictions—as well as reading between the lines of the propaganda we continued to endure.

After the last shuffle, I was the SRO of my cell group. I led my men in continuing to follow the Code of Conduct, as well as the new regulations set forth at Camp Unity. My favorite RESCON to implement as SRO was RESCON 3–Soldier. I would instruct my men to use military formation whenever we were outside the cell. I would make a great show of having my men line up in an organized and unified fashion. They would not move until I said, "Dismissed." This showed the Vietnamese that we were still soldiers committed to our country and our cause. It was a source of great irritation to the guards, which was a great source of pleasure for us.

LOUISE 39

It was September 1972. The children were busy with their school activities, Scout meetings—of which I was the leader—church activities, piano lessons, and sports practices. I was busy trying to keep up with them, as well as to keep all things in order. Most days went smoothly. Most days we were joyful. Some days we were not. Some days the reality of our situation hit me like a blast of cold air, taking my breath away. During the daytime, I did not have time to think about our situation. I did think about Smitty, however.

I watched then seven-year-old Lyle develop friendships with the neighborhood boys, learn to ride a bike, and diligently fold a piece of paper backward and forward until a replica of an airplane came forth. I would smile wistfully at him, happy in the knowledge that he was a contented little boy, and at the same time sad that Smitty was missing all of the ordinary moments that make up a lovely life. And sad that Lyle and my precious girls were missing the great influence that their father would have had on their lives simply by his presence. I missed his wisdom, and I missed his wit. No one could make me laugh the way Smitty could.

At night, the wistful feeling turned to an acute, aching loneliness. But even as I allowed myself to feel it, I would not embrace it. I could not. I had too many responsibilities; too many little lives were counting on me. Once again, I reminded myself that if Smitty could do what he was doing, I could do what I must do.

Over the years, I had felt a strong responsibility and desire to keep

Smitty's presence alive in our children's lives. By now, they did not know him at all. Yes, Robin may have had a few flashes of memory of her father, but Carolyn did not, and of course Lyle had never even met him. Yet each night we all knelt by the bed—me and my three little ones lined up side by side as good soldiers in a spiritual war. We were doing our part to defend Smitty and all the POWs. Our warfare was not carnal, but mighty for the pulling down of strongholds—as the Scriptures say. So each night, in prayer, we pulled down the strongholds of despair and destruction, and we prayed our Smitty home.

To the children, I talked as if Smitty were away on a long assignment. He had a very important job, and our nation was counting on him to do it. Since this was all they had ever really known, the children took this in stride and did their part by praying each night for their father. One day, when Lyle was about five years old, we were playing in the park when an aircraft darted across the blue sky with its white clouds trailing behind. Lyle looked up and pointed. "There goes Daddy," he said. Thankful that this was the picture in his mind of the father he didn't know, I simply said, "Yes, son. There he goes."

One day, as the oppressive summer humidity finally gave way to the refreshing signs of autumn, I received a phone call from my casualty officer in Washington. He invited me to travel to Washington with several other POW wives to participate in talks concerning a plan they had dubbed Operation Egress Recap. We called it Operation Homecoming. The thought of Smitty's homecoming could be likened to the current weather—the oppressive unknown was slowly giving way to a refreshing view of what was to come.

By now, the reports of the war seemed to positively indicate that the POWs might be released in the coming months. How we each longed for that day. But having an inkling of what our men had endured meant that we must prepare carefully to ensure the healthiest and smoothest transition as they were filtered back into a society to which they were no longer accustomed.

As a wife, I was thankful that the United States military was considering the impact of such transitions—especially given the heightened volatile stance of many Americans. Though I never personally experienced the forceful outrage of Americans who were confusedly fighting against the very men who were risking their lives to fight for them, many of my fellow POW wives had. And as shocked as we were when such blatant discontent was aimed in our direction, we had seen this happen gradually. There would be no gradual indoctrination of the current climate for our men, and I cringed to think of the ungratefulness at the least and contempt at the most that these men who had sacrificed so much might experience.

The U.S. military leaders wanted our input for this Operation Egress Recap, and we were very glad to give it. Eight wives flew to Washington to participate in three days of meetings with various leaders of the military. As we walked down the Washington Mall, I was gripped once again with a patriotic force rising in my heart and mind. I took a deep breath of the crisp, cool autumn air and held my head high as I walked past remnants of the latest protest that had signs proclaiming, "Make love, not war" in blood-red paint scattered on the lawn. I was proud of my husband and proud of the brave warriors who had sacrificed everything. I could only hope that these protesters would one day see things from a different perspective. Yes, war is the most complex entity. It is extremely hard to decipher. Yet this I knew with all my heart—our men were the bravest, most honorable of men.

Our meetings took place at the Pentagon. Yes, they wanted our input, but they also wanted to win us over to their view of our husbands' return. Operation Egress Recap had started as a plan in the anticipation of a large-scale release. The early release of three POWs from Vietnam was causing a bit of havoc in their systems. These men appeared intact not only physically but also mentally and emotionally. The job of the leaders of this plan was to make sure that all POWs experienced the healthiest homecoming. Since each man would have had different experiences of torture and tragedy, the plan tried to anticipate the issues that some of the men would likely endure, and it was in our best interest to prepare for that possible reality.

The Operation Egress Recap project was connected to the Navy's Neuropsychiatries Research Center, which was ironically located in an old World War II structure overlooking the Pacific Ocean at Point

Loma in San Diego. The research center was led by a Harvard Medical School graduate, Capt. Ransom J. Arthur. A civilian physician named Dr. John Plag was directly in charge of the project. Dr. Plag explained that there was no way to know the specific condition in which each man would return, and they were therefore preparing for the worst while hoping for the best.

Six months earlier, researchers at the Defense Department's Center for Prisoner of War Studies had collaborated with sixteen learned professionals, including medical doctors, psychiatrists, and psychologists, to create a plan for a mass return of POWs. Combining knowledge from both previous wars and from detailed information about each of the POWs, they recommended what they called "slow decompression" of our released men.

This would involve delaying family reunions, as well as slow integration back into our society. They recommended delayed encounters with any emotional situations, as well as any decision-making positions, including those at home. They believed that continued isolation with gradual integration would be most effective for the medical and psychological health of our men. They feared that many of the men, while looking physically healthy, would be acutely afflicted with "concentration camp syndrome" and might suffer with various symptoms such as fatigue, anxiety, suspicion, memory loss, meekness, and loss of initiative.

"It's important," said one of the Navy doctors, "for you wives to understand this reality: though the three pilots who came back this week are in good physical condition, and though they seem to be emotionally healthy, this will not be the case for all of the prisoners. In fact, we suspect that a great majority will have a much different experience with their return. You must understand that these men were handpicked for early release. We are still dealing with the propaganda of the Vietnamese."

As much as I longed for Smitty to return, I felt the churn of anxiety in the pit of my stomach as I thought of the unknown. The experts warned of deep personality changes that often occur in prison confinements, particularly pointing out that those who had been there eight or more years would most likely exhibit this symptom. This, of course, would soon include my Smitty. The premise of the Operation Egress Recap was to ease the shock and bewilderment that a sudden return to freedom and family could cause.

Most of the wives were won over to a gradual rehabilitation of our men, though the thought of being so near our husbands—finally on the same soil—and yet not being fully able to incorporate them back into our lives was excruciating. Even so, whatever was best for Smitty was best for me.

They explained that all POWs would first be held on hospital ships or in military hospitals in Guam, the Philippines, or Hawaii. Those who required additional medical attention or who had undergone deep personality changes would travel to military hospitals near their families for gradual reintroduction of their loved ones. Much of the work of Operation Egress Recap was directed at dealing with the emotional scars of POWs, some of which might be hard to detect. All the wives of the POWs were interviewed, and group therapy for the entire family was recommended as a means to help restore normal family relationships. A lot would have changed in the years our husbands had been gone. They pointed out that even something as simple as a wife's different hair color or few extra pounds could be an emotional mountain to overcome as our men transitioned back to our families.

The night after our first day of meetings, I stood before the mirror in my hotel room, looking at myself with a critical eye.

What has changed in me? I wondered. *Of course, it is inevitable that the children have changed*, I reasoned to myself. *But have I?*

I looked at my hairstyle that was longer and styled differently than it had been the last time I saw Smitty. I was wearing a teal polyester pantsuit, which was a bit of a change from the stylish cotton dresses of the mid-sixties. Leaning closer to the mirror, I wondered if my face had changed. I saw a few tiny lines in the creases of my eyes. And there was a faint line in my forehead. As I had experienced the changes of time little by little, I couldn't really discern which of those changes would be surprising to Smitty.

Not only did I wonder, *Is he the same?* but I also wondered if he would think I was the same. Deep down I knew I wasn't. I was stronger, tougher, bolder, and more responsible. I could only hope that he would find these changes desirable. Nonetheless, I had no fears. Whatever we faced, we would work through it together.

I knew this would not be the case for everyone. Several of the prisoners' wives had already obtained divorces, and others had told researchers that they were also planning on a divorce but were waiting to break the news to their husbands when they returned. I hurt for all involved when I heard those stories. I had neither the energy nor the desire to speculate or judge their circumstances. I knew only that I was determined this would not happen to Smitty and me. We would find a way through the transition. With the same gut knowledge and determined faith I had utilized when I refused to think he might be dead, I set my sights on learning all I could to make the transition home as smooth as possible. I was positive we could work through whatever was required for us to stay together happily.

◆ ◆ ◆

On the last day of our time in Washington, our group was told that Admiral John McCain Jr. wanted to meet with us. We were overwhelmed. John Sidney "Jack" McCain Jr. was a very busy man. A second-generation admiral, he and his father, John McCain Sr., were the first father–son duo to achieve four-star rank. He had been stationed in Hawaii in the highest position of CINCPAC, Commander in Chief, Pacific Command, and was now back in Washington, working alongside Admiral Elmo R. Zumwalt Jr., who was Chief of Naval Operations.

We were invited to meet in an office in the Pentagon. As he entered the room, we were struck silent, knowing his position of authority. He was obviously very busy, highly focused, and full of energy, but for that hour, he focused totally on the eight wives sitting in that room. He was very interested in how we were faring, his sincere concern highlighting his eyes as he listened to each story. He knew our names and the names of our husbands. He wasn't there to impress or to accomplish a publicity goal—in fact, no news outlet ever knew about this private meeting. He just wanted us to know that he cared and that he understood. We all knew that he also grieved the situation in a personal way, as his own son, John McCain, was a POW with our husbands. He expressed concern for us in a way that only one who knew firsthand the emotions of this experience could do. And he humbly allowed us to express concern for him as well—concern not just for an admiral but for a father who longed for his son to come home.

"I want you to know that I fully believe our men will come out. I believe they will come out well and strong, and we will do anything to get them out," he told us.

The experience was somber and serious, yet it was filled with hope and encouragement. His final words to us meant the most: "I pray for John and all the other POWs every day. And I pray for all of you—the families who are doing their part back home."

Those words and those prayers were a great balm to each of us. We left this meeting feeling encouraged.

As I flew back to Tupelo and to my children, I carried a small souvenir for each of them. And for myself, I brought back renewed hope.

SMITTY 40

I was at Dogpatch for about a year, during which time I had several roommates, including Mo Baker and Al Brudno. Al had not fared well mentally during his time of captivity. He was a very intelligent man and had great moments of being strong, positive, upbeat, and hopeful. This, however, would always be followed by deep pits of sadness, hope-lessness, and despair. As roommates, Mo and I tried our best to talk him out of the darkness, and most of the time he came back around. Mo was worried about the potential for Al attempting suicide during his dark phases of depression. But the latter months at Dogpatch gave him ample reason to hold on to hope.

The daily propaganda of news coming through the PA system into our cells told us of the antiwar activities in the United States. They acknowledged the peace talks in Paris, but their spin was the contrast between how wonderful Vietnam was and how terrible the U.S. was. We read between the lines, though, and as time went on, we would often look at each other and whisper, "We are going home soon!" Those statements seemed to really help Al. He had only been married for two months before he was shot down. He was a brilliant individual with plans to become an astronaut. He had joined pilot training as the most direct route to his dream—until the status of POW delayed his plans.

We knew change was on the horizon, as both the food and treat-ment had gotten better. We realized that the closer we came to free-dom, the better the Vietnamese would treat us so that they could save face with the rest of the world.

In January 1973, the Vietnamese guards once again told us to gather our meager belongings and load up in the back of a truck. It was the same scenario that had played out over and over in the past almost eight years. There was just one difference in this move. For the first time, they did not blindfold us. We knew something epic must be underway. They drove us back to the Hanoi Hilton, where we discovered notices posted in the courtyard of the camp. In accordance with the agreements signed in Paris, the signs were giving us notice of our release. We were going home.

You might expect that there would be cheering and joyful celebrating. There was not. Though there was quiet acceptance, we did not let ourselves show emotion of any kind. First of all, after so many years of propaganda and mistreatment, we did not fully believe what they told us. Second, even if it were true, we would not give the Vietnamese the pleasure of seeing our joy or the opportunity to use it for further propaganda. So we did what we had done for so many years—we waited.

JANUARY 1973
TUPELO, MISSISSIPPI

It was January 28, 1973. The day was crisp and cold, but not so cold as to keep people away. Two hundred or more people had gathered on Jefferson Street in downtown Tupelo for the presentation and planting of two magnolia trees at the local library. I had been invited to participate in the presentation, as these trees were in honor of the POWs. Excitement was in the air, as all had taken a keen interest in the news that was coming out of Paris.

Peace talks had been in the works since April 1965, although significant progress was not made until a May 1968 informal meeting between Averell Harriman, the U.S. emissary, and Xuan Thuy, the North Vietnamese counterpart in Paris. High demands on both sides stalled the progression of the talks until October of that same year. This paved the way for formal peace talks. Five days after President Nixon took office on January 20, 1969, the United States sent delegates to Paris to show the seriousness of their desire for peace. However, the talks proved fruitless and were delayed for four years due to firm disputes on both sides.

Though the problem appeared unsolvable, secret talks between Nixon's National Security Advisor, Henry Kissinger, and Le Duc Tho, a member of the North Vietnamese politburo, the highest political body of the Communist Party of Vietnam, continued. While seemingly deadlocked, Kissinger and Le Duc Tho finally made a breakthrough in negotiations and reached an agreement to end the conflict on October 8, 1972.

In late October, Kissinger publicly revealed the draft of the agreement. However, South Vietnamese President Nguyen Van Thieu was furious over the secret meetings and refused to accept it, which caused North Vietnam to resist talks. However, Nixon's massive aerial bombardment, Operation Linebacker II, got Hanoi's attention after they had withdrawn from the talks, and a monetary pledge for South Vietnam reassured President Nguyen Van Thieu enough to continue negotiations.

News reports boosted our confidence that an agreement could be possible in the near future. I had even received a call from Claude Watkins, who was still serving as my casualty officer, with the guarded encouragement to "keep being patient; release is coming." Pins and needles were my companions for several weeks. But I kept busy with the children, struggling to focus on my task at hand, all the while dreaming of the day when I would see Smitty once again.

I had just joined Mrs. Virginia Robbins—whose son, Doug Clower, was also a POW—as we placed a shovel in the loose soil, symbolically digging the hole that would house the new trees. I hoped these trees would grow deep roots and rise strong and proud, a symbol of the strength the POWs had shown—and, for me, a symbol of the deep roots the children and I had grown in this precious community.

As the ceremony came to an end, Guy Gravlee, a general in the National Guard who lived in Tupelo and had been such a kind support for me, walked up, dressed in his uniform. He said, "I just received a call from Washington, and I knew you would want to know. The peace treaty has been signed. Our fellows are coming home." Oh, the joy! The news quickly spread among the crowd, and the whole lot broke out in spontaneous celebration. There was cheering and laughing—and, for me, streaming tears of joy. Smitty was coming home!

SMITTY 42

FEBRUARY 12, 1973

On the night of February 11, the group of men with whom I had shared a cell for the past week were taken out and led to a large room, where we found piles of new, clean clothing. All the clothing was exactly the same—a uniform of sorts, which included long blue cotton pants, a light brown jacket, and brown leather shoes. New skivvies and socks completed the wardrobe. This was a far cry from our standard red-and-pink-striped pajamas that turned gray within days. I was so used to those pajamas after almost eight years that it took a few moments to settle into the feeling of real clothes.

We were instructed to try on different sizes to find out which fit the best. By now, my weight had climbed to 130. In the last few months, the Vietnamese had greatly improved their menus. Our portions were larger, and the protein content was higher too. All of this was an effort to fatten us up to maintain the facade that we had been treated humanely. We didn't complain though.

My pre-shoot-down weight was 160 pounds, with extremely low body fat, and my lowest weight during captivity was less than ninety pounds. I forced myself to adhere to my own self-prescribed physical therapy, which eventually helped my shoulder and knee to heal, though it took about three years to regain strength and movement. I had to start all over at times when I became extremely sick or injured from torture, but I always forced myself to begin again. It was good for my body, my mind, and my emotions.

After we were fitted with our new clothes, we put our pajamas back on and returned to our cells, with our clothes tucked into matching handbags that had also been distributed. The mood was subdued and stoic. Everyone was pensive. It appeared that what we had longed for was finally coming to fruition, and yet we would not let ourselves be emotional. We were soldiers. We would not give the Vietnamese satisfaction or propaganda of any form. I lay for hours on my concrete bunk, thinking of what was to come, emotionally detached from the reality of it all, yet silently embracing a sliver of hope.

The next morning, I was in the first release of prisoners, selected according to shoot-down date. The guards tried to line us up, but we quietly mingled around, making their job harder and more confusing— one small last act of defiance. Eventually, we all got on the buses. Riding without a blindfold felt strange. We were all quiet as we watched the dank, stone walls and iron gates disappear from sight. It was hard to see hundreds of our fellow POWs left behind, though we were confident now that they too would ride through the gates for a final time.

On the bus, we were quiet and stoic. The seriousness of what was happening was heavy on every man. We drove for less than an hour and arrived at the Hanoi airport. We silently got off the bus and lined up military fashion according to the instruction of our SRO, and then we defiantly marched out to the ramp, knowing this would make the Vietnamese angry one last time. They could do nothing to harm us or break us now. We had survived, honor intact. We acted like the soldiers we were.

One by one we walked to a table where an American officer in dress blues stood, along with Vietnamese officers, including the Rabbit—the sadistic, cruel enemy who enjoyed mistreating Americans. He had no power over us now.

Name, rank, and serial number. I spoke with clarity and dignity. I spoke like a soldier, as did every one of us.

We walked in military fashion as an escort led us to the airplane. We climbed the metal steps, the wind blowing gently, a reminder of the winds of change occurring in our lives. We weren't sure what we would find back home, but we were glad to go.

When the airplane was full, the door closed. Pretty nurses, clean and perfumed, assessed each of the soldiers, but still we maintained our stoic demeanor. The plane taxied out, and still we were stoic. The plane could have turned around, and we would not have shown emotion, so intent were we on acting like soldiers.

A few minutes later, we heard the thump of the retracting wheels, indicating that we were airborne. As if on cue, we finally let go. We cheered and celebrated, hugging nurses and each other. Most of us walked up to speak to the crew—the freedom of that act alone was exhilarating. Eventually, we settled back down—that is until the Captain said, "Feet wet," the universal lingo indicating that we were flying above water. We were no longer over Vietnamese soil.

Another round of celebrating ensued, with cheering, victorious fists raised high in the air, and, yes, joyful tears in the eyes of every man. Air Force Maj. Gen. Ed Mechenbier said it best when he described his own flight out of North Vietnam: "When we got airborne and the frailty of being a POW turned into the reality of freedom, we yelled, cried and cheered."* And so did I.

After an hour-long flight, we arrived at Clark Air Force Base in the Philippines. As we exited the airplane and walked down the metal steps, we were astonished to be greeted by two thousand cheering people waving American flags and holding long signs that read "Welcome Home" and "We Love You." It was surreal and felt like a taste of heaven.

The weather was beautiful on this early afternoon—not a cloud in the sky, nor in our hearts and minds. Our SRO, Jeremiah Denton, was the first man off the plane. At the bottom of the steps, he was greeted by several generals and a Navy admiral. "Captain Denton, would you like to say a word?" they asked as they led him to a microphone.

"We are honored to have had the opportunity to serve our country under difficult circumstances. We are profoundly grateful to our Commander in Chief and to our nation and for this day. God bless America," he said with a strong, clear voice that was soon drowned out by loud cheers from the crowd.

---

* Quoted in Donna Miles, "Operation Homecoming for Vietnam POWs Marks 40 Years," February 12, 2013, www.vietnamwar50th.com/operation_homecoming_for_vietnam _pows_marks_40_years.

After Denton spoke, we lined up in order of shoot-down to exit the plane. I was the sixth in line. Ray Vohden, still on crutches after eight years, had been shot down the day before me, as had Scotty Morgan, who stood just in front of me. Behind me were Phil Butler, Bob Peel, and J. B. McKamey, along with thirty other former POWs who were on the first flight out with me.

Later that day, three more aircraft would land at Clark Air Force Base, bringing a total of 143 soldiers to freedom that day. Within a month's time, 591 POWs returned to the land of the free and the home of the brave. We proudly earned both of those descriptions, having adhered to the Code of Conduct through the darkest trials and the deepest testing.

When asked to comment, I echoed Denton's words in saying, "My only message is 'God bless America.'" When pressed further, I replied, "With six, seven, or eight years to think about the really important things in life, a belief in God and country was strengthened in every POW with whom I had contact. Firsthand exposure to a system that made a mockery of religion and where men were unable to know truth made us all appreciate some of the most basic values in 'God bless America.'"

And bless us God has. God bless America, my home sweet home.

LOUISE 43

On February 12, I sat glued to the television. The release of the first wave of returning POWs—which I had been told included Smitty—was big news in the United States. However, due to the time zone differences between the United States and the Philippines, the broadcast of the return occurred in the wee hours of the morning of February 13. I, along with all three of my children, watched anxiously as Jeremiah Denton walked down the metal pull-away steps. I teared up as he spoke his clear, poignant words. The camera zoomed in as faces began descending the steps. Alvarez, Shumaker, and Lockhart smiled as they met the fresh air and the loud celebratory applause. They were followed by Ray Vohden on his crutches and Scotty Morgan, both shot down the day before Smitty.

My heart beat faster and faster as I strained to see the man at the opening of the plane, still in the shadows. And then there he was. My Smitty. He was alive! Thin, maybe a bit pale, but alive! Eight years seemed to evaporate as I recognized the shape of his face and his familiar movement as he descended the steps. We all cheered, the children screaming and jumping up and down. I stayed glued to my seat, with my eyes cemented to the screen, as I watched every second of the broadcast.

When I at last lay down in my bed—not too long before the sun began its ascent in the sky, announcing a new day, a new life for me and my family—my mind drifted back to that night long ago in Okinawa when I awoke with a start, the sound of Smitty's voice beckoning me from my dream. Soon I would hear his voice once again. This knowledge kept me awake even longer.

FEBRUARY 12, 1973
CLARK AIR FORCE BASE, THE PHILIPPINES

After we made our way through the cheering crowds, we were taken directly to the base hospital, where we went through several days of intensive medical care. They took each of us to a hospital room shared by one or two other POWs. When I walked into my assigned room, I didn't recognize the POWs who were already in the room. Obviously, they had not been in the same cells I had been in, even in Camp Unity, where we were all allowed time together and were housed in cells with fifty or more prisoners each.

Then it occurred to me who they were—the turncoats. The two men who had cooperated with Jane Fonda and the North Vietnamese—the same two who got preferential treatment from the enemy and whose cooperation made living conditions much worse for those of us who resisted being used for propaganda. I had never seen them, but I had heard their voices many times as they recorded their propaganda messages that were played over the PA system in the camps.

Just as the realization of who they were hit me—just as my blood began to boil—and before I had a chance to say or do anything, two nurses quickly came in and took the two turncoats to another room away from all the other POWs. The look on their faces told me they understood the situation. I was glad to see them go.

Another face entered my hospital room that I was both surprised and excited to see. It was Rudy D'Urbano, an old friend and fellow pilot who had volunteered to be my escort home. Each of us was assigned an escort officer who would help us navigate these uncharted waters–bridging the gap between our former life of trauma and our future reunion with family and life in the United States.

Much had happened in the past eight years, I quickly surmised, as we heard bits of information such as the assassinations of Martin Luther King Jr. and Robert Kennedy, the surprising moral changes introduced in the 1967 "Summer of Love," and the mind-boggling "one small step for a man, one giant leap for mankind" historic walk on the moon by Neil Armstrong and Buzz Aldrin.

Rudy also came to assist me in my greatest step of repatriation–contacting my family, who were now anxiously awaiting a phone call. When it was my time to call, I felt only a slight hesitation. I had not talked to Louise in almost eight years–2,871 days to be exact. And in all of those years, I had received only twelve letters and two packages from her, though I was confident she had sent many more.

I was alone with Rudy in a small conference room, and a beige rotary phone sat on the table between us.

"Are you ready, Smitty?" he asked carefully.

I gave him a nervous smile and replied with as much confidence as I could muster, "I'm ready."

He dialed the number–first the country code, then the area code, then the local number. With each number the round dial spun back into position, the sound echoing in the small room. Then from across the table I heard ringing–the tinkling of connection that had long been forbidden.

A female voice promptly answered. "Hello?" Louise. I would never forget that voice.

"Louise, this is Rudy D'Urbano," he began.

My heart pounded in my chest. Our test of "for better, for worse" was about to be revealed.

The next day, I sat joyfully in the living room with the kids surrounding me, as well as Janice and her whole family. Up and down I went, time after time, as the phone started ringing off the wall. I had been told that Smitty would soon be calling, and I was anxiously waiting to hear his voice once again. Eight years. Eight years. That's what kept rolling over and over in my mind. What would it be like to hear his voice after eight long years? I thought of the Thanksgiving dinners he had missed, as well as the delight of Christmas morning with our children. He would have loved to dress up like Santa Claus with a hearty "ho ho ho"—which in the coming years he would embrace with gusto.

My girls did not remember his voice, and Lyle had never heard his voice, yet his "voice" was a precious presence for all of us, as I had been determined to keep his voice alive in our home. The children knew all my favorite Smitty stories, including the ones about the many pranks he loved to play on their Aunt Janice. They knew that he called me Jane and I called him Tarzan. They knew his likes and dislikes, his favorite foods and pastimes. To the best of my ability, I made sure they knew him. Yet they did not know his voice. But I did. And I was about to hear it once again.

The phone rang again, and again as I jumped up to answer, I was greeted with the familiar sound of dear friends wishing me well and wanting to join me in celebration. I greatly appreciated their calls, though at the time I hung up quite rudely for a Southern lady. Before the days of call waiting or caller ID, phone calls were met with either a solid ring or the annoying beep of a busy line. I was determined that Smitty would not hear that annoying beep, so I practically hung up on most of the callers with a hasty message: "I'm sorry; I can't talk now. I'm waiting for Smitty to call!"

After seemingly dozens of calls, the phone rang once again, and once again the voice was not Smitty's.

"Louise, this is Rudy D'Urbano." Rudy had been a dear friend of Smitty's since their days in aviation pilot training. I knew he would want to get an update on Smitty's homecoming, but now was not the time to give it.

"Oh, Rudy, I really appreciate you calling, but I can't talk now," I hastily said as I prepared to hang up the phone.

"Wait, Louise! Don't hang up. I'm with Smitty now. He is sitting right here. Let me give him the phone."

My heart pounded in my chest, and in the seconds it took him to hand the phone to Smitty, I sent up the same prayer I had been praying for many days: "Lord, please let him say something that lets me know that he remembers as I remember and still feels the way I feel."

I could hear the sounds of the phone changing hands, and then a voice spoke—the voice I knew so well.

"Hi, Jane; it's Tarzan," he said spontaneously. And in those light-hearted words, I knew that God had heard my prayers. Smitty remembered as I remembered. I laughed and cried. His voice was warm and filled with humor. The conversation was us. I knew that whatever adjustments we faced, we were going to be just fine. Much better than fine, in fact.

After I hung up the phone, I let out a deep sigh of relief. It was as if I had been holding my breath for eight long years and I could now breathe deeply—unhindered and without restraint.

214

FEBRUARY 12–15, 1973
CLARK AIR FORCE BASE, THE PHILIPPINES

The next couple of days were filled with medical tests—from blood work to physical inspection, from mental capacity tests to psychological testing. During the testing process, Mo and I tried our best to warn the doctors about the mental state of Al Brudno. We repeatedly told them he was not okay and tried to describe what we had witnessed as his roommates when we were at Dogpatch. But Al was on a high at that time, so relieved to be freed. His intelligence also helped to mask the deep mental brokenness he consistently dealt with. Our warnings were not heeded, and within days, Al was on a plane headed back to the United States to his wife.

Though many of my brothers came back on crutches, still dealing with shoot-down or torture injuries or with the effects of illnesses from vitamin deficiencies, I was fairly healthy upon inspection. I attribute that to good, healthy genes and adherence to the strict exercise regime throughout my years of captivity, with the exception of the year I was too sick to do so.

In every camp, no matter how small my cell, I forced myself to spend time each day in self-imposed exercise routines. At one point, I required of myself three hundred sit-ups each day—that is, until the hard concrete floor caused sores on my backside. I lowered the number to accommodate that painful issue. I then started doing three hundred V-ups to help manage the sores. I would lie on my back, raise my legs, and touch my toes, using the same muscles as a sit-up without aggravating the sores on my backside.

Next, I turned my attention to countless push-ups—clapping my hands between each of the fifty reps. I would then touch my chest to the ground and back up for another fifty reps. My concrete bunk served as a step machine, as I forced myself to step up and back down over and over on the bunk about fourteen inches from the ground.

My next exercise included running in place while jumping up on my right foot, after which I would go back down and let the left foot lead. I would do this until I was huffing and puffing—usually two hundred reps, twenty-five with one foot, twenty-five with the other, alternating until I reached my goal. In most of my cells, there were small ledges over the doorway, which served as a challenging source of pull-ups, my fingers wrapped as tightly as possible on a 3/4-inch ledge. Those were kind of tough. Squat jumps were a great source of cardio, so much so that after my release, I could easily run five miles, though I had spent most of the past eight years in a seven-by-seven-foot cell.

In addition to the medical and psychological tests, we were extensively debriefed about our experience, particularly concerning any names we knew of fellow POWs. After being given extensive physical, mental, and dental exams, as well as good food to fatten us up, we were finally fitted for new uniforms. It was a proud moment in my life when I once again wore clothing that reflected and represented my devotion to the United States.

Though I had been told that it could be up to two weeks before I returned to the U.S., within three days, I was released to go home. *Home*—and all that this word encompassed—was finally within my reach. My heart pounded with anticipation.

SMITTY 47

FEBRUARY 15, 1973

When the plane touched down at Travis Air Force Base in Sacramento, California, I breathed a deep sigh of relief. American soil! It had been more than eight years since I had been on American soil, and the feeling this brought is hard to describe. We had a short layover at Travis, and while the plane to Maxwell Air Force Base in Montgomery, Alabama, was being readied, those of us who were heading in that direction waited in the lounge area.

The military was very protective of people getting near us at that time, so I was greatly surprised when I looked up and saw a very familiar face heading toward me. It was Col. Frank Masters (ret.). I had gotten to know him as a dear friend when he was the base commander during our time at Bainbridge Air Base, the flying school for USAF Air Training Command in the 1950s. Somehow Frank had found out we would have a layover at Travis and had traveled a great distance to see me, even though he knew it would be only for a brief time. I was totally surprised and filled with joy to see my good friend once again after so many years.

Our visit was cut short when it was announced it was time to board the plane to Alabama. This was the last flight on my long journey home—so much longer than I could have ever imagined when I set out for Korat so many years before. At that time, I had told Louise good-bye in the middle of the night, thinking I would see her in two weeks. Due to the delay in the flight to Alabama, it appeared I would finally be returning to her in the middle of the night many years later.

As I felt the familiar jolt of being airborne at last, my mind, heart, and emotions were all over the place. Many have asked me what I was feeling. My reply is that I was feeling nervous and anxious, joyful and euphoric—and really, any feeling between that wide scope of emotions.

The flight from California to Alabama was long. I had time to wonder and time to worry. What had changed over eight years? How would things be different between Louise and me? How would the children receive me after such a long time? And Lyle—how would he react to a father he had never met? I tried to picture what they would look like now. Robin was now twelve, almost thirteen. She was a young lady. Carolyn was eleven and following quickly behind her sister in maturity. How much I had missed! And Lyle. My son. What was he like? Would he accept me not just as a father but as a daddy? Oh, how I hoped he would!

It was 2:00 a.m. when we began our descent at Maxwell Air Force Base in Montgomery. I didn't know who would be there to greet me. I was sure Louise would be there, but I wasn't sure if the children would accompany her or not. A few days alone with Louise sounded wonderful, but I was also anxious to see the children, as well as other family and friends.

As the wheels touched down with a thud, my heart pounded in the same way. There were twenty of us on the airplane, and I was the senior ranking officer of the group, so I was to be the first one off the airplane. I hardly felt the cold night air as I descended the metal steps of the plane. I was surprised to be greeted at this late hour with cheers and applause as two hundred people waved flags and held signs that read "Welcome Home." Base personnel lined the perimeter, and civilians in Montgomery who had heard of our return lined the fence, all being held back by the Air Police. After I descended the steps, my escort led me to a microphone and asked me to say a few words. The moment was so surreal that I don't remember what I said. However, I am certain it included the words "God Bless America."

As I spoke to the crowd, I didn't realize that a blue sedan had pulled up right behind me. When I finished speaking, I turned around and immediately saw that the sedan held my great treasure. My Louise was just steps away from me! I quickly bridged the distance between us and got into the sedan, indescribable joy filling every one of my senses. She had never looked more beautiful.

We didn't speak many words on the short drive across the base to the Visiting Officer Quarters where we would be staying. We were speechless with joy and emotion that had been held back for years, but our embrace spoke volumes. I was finally home!

Louise was able to quickly prepare me for the great party awaiting me at the VOQ. The children were there, as were Janice and Dick and their children. Louise's mom and her grandmother were there, and so were my parents and my brother, Joe. My parents! They had both lived to see me return. Later, I would find out what a battle my father fought through cancer treatments in order to see this day become a reality—but he was alive, and he was there! Another wave of joy overtook me, and along with it a wave of nervousness as I exited the car and made my way to the room where my family was waiting.

As I stepped into the quarters, both Robin and Carolyn squealed and came running to jump into my arms. "Oh, thank you, Lord—they haven't forgotten!" I breathed a prayer of gratitude. They had grown to be lovely young women. I was overcome with emotion, and tears of joy rolled down my face.

Then there was Lyle. I picked him up and hugged him for a long time. It didn't bother me that he didn't hug back. I knew it would take a little time. Though I knew Louise would have talked about me, the man picking him up was still a stranger.

And then a flood of family gathered around to embrace me. Loud laughter and flowing tears—the perfect combination of emotions filled the room. I was delighted to see every person there, especially Mom and Dad. I can't describe the feeling of hugging them and being hugged by them. I had worried about their health, worried that I would never have another moment with them on this earth, yet here we were in a tight embrace, with tears flowing down our cheeks.

I was also thrilled to see Louise's mom and grandmother, with whom I had always had a good relationship. Grandmother Rindeleau was a proper lady, but somehow she seemed to connect with me, rough edges and all. That night she pulled Louise aside and told her,

"You know, I have accomplished everything I have ever wanted. And now I have seen everything I have ever wanted to see in my life—now that our Carlyle is home." These rare, tender words would be a source of great comfort when three weeks later she passed from this life to the next.

The whole room was almost chaotic with talk and laughter. When we all finally settled down a bit, I went to my bags and began pulling out the gifts I had purchased for everyone with the money I had received as an installment of my back pay while I was at Clark Air Force Base in the Philippines. I had bought very nice gifts of watches for the men and pearls for the women. Robin and Carolyn received necklaces, and Lyle received a miniature airplane. Louise, of course, received my best gift—a beautiful Mikimoto pearl necklace and pearl ring. She still treasures them today.

And they all had gifts for me. I must confess that my favorite gift was from my sister-in-law Janice. We had a longstanding tradition of exchanging crazy gifts. Her gift to me that night was a large, beautifully wrapped gift box—filled with dry, white rice. We all had a good, hearty laugh. When I gave her a velvet box, like those who had received pearls, her face dropped and turned white, obviously fearing I had not adhered to our tradition. She carefully opened the box and pulled out a huge pair of men's boxer shorts! I had crammed them into the velvet jewelry box. We all burst out into laughter once again.

After about thirty or forty minutes, while I sat in the large easy chair, opening yet another gift, I looked around for Lyle and found him in a corner, just watching me. I turned and opened my arms toward him, and he came running, jumped into my lap, and threw his arms around my neck in a big hug. I tossed another grateful prayer heavenward as I hugged him: "Oh, thank you, Lord!"

In my years of captivity, I had learned over time to have no emotions, at least not to demonstrate them while held prisoner. What an indescribable feeling to finally let go and allow myself to *feel* once again. Seeing Louise, my children, and all of my dear family elicited a release of emotion I had held in for years. It felt like heaven on earth.

Having stayed up for most of the night, we all met for a late brunch the next morning, and then everyone began their journey home, except for Louise and me. We stayed at Maxwell for three more days of debriefing and reconnecting with each other. When we finally pulled into the driveway of our home on Madison Street in Tupelo, I realized what a miracle this reunion had been. Looking back, I still see it as an amazing miracle. Truly, we didn't miss a beat. We just started over where we had left off. It was if I had simply taken a walk around the block.

LOUISE 48

MAY 1973
TUPELO, MISSISSIPPI

I looked through my closet for the third time, knowing I would find nothing there for the important event ahead. Formal wear was not readily available in our small town, and I had exhausted all the local options. I walked over to the dresser and picked up the invitation. The engraved text and heavy cream paper, along with the words "President of the United States" and "White House," emphasized the importance of the evening to come. Decision made, I walked straight to the phone in the hallway and pulled the long, curled cord tight as I sat on the sofa.

As soon as Janice answered, I said, "Are you up for a road trip to Memphis?"

"You know I am."

The next day, we were headed up Highway 78 toward Memphis, Tennessee, the closest metropolitan city in our area. We chatted as only sisters can do, the sound of the latest hits from the radio playing as background music.

"Oh, I love this song," I said as I turned the knob on the radio to increase the volume. Janice and I sang along with Tony Orlando and Dawn as they belted out their hit, "Tie a Yellow Ribbon Round the Ole Oak Tree." In the previous month, the song had reached number one on the Billboard charts in the U.S. and stayed there for four consecutive weeks. As we sang, I thought of the lyrics and of how applicable they were to our experience with Smitty's homecoming.

The song was from the point of view of someone who had "done his time" and was returning home, uncertain if too much time had passed for him to be welcomed back. He writes to his love and asks her to tie a yellow ribbon around the oak tree if he would be welcomed back. If he didn't see a ribbon, he would remain on the bus, knowing that their time together was over. To his surprise, there was not just one ribbon, but one hundred yellow ribbons tied around the old oak tree.

The original idea of the yellow ribbon was most likely from the nineteenth-century tradition of wives tying yellow ribbons in their hair as a symbol of their devotion to their husbands in the United States Cavalry. According to the coauthor of the song, L. Russell Brown, he and Irwin Levine wrote the lyrics based on the old folk tale of a Civil War POW who wrote to his girl that he was returning home from a POW camp in Georgia.

Yes, it was a fitting song for Smitty and me, and I would have gladly tied a hundred ribbons around a tree if that would have assured him of my devotion. Sadly, that was not the case with many of the wives of the POWs. A dozen or more POWs were divorced while in captivity. Many others received the news that their wives had moved on when they returned home. In fact, the stories of such difficult relationships were widely published.

On March 6, 1973, the *New York Times* printed a piece titled "P.O.W. Wives Who Chose New Life Face Dilemma."* Some of the wives interviewed remained anonymous, yet told stories of new loves, new interests, or even new independent personalities. For many, too much time had passed. One such case cited was that of Commander Ray Vohden and his wife, Bonnye, who were from Memphis. After six years as a POW, Vohden wrote home, urging his wife to "make a new life." A year later, Bonnye filed for divorce. However, before divorce proceedings were final, peace talks were resumed, a cease-fire was called, and word came that her husband would be one of the first prisoners released. As soon as Ray, badly wounded and on crutches, arrived at Clark Air Force Base in the Philippines, he called his wife,

---

* Steven V. Roberts, "P.O.W. Wives Who Chose New Life Face Dilemma," *New York Times*, March 6, 1973, www.nytimes.com/1973/03/06/archives/po-w-wives-who-chose-new-life-face-dilemma-well-work-it-out.html.

deeply upset, and she agreed to drop the divorce proceedings. She publicly stated that they would work things out day by day.

However, shortly afterward, Commander Vohden announced at a press conference that he was taking a trip–alone–to try to enjoy life, acknowledging that things were not the way he left them. The publicity surrounding their divorce gave voice to many opinions, and their situation was discussed widely in Memphis, as well as throughout the country. I was saddened for the men who had endured so much to come home to further grief, and I wished that everyone could experience the kind of joyful reunion Smitty and I had.

We arrived midmorning at the dress shop in Memphis and were greeted by a lovely older German lady. It did not take long to find the perfect dress. It was a floor-length, sleeveless, navy blue dress with a beautiful, large white collar. Both Janice and I agreed this was the dress; however, there was one problem. The dress fit like a glove, with the exception of the low cut of the V-neck in front, which was far too revealing for my conservative taste. Janice suggested we take a piece of the white lining and attach it in the V of the neckline to make it more modest. Our outspoken German saleslady agreed–until we told her our timeline. The event was fast approaching, and I needed the dress within a few days.

"Oh, no. I can't do dat," she said in her heavily accented English.

"Oh, please, ma'am. My husband has just returned from North Vietnam. He was a POW for eight years, and we have been invited to the White House for dinner."

"Vas you a good girl while he vas gone?" she asked suspiciously.

"Oh, yes! I surely was!" I replied sincerely.

Janice spoke up to confirm, "She was a *very* good girl."

"Okay, if you vas a good girl, I fix your dress; if you vasn't a good girl, I vhip your fanny."

Two days later, my beautiful navy dress, fitted yet flowing, with the white collar and new V-neck insert, arrived in Tupelo on the Greyhound bus.

Of my closest POW friends, only Ron Storz did not come back alive. Other KIA brothers did not return, and we grieved for the loss of their lives and the heartache of their families. The rest of my closest brotherhood survived and returned home, perhaps a bit scarred, but intact. The physical ailments healed, and so did the mental and emotional ones. It helped that we stayed in contact with each other—no one else could possibly understand what we had gone through. If a thousand books were written, they still could not contain the true expression of the experience we all shared.

But with these brothers—well, I don't have to put it into words. I don't have to try to explain or describe or remember or decipher. They were there. They know the sounds I heard and the sights I saw. They know the feeling of the ropes and the belts and the fists. They know the tastes of the watery soup and the strange, foreign vegetables. They know the longing for home and family. They know the comfort of faith and the pride of country. They know the hurt of rejection and the confusion of being misunderstood. They know the brotherhood born through adversity. They know the Tap Code.

Oh, the comfort I felt when I was reunited with these brothers in the first reunion of all the POWs just three months after our homecoming. Louise felt it too, for she had experiences that only the wives of the POWs could truly understand.

On May 24, 1973, we were invited by President Nixon as he hosted all the POWs to a "welcome home" dinner on the south lawn of the

White House. One hundred twenty-six tables seated thirteen hundred guests, including the POWs and their wives, U.S. military leaders, and many movie stars and celebrities such as Bob Hope, John Wayne, Phyllis Diller, and Sammy Davis Jr. To this day, it remains the largest dinner event held on White House grounds.

We all looked radically different from the last time we had been together. Though we were still a bit thin from the years of malnutrition, three months of home cooking had added needed pounds, and three months of family had brought the look of relief and joy to hollow eyes. Since it was a formal affair, we were dressed in crisp military dress, which was a far cry from the dirty, gray striped pajamas to which we had grown accustomed. Some still limped or walked with crutches, but all heads were held high with patriotic pride. There would still be mountains to climb as we journeyed through years of acclimation and transition, but on this night, we were overjoyed to be with each other and with our loved ones—a combination that had long been withheld from us.

The evening was surreal. Dignitaries and movie stars were at every table. Henry Kissinger and Senator John C. Stennis sat next to us, which thrilled Louise, as she was finally able to thank the Senator in person for the help he had given her with the VA loan. I looked over and saw fellow pilot Mike McGrath chatting with Jimmy Stewart.

Everyone was seated at round tables with crisp, white tablecloths and beautiful floral arrangements in the center of each table drawing our eyes upward to the gilded chandeliers hanging from the ceiling of the white tent. I looked down at the beautiful White House china and crystal and thought of the tin cup and flimsy metal plate I used throughout my years as a POW. I tasted the all-American cuisine—Seafood Neptune, roast beef, and strawberry mousse—and savored each bite, thankful that there was no rice or cabbage soup on the menu. The sound of the Air Force Strolling Strings made the event sound heavenly as they performed classical music as well as popular current tunes, which, though well-known to our wives, were new to all the POWs.

Though the night was overflowing in memorable moments, the most moving of all was when the POW choir rose to sing the POW hymn that Air Force F-105 pilot James Quincy Collins had secretly written—on a piece of toilet paper with a fish bone as a pen and the red dye from a diarrhea pill as ink—while in captivity. Thirty-five of my brothers rose to sing the words we all wholeheartedly believed:

Oh God, to Thee we raise this prayer and sing
From within these foreign prison walls.
We're men who wear the gold and silver wings
And proudly heed our nation's call.
Give us strength to withstand all the harm
That the hand of our enemy captors can do
To inflict pain and strife and deprive every life
Of the rights they know well we are due.
We pledge unswerving faith and loyalty to our cause,
To America and to Thee. Amen.

As was the custom, the President rose to propose a toast. He told us he had consulted senior officers to ask for their wisdom concerning to whom he should propose the toast. To a man, they each said, "Don't propose it to us. We have been toasted, and we appreciate the great welcome we have received." Most suggested that the toast be aimed toward those still missing in action or killed in action, or those who served in Vietnam or were still serving all over the world. These brave ones he did mention with heartfelt gratitude in his speech. But the toast was reserved for a select group of courageous, tenacious individuals who suffered almost as much as the POWs did.

"And now I do come to the moment, and I propose the toast," he said. "It is traditional on occasion to propose the toast to a lady rather than to a man, and on this occasion, I think of the First Lady and of many first ladies. Of course, traditionally the wife of the President is the First Lady of this country. I can tell you, as I look back over those months and years that we have met with the wives and mothers of those of you who were prisoners of war, they were and are the bravest, most magnificent women I have ever met in my life. And now, if they will give me my official toasting glass, I will propose the toast. If all of the gentlemen will please rise—tonight, as President of the United States,

I designate every one of the women here, the wives, the mothers, and others who are guests of our POWs—as First Ladies. Gentlemen, to the First Ladies of America—the First Ladies."*

We all rose and raised our glasses to our faithful, brave women who worked diligently and prayed faithfully until we could be together again. I smiled down at my Louise as she sat, full of joy, beautiful in her blue evening gown, and I felt an overwhelming sense of gratitude for her and for our life together.

As we took our seats, President Nixon continued a good-natured speech in which he recognized a hero in his own right—Bob Hope: "And now, ladies and gentlemen, we come to the real reason that it was essential to bring you back and bring this war to a conclusion before the end of this year," Nixon quipped. "The reason is that I made a promise to Bob Hope."

Nixon continued. "Bob Hope told me, when he was in the White House a few months ago—this was before we knew you were going to return—that he had spent the last 20 Christmases outside of the United States, and the last 12 of them in Vietnam, and he said, 'Mr. President, next Christmas I would like to spend Christmas with [Mrs.] Dolores [Hope] at home.'"

We all laughed and cheered, thankful that we had something to laugh about. I looked around at those seated at nearby tables—Shu and Scotty Morgan, Chuck Boyd, George Hall, and Robbie Risner. Bud Day, John McCain, Lee Ellis, and Ray Vohden were there too. Every POW who returned home was present at that great event, with the sad exception of thirty-four of my brothers who were still receiving medical care.

Over the years, we've had many reunions, some large, some small. Each has been infused with the understanding of shared experiences, the joy of survival, and the relief that we did, indeed, return with honor. Despite the opinions or views of some of our U.S. citizens, we knew the truth. Within the restrictive walls of the Hanoi Hilton, as well as every other prison camp, there could be found resilient spirits that, though refined by the fire of adversity, could not be broken.

---

* Richard M. Nixon, "Toasts at a Dinner Honoring Returned Prisoners of War," May 24, 1973, www.presidency.ucsb.edu/documents/toasts-dinner-honoring-returned-prisoners-war.

JUNE 1973
MONTGOMERY, ALABAMA

I got the call at 8:30 in the morning relaying the horrific news that Al Brudno had taken his own life. It had been four months since we had returned, and most of us had been busy reconnecting with our families. Al did not reconnect very well. In fact, he returned to find out that his newlywed wife had developed a very different view of the war for which he had sacrificed so much. These differences were merely symbolic of the differences they now faced as a couple.

Looking back, it's understandable how they grew apart. Being married for only two months and then separated for years did not provide an enduring foundation. This blow was the last break in an already fragile mental health situation. He used his intelligence to ensure his act was final—he took an overdose of phenobarbital, a strong sedative, which killed him instantly, quietly.

Within days, the POWs were being reevaluated. I and others in our area were summoned back to Maxwell Air Force Base in Montgomery, Alabama. The oppressive Southern heat had made an early appearance that year, and I sat waiting for hours in a room with no air-conditioning. Finally, I was called into the evaluation room. I was mad as a hornet. My anger stemmed from the fact that our warnings had gone unheeded. We had tried to tell those in charge that Al was not okay. Grief and anger filled my heart that day, and the heat and the long wait fueled my fire.

When they finally called me back, they asked me to fill out a mountain of psychological evaluation forms. I looked through the forms, my anger growing. I stood up and ripped the papers in front of the evaluator.

"Look, this may be to my detriment, but I am not doing this. I am fine. Al Brudno was not fine. I tried to tell you that, but no one would listen. And now look what happened. You've made me wait for hours in this place. I've wasted all the time I'm going to waste. Eight years of wasted time. Time is precious."

I turned around and walked out the door. They must have taken my abrupt response as righteous indignation rather than mental instability, because they never called me back.

Al Brudno was killed in action. If not for the ill treatment he received in captivity, he would have had a brilliant career as an astronaut, I am certain. Al's brother, Bob, worked tirelessly so that Al Brudno's name would be honored. For decades, this honor—tangible through the etching of his name on the Vietnam Veterans Memorial Wall in Washington, D.C.—was denied him and his family. Suicide was not considered a condition of honor, nor was it considered a means of death as a direct result of military service.

In 1998, Bob made a request to the Vietnam Veterans Memorial Fund, just as Al's widow, Debby, had previously, that Al's name be put on the wall. Both requests were denied. But Bob did not give up, and in 2004, he recruited the help and testimonies of many of us who knew Al, as well as his medical records from both before and after captivity. Finally, Bob went to the Air Force, who ruled that his brother's death was a direct result of injuries suffered during the war. After much pressure and persuasion, the administrators of the Vietnam Veterans Memorial Fund finally agreed.

In May 2004, Bob Brudno stood next to Debby Brudno, symbolic of a healing wave held back for decades, as the stonecutter revealed the newest name etched in the granite wall: E. Alan Brudno. My friend was finally honored, and his name will forever be remembered for the sacrifice he made for his country.

OVER THE YEARS

Over the years, we have made great efforts to keep in contact with our dear friends and fellow POWs, as well as those who were never POWs yet played an important role in our military journey. We have been committed to several types of reunions. First are the annual POW reunions, with a big reunion every five years. The last one we attended was in Frisco, Texas—our forty-fifth reunion. These reunions have afforded me the opportunity to stay in touch with many of my POW brothers like Ev Alvarez, Robbie Risner, Chuck Boyd, Doug Clower, Jerry Driscoll, Bob Shumaker, Hayden Lockhart, Mike McGrath, Scotty Morgan, Bob Peel, Larry Guarino, George Hall, Pop Keirn, and Gene Smith—those you have read about in this book, as well as many others to whom you have not been introduced. Oh, that I had the time and space to write of each of their heroic instances of endurance and strength.

We've also had the opportunity to attend many of the Freedom Flyers reunions, which began in 1975. Put on by the Flying Cheetahs—the 560th Flying Training Squadron, this reunion began when we were invited to Randolph Air Force Base, outside of San Antonio, Texas, and given the opportunity—if we were physically able and wanted to—to fly once again.

During the Vietnam War, it was the tradition of the pilots to fly their last flight in Vietnam as their "Champagne Flight." The pilots were met by their fellow pilots and friends, and a great celebration would ensue, honoring them and their safe return. As POWs, we never were able to take our "Champagne Flight." So when given the opportunity to do so, many of us jumped at the chance. This reunion has the longest history of any annual reunion.

There have also been reunions of the pilots who flew the F-105. It was at one of these reunions that Louise had the great joy of seeing her dear friends Patti McCoy and Shirley Meyerholt. It had been at least a decade since they had last seen each other—the day they had escorted her to the plane that would take her home to the United States with three small children. In contrast to that sad day, their reunion in the hotel lobby was filled with love, laughter, and great joy.

Another reunion that stands out in our memory was put on by Ross Perot, the Texas billionaire. In 1974, Perot was awarded the Medal for Distinguished Public Service by the Department of Defense for his efforts on behalf of the POWs. His purpose in that arena began by a chance meeting with one of the POW wives and her son—who had never met his father, Jerry Singleton, due to his confinement in the prisons of North Vietnam. The encounter with this family, whose experience mirrored that of Louise and Lyle, changed the life and purpose of Perot and in turn made a difference in all of our lives.

When the POWs returned home, Perot set out to show his faithful support. At a cost of more than $250,000, Perot invited every POW who had spent time in Son Tay, as well as all the Son Tay Raiders, to finally have a chance to meet. The Raiders were now serving as Green Berets in army bases all over the world. Mr. Perot flew all of them, along with their wives, back to the United States at his expense. He then flew all the POWs and our wives to meet the Raiders in San Francisco, where we were treated to a luxurious weekend at the beautiful Fairmont Hotel. When the invitation had arrived, Louise quickly asked Janice to keep the children, and she readily agreed.

There were fifty or more POWs with their wives, and 150 Raiders with their wives. We filled the hotel and enjoyed being entertained by other guests, including Ernest Borgnine, Sammy Davis Jr., John Wayne, and Diana Ross and the Supremes, all of whom provided wonderful entertainment each night. Joe Louis—the Brown Bomber—elderly and in a wheelchair, made the effort to be there and shook our hands. On the one free night we had, Perot had arranged for a team

232

of concierges to plan our evening, which had been covered by $200 in cash we had each been given.

In those early days after our return, none of the POWs had slept much, since we were determined not to miss a moment of joyful living. I was downright hyper and didn't want to miss a thing. Louise and I went on wonderful, long walks on the streets of San Francisco at three and four in the morning. We could not get enough of experiencing life together again.

The city of San Francisco wanted to have a parade of the POWs and the Raiders, but there was a bit of concern about antiwar protesters. Ross Perot responded, "Don't worry. If there's trouble, the Raiders will protect the POWs. It's what they were trained to do."

The mood throughout the weekend can only be described as euphoric. As the POWs and all of the wives ascended the steps of the trolleys that would carry us in the parade, the Raiders lined up in front and back, marching proudly around us. The celebrities joined in the old-fashioned ticker-tape parade, and we were all covered in confetti. Thousands came out to cheer for us as we made our way through the heart of San Francisco. Throughout the great crowd, we saw only one antiwar sign. The American people—even those opposed to the war—were overjoyed that the prisoners were home at last. Although the war had been a hotbed of differing opinions, the POWs turned the nation toward a euphoric, patriotic resurgence.

The prisoners were still adjusting to being back at home, and throughout the weekend we exhibited this fact through one obvious act. Day and night, you could hear tap, tap, tapping on the walls of the Fairmont Hotel.

SMITTY 52

As the years passed, I kept my vow to never waste time again. My utmost priority was my family, and God truly did restore to us the years the locust had eaten, as promised in the Scriptures. Upon my release, I attended the Air War College in Montgomery, Alabama, and was selected to stay on the faculty for the next five years as chief of curriculum planning. Our years in Montgomery were fruitful and memorable, and the girls graduated from high school there, though Tupelo was always considered home.

During my Air Force career, I had earned a bachelor's degree and an MBA at night schools. Decorations during my Air Force career included two Silver Stars, three Legions of Merit, the Distinguished Flying Cross, two Bronze Stars for valor, two Air Medals, two Purple Hearts, and two Commendation Medals. While honored and grateful for all of these distinctions, I am most thankful to know deep in my soul that with God's help and strength, I returned with honor, having kept the Code of Conduct.

When I retired from the Air Force in August 1979, I entered directly into the University of Mississippi School of Law, joining the Mississippi Bar in December 1981. My post–Air Force employment included banking, law, and marketing. I retired in 1997 at the age of sixty-eight but have since made a full-time job of doing volunteer work, flying, traveling, golfing, reading, and carrying out other pursuits for which there just never seems to be enough time. To my dying breath, I will seek the purpose and pleasure of each day.

On my eightieth birthday, April 11, 2009, I was asked to give a speech at Veterans Park in Tupelo. I had been free from captivity for thirty-six years. Tupelo, the town that had embraced my family in the years I was a POW, had now become my town—my home. With the exception of the few years in Montgomery, Louise and I have lived in Tupelo together for forty-five years. All of our children returned to Tupelo to live after obtaining their college degrees, which has afforded us the great gift of living near our grandchildren. The honor of being a part of the lives of the next generation is beyond description.

The good people of Tupelo—and the whole of North Mississippi—often have events to commemorate and honor veterans. A huge sprawling area of 206 acres was dedicated as Veterans Memorial Park. It is a place where families can congregate and feed the ducks at the lakes, swim at the 43,000-square-foot Aquatic Center, and learn important historical facts about the wars in which American soldiers sacrificed their lives for the sake of the freedom of their fellow citizens.

The latest addition to Tupelo Veterans Memorial Park is an exact replica—at 60 percent size—of the Vietnam Veterans Memorial Wall located at the National Mall in Washington, D.C. In 2011, Janie Alexander and Barbara Rushing spearheaded a movement to build the wall and spent their boundless energy raising funds and enthusiasm. The replica of the Maya Lin–designed wall was a million-dollar project, supported by the Mississippi Legislature, the VVA Chapter 842, the Marine Corps League Detachment 1220, and generous donors from the community. Now I have ready access to visit the wall and see the names of my 58,318 brothers who were killed in or are still missing due to the Vietnam War.

I was asked to give a speech as a representative of the great family of veterans who have faithfully served our country. I can't say I was nervous, for I had given countless speeches and interviews over the years since my release. But this hometown speech felt important, and I felt the weight as I anticipated the opportunity to relay words of inspiration.

I walked up the steps of the temporary stage that was set up next to an actual Air Force F-105 Thunderchief—the same type of plane I had flown in the Vietnam War and the same type of plane that had been shot down in enemy territory. When interviewed about the plane for the local paper, I explained that the F-105 was similar to what I flew, but not the exact aircraft. "The one I flew," I explained, "is in little bitty pieces."

I raised the microphone just a bit, to accommodate my five-foot-ten-inch height, which was still to diminish with age. The typical squeal of the sound system forced the attention of my listeners, and then, with the crowd's silence as my backdrop, I began my speech.

I am honored to be here today as a representative of the veterans who have served their country. And it is so fitting that we are assembled here in a beautiful park dedicated and built by concerned people to honor veterans. And veterans know there is no greater responsibility—or privilege—than the defense of the freedom of the United States of America.

Where did those freedoms come from? Every American is familiar with the opening sentence of our Declaration of Independence: "We hold these truths to be self-evident, that all men are created equal, that they are endowed by their Creator with certain unalienable Rights, that among these are Life, Liberty, and the pursuit of Happiness" . . .

In my view there are two essential elements of responsibility for defending our freedoms—moral fabric and physical strength.

Since this is Easter weekend, our whole nation takes time out to remember one of the most important Christian holidays. Yet on the moral fabric scene, during the last fifty years, I have observed a deterioration of our underpinnings, with violence, drugs, and corruption rampant. We have also seen God taken out of our schools, our courtrooms, and our workplaces. We have left the standard. We have chosen our own path. Yet in spite of this, I am still very proud to call myself an American.

The armed forces of the United States have provided the physical strength to achieve other aims. America has the greatest resources on planet Earth for helping those in need. We are feeding starving families in Africa, Asia, and elsewhere. We free those who were once captives. We promote democracy, liberate people, help them, and support them. We have sacrificed our own sons and daughters so that the world can know peace, prosperity, and happiness. And the armed forces ensure that no foreign government will ever be able to enforce their rule upon our people.

We must remember it is the soldier, not the reporter, who has given us freedom of the press. It is the soldier, not the poet, who has given us freedom of speech. It is the soldier, not the campus organizer, who has given us the freedom to demonstrate. It is the soldier who salutes the flag, who serves beneath the flag, and whose coffin is draped by the flag. And it is the soldier who allows the protester to burn the flag.

In conclusion, I have no idea when and how our nation will turn around the moral decay that has occurred. I only know it is an absolute necessity. The other part of our greatness—the physical strength—is represented by our armed forces, for which there is no better example on earth than their dedication, courage, and honor.

We are a peace-loving nation. No one wants war, especially the veterans who have experienced it. But when provoked, we are a nation of warriors, meeting the challenges just like our courageous soldiers fighting right now in Iraq and Afghanistan. God bless the men and women of our armed forces, our veterans, and the United States of America.

As I walked away from the podium to the sound of applause, I couldn't help but think of the sacrifice of my brothers with whom I had served. This brotherhood lies like a weight of holiness that is hard to describe to those who have not experienced it. I can honestly say the net effect of my captivity has been positive. I and my family would have never chosen the path we walked, but the positives by far outweigh the negatives. It is the woven fabric of my life; without those eight years of captivity, I would not be who I am. My children would not be who they are—my grandchildren as well. Because of my captivity, I have a greater understanding and appreciation for our country and its freedoms. I appreciate life more, especially my family. I am more patient now, and I know that those eight years gave me time to sort out for myself the really important things in this life—especially my relationships with God, country, family, and friends. Life has been wonderful for me, and I am eternally grateful for every part of it.

53

2019

I celebrated my ninetieth birthday this year. What a gift life is! What an honor to live such a long and wonderful life. My health is excellent, and my soul is even better. I have been participating in an annual study of the effects of my years as a POW for the past thirty years. Each summer, Louise and I travel to Pensacola, Florida, to participate in the voluntary study with 180 other POWs. It is a very extensive physical exam, with thorough blood work and testing of every kind. The information gathered is compared to that gained from other groups of pilots and peers who have not been in the prison camps of North Vietnam.

By God's grace, even at age eighty-nine, I passed the tests with flying colors. Last summer, June 2018, the chief flight surgeon, Army Col. Albano—who is the head of the Naval Air Study and who evaluates all the reports—called us in for a debriefing of the findings. My particular results included a blood pressure of 120/68, a little bit of high cholesterol, and 20/20 eyesight. Thanks to cataract surgery in both eyes, my eyesight has been restored to pilot vision.

"Col. Harris, I am pleased to announce that you have passed the Naval Aviators physical exam. Now, you *are* going to need a waiver for your slight hearing loss, but that shouldn't be a problem," Col. Albano quipped.

After hearing me brag about my good reports all the way home, Louise—in her perfect, sassy way—commented, "Oh, my stars. I'm not going to be able to put up with you now."

While we were in Pensacola for my checkup in 2013, we received the word that Bud Day, my fellow POW and dear friend, had just been admitted to hospice care. We knew he had been fighting cancer, but a fighter was indeed what he was, and we were saddened to know that the end of his stellar life was fast approaching. We quickly changed our plans and drove to his home in Shalimar, Florida, to visit with him and his wife, Dori.

Bud was a great man. He was a fierce resister during our years of captivity and was the one to stand up and lead the men of Cell 7 in Camp Unity in the highest level of resistance by singing "The Star-Spangled Banner" as Robbie Risner and the others were led away to isolation after the church service. He continued to be a leader among veterans as a lawyer when he fought and won the case that made it possible for veterans to receive their promised health care insurance. He won this historic case, but when the Department of Defense realized the expense this would entail, they overturned it and pushed it to a nine-judge panel in appeal. This time Day lost the case, though even in this, he acted with honor and valor.

Day had been awarded the Medal of Honor, which meant a great deal to him and all of us who understood its significance. Though a very humble man, he routinely kept the medal in his pocket when he tried cases on behalf of veterans. However, when he approached the panel of military judges, he took the medal out of the pocket of his simple gray suit and put it on. At first, there was silence, but soon the sliding of chairs was heard throughout the room as all nine of the judges rose to their feet to salute this giant of a man.

It was a foregone conclusion that the cost was too great, and therefore Bud lost the case on appeal. However, due to the public pressure on Congress through the publicity this created, the appropriations were passed anyway, and veterans got the medical coverage we so deserved.

Always a fighter, just one week prior to being placed on hospice, Bud, from the confines of his wheelchair, had tried the case of a military soldier who had been denied benefits—and he won.

We thought of this and many other Bud Day stories as we made our way to his home on the water in Shalimar. When we entered, we were greeted by Dori, who led us to their bedroom, where a hospital bed had been set up. Bud was lying weakly in the bed, with oxygen mask intact, but sat up to greet us—as a perfect gentleman. The four of us talked briefly, and then the women seemed to quietly disappear from the room, giving Bud and me time together.

We both knew this was the last time we would see each other on this earth. We chatted lightly for a moment, and then Bud grew serious. He looked me straight in the eyes and said, "Smitty, I want to thank you for introducing the Tap Code. It made all the difference in our communications network and was a lifeline for all of us." It was a powerful moment I will always cherish, quickly topped by an even greater act that will stand out as one of the most significant events of my life.

Bud grabbed my hand, turned it over, and on the back of it began to tap.

Tap tap, tap tap—the letter G.

Tap, tap tap—the letter B.

Tap tap tap tap, tap tap tap tap tap—the letter U.

GBU. God bless you—those words tapped countless times by POWs to offer strength and understanding to each other. It was a symbol of our shared experience and a mark of our brotherhood.

Stunned, I could barely speak, but I managed to thank him for those blessed words and to tell him that I loved him. I know I will see him again, when I will one day follow his lead through the gates of heaven and experience a reunion even grander than those I have written about here.

Yes, God has blessed me indeed. And to you, my friends, who have taken the time to read this book and walk this journey with me and Louise, I say: GBU.

EPILOGUE

Robin Harris Waldrip
Daughter of Smitty and Louise Harris

THANKSGIVING 2018
TUPELO, MISSISSIPPI

French linens, Great-Grandmother Rindeleau's formal china, Grandmother Harris's lead crystal water goblets and wine glasses. Twenty sterling silver place settings, candles, and an arrangement of white roses (another of Mom's talents) centered beneath a crystal chandelier. The table stretched to its maximum capacity with another table pressed against it, dressed in the same finery. The aroma of turkey and dressing, sweet potato casseroles, roasted green beans, ambrosia, Waldorf salad, cranberry salad, rice and gravy, homemade rolls.

I place the final crystal compote on the table ever so gently, knowing I'm holding a fragile, dearly loved piece of history—our history. I dim the lights, as instructed, and light the candles.

The planning, the labor, the hours of baking that went into this scene—I am amazed at Mom's efforts. She must be exhausted. So much love, so much life, documented around this table—and she is our glue.

A cacophony of sound comes from the kitchen; but in this moment, every distraction falls away as I peruse the scene. The flicker of candlelight, the silvery gray silk drapes, and the sparkle of the tablescape engulf me in a sacred vision, carried back to a little table for four, laid out with the same care and attention to detail. I sense the presence of the Maestro, the Master Conductor, suspended over our stories, arranging the most beautiful symphony out of chaos.

Jarred back to the present by the sound of our family entering the dining room, every person talking at once, a melody—indistinguishable and barely audible—rings in my ears. I can't make it out, but it's there, and I'm keenly aware that our sovereign God has taken our discordant notes and composed the most beautiful arrangement. We each take a hand, heads bowed, a prayer offered up. "In Jesus' name. Amen."

A dozen conversations ensue, laughter, "pass the gravy," a fork falls on the Aubusson rug. My granddaughter, Mary Lyle, crawls under to retrieve it and can't resist the opportunity to tickle a foot. A startled shriek, squeals of delight. The melody of our family's song rises an octave once again. Our family. Our family.

Clink, clink, clink. Dad's spoon touches his crystal goblet. Our rowdy group embraces silence. I pull Mary Lyle into my lap. All eyes on Dad, and he begins. We anticipate his usual toast.

"I want to thank Louise—your 'Khaki,' my 'Jane'—for this beautiful meal. As always, sweetheart, you outdid yourself."

Our eyes drift from one end of the table to the other—and rest on Khaki. Snow-white hair framing her lovely face, her sea-green eyes shimmering as a tear threatens to escape, an adoring smile, a quivering chin.

She stares lovingly at him. Dad continues. "As I look around this table, I can't believe I'm here. For eight long years I prayed to God, begging him for relief—I asked for my chains to be loosened so the oozing sores on my wrists would heal—with no reply. I begged to be rescued so I could see Louise and my two girls and meet our new baby—no reply. I cried out in anguish as my stomach wrenched with hunger pains. I shook in fear as the key clanked open the door of my cell—knowing another 'fact-finding' torture session was coming. My requests, my cries, though not answered tangibly, did seem to bring a measure of peace—and, I dare say, hope.

"Yet in my wildest imagination, in my sweetest dreams, I could not have fathomed the blessings waiting for me, the restoration that would come. God did exceedingly more than I could ever have hoped for or dreamed. As I look around this table at each of you, I stand in awe. Not only are my chains loosened; they are gone! Not only was I rescued; I was restored. Not only did I see my wife and girls; I met my son! And my grandsons and granddaughters, my great-grandchildren, and your wonderful spouses. Not only did God deliver a meal; he set a table before me in the presence of my enemies in North Vietnam with a bug or a bowl of greasy rice—and now . . . all of this. That we would all live here and love each other is the greatest gift. God answered my prayers more extravagantly than I could have ever imagined. I'm so grateful—I love you all—and I love God. Cheers. Cheese," he concludes with our old family joke.

We lift our glasses. I lift my gaze and look at each dinner guest through water-soaked eyes. No dry eyes—not even the teenage boys and the grown men can hold back their tears. I breathe in deeply, wanting to savor, to treasure this moment.

Another shriek breaks the silence as Baby Sam slides under the table with his cousin. The choked emotion, the touching tribute, morphs into laughter and multiple conversations again. *Thanksgiving*— never has a word carried more weight, had more meaning.

Lord, we are thankful!

AFTERWORD

Sara W. Berry

DECEMBER 2, 2018
TUPELO, MISSISSIPPI

I sat with my friend Robin Waldrip as we talked home decor and paint colors, casually sipping our hot afternoon coffee. We had known of each other for years, as we both lived in the idyllic town of Tupelo, Mississippi, and shared many common interests, not the least of which was love of God, country, and family.

Both her sister, Carolyn, and her brother, Lyle, and their families had been my kind neighbors for years. I had watched from afar as snippets of her family's tremendous story came to me through newspaper articles and my children, who were in school with her nieces and nephews. Her dad, Col. Carlyle Smith "Smitty" Harris, had been held captive as a POW for almost eight years, and he was well respected in our community. I knew bits and pieces of his story, but I had never met the man himself.

On this day in my living room, Robin began to share more details of her family's story, and I was fascinated. Having read some of my books, Robin asked me if I would consider writing the story in book form. Though flattered, I immediately thought, *Me? What do I know about the Vietnam War?*

I was not yet born when Smitty was shot down in enemy territory. When he was suffering torture and malnutrition, I was growing up in a loving family, filled with joy and making fun memories, in an even smaller town fifty miles down the road from Tupelo. When Smitty returned home, I was finishing kindergarten. As a writer, I was drawn to this story like a moth to a flame, yet I still wasn't convinced I was the one to write it.

"You write it, Robin. I have read some of your writing. You can do it! I will help you!"

"It needs to be written by someone who is not so close to it. Someone who can see all the details from far away," she explained. "At least pray about it."

I agreed, and we even prayed together right there at my dining room table.

That night, I reached for my Bible and turned to the scheduled reading, which included Jeremiah 30. By the end of the chapter, I was thunderstruck at what I had read.

This is the word that came to Jeremiah from the LORD: "This is what the LORD, the God of Israel, says: 'Write in a book all the words I have spoken to you. The days are coming,' declares the LORD, 'when I will bring my people Israel and Judah back from captivity and restore them to the land I gave their ancestors to possess,' says the LORD."

Jeremiah 30:1–3

Stunned, I continued reading as I made my way to chapter 31, verse 8: "See, I will bring them from the land of the north and gather them from the ends of the earth." Verses 16 and 17 continued in this theme: "'They will return from the land of the enemy. So there is hope for your descendants,' declares the LORD."

These words written thousands of years before seemed a mirror image of what little I knew of the story of Smitty and Louise Harris.

"Okay, Lord. I will do my best," I prayed.

I will never forget the first of many days I spent on Smitty and Louise's sofa in north Tupelo. Smitty, now ninety, and Louise, eighty-one, are as sharp and witty as any persons decades younger. Though they sat on opposite couches, I noticed how they looked at each other, as if they were speaking in unison, as one told a snippet and then allowed time for the other to speak. With her beautiful, clear blue eyes and pure, soft white hair, Louise seemed as if she were holding Smitty's hand just by the way she looked at him across the room when he spoke.

"We get along very well," Louise commented one day. "We never argue. Why would we waste time on that?" she said, as if it made perfect sense. That small piece of wisdom has etched its way into my own life.

When the inevitable delays in writing came, they were filled with grace and patience. Smitty and Louise approached this project as if they were delighted to share but unconcerned when or if it ever happened. They told me their story with great detail and superb memory. I marveled at their grace. I marveled at their healing. And I marveled at the many times they insisted that the main objective was for people to see that the overall effect has been positive on their lives and the lives of their children and grandchildren. "We are truly blessed in every aspect of our lives. God's been good to us," they repeatedly told me.

I took the beginnings of a brilliant account of Smitty's experiences that he had started writing in the late 1970s but never finished, and I wove in many more details, scenes, and memories that Smitty and Louise told me as we sat in their lovely home. From there I researched websites and articles and read many wonderful books by other POWs. I even had the great honor of having access to the two-volume professional study titled *Vietnam POW Camp Histories and Studies*, prepared by the Air War College, which was classified information until February 22, 1978.

Though written in story form, this book you hold in your hands is entirely true.

Col. Larry Guarino spoke of Smitty and the Tap Code in his book *A P.O.W. Story: 2801 Days in Hanoi*, saying, "Neither Smitty Harris nor any of us realized that this would be the most valuable life- and mind-saving piece of information contributed by any prisoner for all the years we were there."[*] After reading *Tap Code*, I hope you will be

---

[*] Col. Larry Guarino, *A P.O.W. Story: 2801 Days in Hanoi* (New York: Ivy Books, 1990), 40.

inspired, as I have been, to emulate the grit, honor, and courage of both Smitty and Louise. Through learning both sides of their story, lived out on opposite sides of the world, I believe you will not only learn important details of American history but also see a glimpse of true and enduring love.

As I tearfully told them one day after a lovely session at their home, I am profoundly honored to have been given the opportunity to help them tell their inspiring, life-changing, true story. It is my great desire that this book will bring honor to both of them, their family, our military men and women in all walks of service, and their families. Most of all, I hope to bring honor to God, who has set me free from my own captivity, just as he has every believing soul. To him be the glory.

ACKNOWLEDGMENTS

CARLYLE "SMITTY" HARRIS AND LOUISE HARRIS

We wish to gratefully acknowledge Zondervan for taking on our project so personal to us but hopefully meaningful to others.

The wonderful support and encouragement we have received from all to whom we have made requests—for permissions, clearances, approvals, and help—has been extraordinary. The Department of Defense, the Smithsonian, the United States Air Force, and the many dear friends who happily gave consent to use their precious work means more to us than we could ever express. GBU!

Most importantly, we wish to thank our wonderful children—Robin, Carolyn, and Lyle—and their dear, dear children for their enduring love and all the joy they bring us each and every day. A special thanks to Robin for finding Sara W. Berry for us. Without her, this book would not have happened.

We are grateful to our nation for the opportunity of the wonderful life we have been privileged to lead. God Bless America!

SARA W. BERRY

I am profoundly grateful to Smitty and Louise Harris for trusting me to help them share their story. This opportunity has been one of the greatest privileges of my life.

With great gratitude I wish to thank Andy Rogers and the wonderful team at Zondervan, who not only believed in this story but also led us through the publishing process with enthusiasm and kindness.

I would also like to acknowledge my many faithful friends who have prayed for this project and given incredible support along the way. In particular, I want to thank my parents, Kenneth and Nancy Ann Williams; my friend and editor extraordinaire, Mary Jo Tate; and especially my dear friend Robin Waldrip, who extended the invitation to be a part of this worthy endeavor.

Most importantly, I would like to acknowledge my family for their unconditional love and support. To my wonderful husband, Mont—you are my steady support, the one who makes me believe I can. And to my amazing children, Katie, Owen, Ellie, Drew, Joseph, Troy, Rorie, Joshua, Sally, and Charlie—you are my great joy. I pray you will lead others in your generation in an attitude of gratitude for our great nation.

Finally, to Jesus: "Not to us, LORD, not to us but to your name be the glory, because of your love and faithfulness" (Psalm 115:1).

TRIBUTES

Smitty, 2019

I wish I had the time and space to tell all the stories of brotherhood that I've had the great honor to experience in the forty-six years since my captivity ended. I have been blessed indeed with strong friendships that few have ever experienced. Truly, if anyone is allowed one or two of these types of friends over a lifetime, they should consider themselves blessed. I, however, have had an abundance of such friends. Of the roughly 660 men who were released with me, about 230 of them have passed away, or as we like to say, "They have flown west."

Now, more than four hundred form our current brotherhood, and we have a bond with each and every one, resulting from our POW experience and the shared pride of coming home with honor. Though the list will certainly be incomplete, the names below are just the ones I call my closest friends because they had been my cellmates as POWs, or I have gotten to know them and their families very well at our many reunions—roughly two per year—during the last forty-five years.

Of the ninety-two names on this list, there are twenty-eight, marked by an asterisk, who have "flown west."

Ray Alcorn	Bob Barnett	Dick Bolstad*
Ev Alvarez Jr.	Bill Baugh*	John Borling
Bill Arcuri	Jim Bell*	Chuck Boyd
Mo Baker	Red Berg	Mike Brazelton

Al Brudno*	Will Forby	Ray Merritt*
Al Brunstrom	Dave Ford*	Tom Moe
Herb Buchanan	Ralph Gaither*	Scotty Morgan
Bill Burroughs*	Paul Galanti	Bob Naughton
Bill Butler*	Dan Glenn	Bob Peel
Ron Byrne	Wayne Goodermote	John Pitchford*
Fred Cherry*	Dave Gray	Bob Purcell*
Larry Chesley	Larry Guarino*	Jim Ray
John Clark	George Hall*	Jon Reynolds
Doug Clower*	Tom Hanton	Robbie Risner*
James Quincy Collins	Dave Hatcher*	Wes Schierman*
Tom Collins	John Heilig	Bruce Seeber
Ken Cordier	Roger Ingvalson*	Bob Shumaker
Render Crayton	Gobel James	Jerry Singleton
Mike Cronin	Julius Jayroe	Gene Smith
Tom Curtis	Bob Jeffrey	John Stavast*
Max Dat Nguyen	Jay Jensen*	Bob Stirm
Bud Day*	Sam Johnson	Ron Storz*
Myron Donald	Paul Kari	Leroy Stutz
Bob Doremus	Pop Keirn*	Dwight Sullivan
Jerry Driscoll*	Denver Key	Orson Swindle
Dick Dutton*	Jim Lamar	Dave Terrell*
Bill Elander	Laurie Lengyel	Jack Van Loan
Lee Ellis	Hayden Lockhart	Dick Vogel
John Fer	Tom Madison*	Wayne Waddell
Ken Fisher	Ron Mastin	Jim Young*
Ken Fleenor*	Mike McGrath	John Yuill
Fred Flom	J. B. McKamey*	

RESOURCES

Coram, Robert. *American Patriot: The Life and Wars of Colonel Bud Day.* New York: Little, Brown, 2007.

Gargus, John. *The Son Tay Raid: American POWs in Vietnam Were Not Forgotten.* First Edition. Texas A&M University Military History Series, Number 112. College Station: Texas A&M University Press, 2007.

Guarino, Larry. *A P.O.W.'s Story: 2801 Days in Hanoi.* New York: Ivy Books, 1990.

Howes, Craig. *Voices of the Vietnam POWs: Witnesses to Their Fight.* Oxford: Oxford University Press, 1993.

Myers, Armand J. et al. *Vietnam POW Camp Histories and Studies.* Two Volumes. Montgomery, AL: Air War College, Maxwell Air Force Base, 1974. Unpublished study of Vietnam POWs, unclassified February 1978.

Risner, Robinson. *The Passing of the Night: My Seven Years as a Prisoner of the North Vietnamese.* New York: Random House, 1973.

Rutledge, Howard and Phyllis. *In the Presence of Mine Enemies, 1965–1973: A Prisoner of War.* With Mel and Lyla White. Old Tappan, NJ: Revell, 1973.

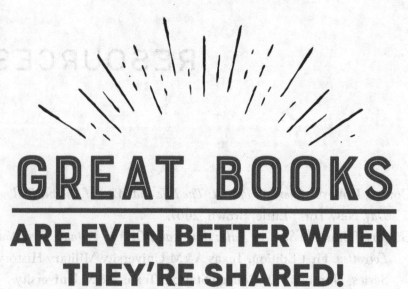

GREAT BOOKS

ARE EVEN BETTER WHEN THEY'RE SHARED!

Help other readers find this one:

- Post a review at your favorite online bookseller

- Post a picture on a social media account and share why you enjoyed it

- Send a note to a friend who would also love it—or better yet, give them a copy

Thanks for reading!